Ailsa, Inc. 2006 reprint edition of "Golfing By-Paths,"
originally published by Country Life Limited, London, 1946.
ISBN: 0-940889-68-4

FLAGSTICK BOOKS

edition of

GOLFING BY-PATHS

by
Bernard Darwin

Foreword by Michael Beckerich

Publisher's Note

As you know, Mike Beckerich owns and runs The Classics of Golf. The Flagstick Books that I produce go first to you, the subscriber, and then into the Classics of Golf library, so that all of your needs—replacements books, extra copies, gift books, etc., whether of the original Classics of Golf series or the Flagstick editions—can be met through the website: theclassicsofgolf.com.

Beckerich has done a splendid job trying to find a larger market for the Classics, and he has produced two new books himself: a biography of Tillinghast and a history of the U.S. Amateur championship. Both are very fine. He has also embraced an important mission of The Classics of Golf and that is to bring out and keep in print the works of Bernard Darwin and Herbert Warren Wind. They are the twin pillars of every golf library. The latest addition to the Darwin collection, *Golfing By-Paths*, was brought to my attention by Beckerich, and I thought he was the ideal person to do the Foreword.

How did Darwin write entertainingly about golf during the war years in Britain when there was virtually no tournament golf at all? He explored the by-ways of the game and discovered some of his most original topics.

One more thing. *Golfing By-Paths* was published immediately ater World War II in 1946 "in complete conformity with the authorized economy standards." You will find a few misprints and some uneven printing. The irony is that the photographs were reproduced sharper than normal, and they are a world of entertainment in themselves. We have changed nothing. Here is the flavor of the real thing.

Robert S. Macdonald

FOREWORD
by
Michael Beckerich

Sometimes you do get more than you pay for. I am not speaking just yet of the fine volume you hold in your hands, though it is an exceptional example of exactly that. I'm talking about how I came across this rarity by the great Bernard Darwin.

Back in 2003, while attending a meeting of the Golf Collectors' Society in Jacksonville, Florida, I passed a table where an older man, who struck me as a veteran of these shows, was offering an array of collectibles. He asked if I had seen his stack of free books. Drawing a smile of interest from me, he casually fanned five books across the table. I immediately was drawn to a timeworn hardcover with the name Bernard Darwin printed on its stained, pale blue cover.

As publisher of the Classics of Golf and lover of golf literature, I am fairly conversant with the works of B.D. Classics of Golf offers the most complete set of Darwin's works available anywhere — 14 titles, ranging from recently assembled anthologies to books originally published between 1910 and 1955. Yet here on this table, abandoned, was a title I was not familiar with: *Golfing By-Paths*.

"It's not in good shape," the seller admitted, as I thumbed through the yellowed pages. "I was just hoping that a guy like you would stop by and give it a home."

"Well," I said, "I'm not getting a Bernard Darwin treasure for free. I insist on paying you something for it." The man protested, but eventually I persuaded him to accept a token sum.

That night I started reading the book, and was overwhelmed. Here was Darwin, the essayist praised by Herbert Warren Wind for the consistently "relaxed vitality" of his voice, keeping the flame of golf alive during the privation of the war years, 1939–1945. Everything was rationed, not least golf balls. The major championships were suspended. Few people, Darwin included, had the opportunity to play. But in these columns gathered from the English weekly *Country Life*, for which he wrote for decades, Darwin celebrates the traditions and camaraderie that makes golf part of the fabric of English life.

I shared the news of my discovery with Robert Macdonald, founding publisher of Classics of Golf and now publisher of Flagstick Books. He hadn't heard of *Golfing By-Paths*, either. That phone call set in motion the process of republishing this long-lost volume.

Though 58 "new" Darwin essays are reason enough to rejoice, the 33 photographs that accompany them tip the book right off the charts in terms of value. The crispness and clarity of these images is simply amazing. Even the 1892 group portrait of the golfers of Aberdovey (following page 84)—among whose number is Darwin himself, winner of the outing's Scratch Medal—is so detailed you can study at length the faces of these proper, tweed-suited Victorian gentlemen.

Many of the photos are close-ups, showing the grace and grit of the golfing greats. No finer example exists than the picture of the brilliant English champion John Ball hitting out of the water at St. Andrews (following page 68). It has everything: Ball in the foreground, his back to the camera, right shoulder dipped, up to his ankles in water, the photo snapped just a split second after impact. The camera has arrested the huge splash of water, taller than the golfer himself, kicked up by the shot. In the distance, standing perilously close to the line of play (some things never change) the expectant gallery hovers.

But, finally, this book is about the balm of memory. In October of 1940, Darwin evacuated his home in Kent, near London, with "its broken windows and its grand new impromptu bunkers" and moved to relative safety in the Cotswolds, where he wrote the essays in this book. He rarely refers directly to the war, but when he does, he deftly brings the focus back to golf.

For example, in a piece called "Noises Without," he reports that a club near London is said to have adopted a local rule allowing a player to replay his shot with a one stroke penalty if his "stroke is affected by a simultaneous explosion of a bomb or shell or by machine-gun fire . . ." Comments Darwin,

> "I sincerely hope it is true, and more so as the rule shows a proper mixture of the Spartan and the modern spirit. It acknowledges that bombs are altogether out of the common and that some allowance is to be made for them; at the same time, to have a second shot is so outrageous that the player must be prepared to pay for it; no number of wild Germans is to be allowed to make the game wholly farcical."

He goes on to recall the effect on Bobby Jones, Joyce Wethered and J.H. Taylor of noises that erupted as they were about to swing in important matches.

Golfing By-Paths shows us Darwin in a Proustian mode, recalling sunnier seasons with the sometimes uncertain hope that they will return. In "The Golfer's Lunch," he takes a sentimental tour of signature dishes he has enjoyed at lunch in the famous golf clubs of England and Scotland. There was the "scrumptious" fried sole at Addington and Mid-Surrey, the potted shrimps at St. Annes, Formby, Hoylake and St. Andrews. It's a world-class piece, in which he goes to lengths to be generous to all. The difficulties facing the membership and club secretaries to preserve the mosaic of social graces associated with "a day at the club" weighs heavily on Darwin's mind.

This essay can make you hungry. At the end, ever self-effacing, Darwin writes, "I am not really so greedy as I may appear, only grateful to many people for many kindnesses and much hospitality."

These many years later, we are happy, a smile on our faces, for the kindnesses and hospitality that always await us in the company of this most endearing writer.

HOMEWARD BOUND AT ST. ANDREWS

Sport & General

GOLFING BY-PATHS

BY
BERNARD DARWIN

LONDON: COUNTRY LIFE LIMITED
2-10 TAVISTOCK STREET, COVENT GARDEN, W.C.2

First Published, 1946

THIS BOOK IS PRODUCED IN
COMPLETE CONFORMITY WITH THE
AUTHORISED ECONOMY STANDARDS

MADE AND PRINTED IN GREAT BRITAIN BY
WYMAN & SONS LIMITED, LONDON, READING AND FAKENHAM

CONTENTS

	PAGE
INTRODUCTION	ix
SPLENDOURS AND TRAGEDIES	1
WHAT A MATCH!	4
THE FOURSOME	7
THE GOLFER'S LUNCH	10
HISTORY REPEATS ITSELF	13
MR. WINKLE	16
A PILGRIMAGE	20
DRIFT AND DRAW	23
OUT AT ELBOWS	26
HAROLD HILTON	30
SOME HILTONIANA	34
"O SWEET, O LOVELY WALL"	37
"UNFAIRNESS"	41
ON THE SKY-LINE	44
CONSOLATIONS OF SHORTNESS	48
"OF PERSONS ONE WOULD WISH TO HAVE SEEN"	51
A GOLFER'S GOLFER	55
THE ANÆSTHETIC OF DON'T CARE	58
DALE	61
MY FIRST OPEN	64
THE MOST EXCITING	68
ELEVEN AND THIRTEEN	71
WRY NECKS	76
A PREHISTORIC PEEP	79
WRITING IT DOWN	82
LONG SWINGS AND SHORT	85

v

CONTENTS

	PAGE
A Game of Choosing	89
Favourites	92
A Putting Challenge	96
Back to Macedon	100
A Choleuse Plays Golf	103
A Match in Italy	107
Past Days in the Sun	110
The Allies	114
The Secret of Style	118
Off the Socket	121
My First Amateur	125
The Seventeenth Hole	128
" A Congenial Companion "	132
Battles Long Ago	135
Fossils of the Past	139
On Throwing Clubs	143
A Hoylake Friend	146
Par to Win	149
Gestures	153
Tactics	157
You Never Can Tell	160
Back to School	164
Noises Without	167
The Illustrious Obscure	171
The Young Idea	175
Assorted Rough	178
Golfing Views	182
To the Nineteenth	186
A Club of Character	190
The Hedge-Golfer's Farewell	193
Forward Tees	196
On Giving Up	199

LIST OF ILLUSTRATIONS

Homeward Bound at St. Andrews - - - *Frontispiece*

Following page

Burton at the corner of the Dyke - - - - - 4

Cotton with J. H. watching him - - - - - 4

The 5th Green at Mid-Surrey. Taylor and Braid *v.* Cotton
and Compston - - - - - - - - 20

Father and Son : Old Tom Morris and Tommy - - 20

On the Alps Green at Hoylake - - - - - 36

Leo Diegel in the Ryder Cup Match at Moortown - - 36

Harold Hilton at Sandwich in 1914 - - - - 52

Unorthodox but effective. Charles Stowe of our winning
Walker Cup side - - - - - - - 52

James Bruen the Infant Phenomenon - - - - 60

Rex Hartley at Sandwich - - - - - - 60

Dale Bourn at St. Anne's - - - - - - 60

James Braid on his own Heath - - - - - 60

The Maiden Green at Sandwich - - - - - 68

John Ball playing out of water at St. Andrews - - - 68

At Aberdovey's First Meeting in 1892 - - - - 84

On the 4th Teeing Ground at Gleneagles - - - 84

A Typical Sunningdale View. The 4th Green with the
5th and 6th Holes in the distance - - - - 100

George Duncan Putting - - - - - - 100

Plenty of Trouble. On the Links of the Royal Lytham
and St. Anne's Club - - - - - - 116

The Winner almost Home. R. A. Whitcombe's brassey
shot to the 17th at St. George's in 1938 - - - 116

viii LIST OF ILLUSTRATIONS

Following page

Jerome Travers with his faithful driving iron - - - 132

An Uncrowned King, Jack Graham - - - - 132

Going to the Road Hole at St. Andrews - - - - 148

A Typical Bobby Finish - - - - - - 148

Francis Ouimet at Garden City, 1913 - - - - 164

Cyril Tolley in 1938 - - - - - - - 164

The Last Putt. Walter Hagen winning the Championship
at St. George's in 1928 - - - - - - 180

Lady Heathcoat-Amory (Miss Joyce Wethered) Driving - 180

Driving to the 7th Hole at Sandwich - - - - 180

North Berwick Law looking down on the Links - - 180

Miss Cecil Leitch at Troon - - - - - - 188

The Big Bunker at the 4th Hole at Westward Ho ! - 188

INTRODUCTION

ALL the papers in this book have appeared in *Country Life*, and all but the first during the time of the war. That single exception refers to the Open Championship of 1939, and I have included it as a reminder of happy times that are past and are now, thank heaven, in process of returning. The *News of the World* tournament was played once in war time, in the spring of 1940, and then, incidentally, produced one of the greatest matches I ever saw, between Cotton and Padgham. Of that too I have included some account. I must not, and do not, forget the many exhibition matches by which Henry Cotton and his brother professionals raised large sums of money for the Red Cross and other good causes. They served their purpose to admiration but were hardly memorable in themselves, and in any case I must confess to having seen only a very few of them.

Golf, in so far as it has been played at all, has been a purely private game, giving air and exercise and a brief surcease from hard work and anxiety. It has not been taken too seriously, as was right and proper, and has been played with a sense of proportion and a sense of humour which many of us have been conscious of lacking in peaceful times. Even of this mildest golf I have myself played or seen but little, partly owing to my own incapacity, partly because I have chanced to be largely in golfless places. Two or three brief and ecstatic little holidays by the sea have made up almost the sum total of my golf. Otherwise I have been what in one of these papers I have called a hedge golfer, playing a few solitary shots now and again in some kindly meadow not yet ploughed, where there was a fair chance of not losing the all too precious ball.

I say this not egotistically but in humble propitiation and in order to explain why I have had to delve so largely into the past. As far as I am concerned this has been a pleasure, if sometimes so sensitive a pleasure as to be akin to pain. For my

ix

readers perhaps the pain may predominate, though I hope not. To the younger of them some of my memories may seem a little musty, referring as they do to those who to them are but historic names. I am afraid that is almost inevitable since to each one of us the most towering figures must be those of his own youth. The hero must be older than the worshipper or at least his contemporary. Once we grow older than those we admire they approach more nearly to life size. I can never quite believe that the great players of to-day, and they are great, can be to the modern youth what John Ball was to me. My mind accepts it as a fact that they are, but my heart refuses its assent. So if I have occasionally grown too lyrical over the past I trust it will be attributed not to malignant prejudice but to a common and amiable weakness.

In writing week after week I have owed much to a number of kind correspondents. Some of them have been younger friends of my own who have constantly warmed my heart by letters from different theatres of war, as witness the account of the epic contest at Uglino. Several others, some of them personally unknown to me, have written telling me of interesting or amusing things. They have not only been of much practical help when there has been a grave deficiency of straw for brick-making; they have encouraged me with the hope that they are still a little pleased to breathe the air of the links in however diluted a form. Till I re-read my files of *Country Life* I did not fully appreciate how often I had been in their debt, and to one and all I now offer my sincere thanks.

The articles appear here almost exactly in their original shape. I have made very slight alterations only when some reference to dates has become superfluous or when I appear regrettably to have said the same thing more than once. This, in the words of Michael Finsbury, is "a thing that may happen to anyone," and indeed after a decent interval it might escape detection, but I have conscientiously excised the more obvious repetitions. I have not adhered to chronological order but have rather tried to give the reader some "fine confused eating." After the powder of a mildly didactic paper comes the more personal and frivolous jam; the ancient and the modern alternate discreetly. If the reader cannot endure Mr. George Glennie or the Rev. J. G. McPherson, which I take leave to think bad taste on his part, he can skip to the newer champions next door.

Already, as I write these words, golf is alive again. Witness the spate of professional tournaments during the later days of the past summer, and in particular that at St. Andrews, which saw the Old Course a sterner and more glorious test than it had been for many years. The battlefields for the championships have been appointed; the undergraduates are once more playing their matches; in short, the game is getting into its stride and all we need is some more golf balls with which to play it. I can only hope that however badly they may play at first, a few golfers may be in so happy a temper at beginning again that they may look indulgently on this little book's imperfections.

B. D.

SPLENDOURS AND TRAGEDIES

OST Open Championships end in one of the early starters on the last day setting up a mark which his pursuers, one after the other, just fail to hit. That makes for long drawn-out excitement, but it is never quite so exciting, though fully as agonising, to see a putt missed as to see it holed. This Championship at St. Andrew's in 1939 held for the spectators the pleasanter thrill of seeing a man come up from behind and, knowing what he had to do, do it. Moreover, Burton did it not only to win the Championship for himself, but to save it crossing the sea to America where it was most assuredly going if he faltered.

When Bulla had finished and Shankland, following on his heels, had had a putt to tie and missed it, everybody grew busy with arithmetical calculations and very depressing they were. Whitcombe had a 72 to tie, so had Rees, so had King; but a 72 in a stiff west wind in the last round, with huge crowds spreading across the course, was a very great deal to ask. A more hopeful speculation, only to the extent of one stroke, was Burton's 73 to tie, but Burton had rather thrown away his chances in the morning with a 77 and had begun his last round with three putts. Everyone was decidedly gloomy, and then came a real ray of hope: Burton had reached the turn in 35, and a 38 home was very far from impossible. Besides, Burton had the wind on his right coming home, and he is generally supposed to like a hooky wind better than a slicy one. There followed another period void of news, and then by a field telephone came the glorious intelligence that he wanted two fours and two fives to win. The four at the home hole with the wind behind was easy: he could afford an unambitious 5 at the Road and one more 5 at either the fifteenth or sixteenth. At this point I rushed, or rather hobbled out and saw the crowd sweeping across the links, breaking every now and

2   GOLFING BY-PATHS

again into a charging run, in a positively terrifying manner. Burton had got his 4 at the fifteenth, but the sixteenth cost him the one additional 5 he could afford, and it had been a very dubious 5, with a wild hook from the tee, a shaky, fluffy little chip, and only a most gallant last putt to redeem it. The seventeenth made us all happy, but it was an awful moment when we waited for the second shot. The ball ended in the ideal spot, and it was now a case of "nothing but a stroke of apoplexy." Golfing crowds will cheer the shortest putts, but they do not often cheer plain-sailing drives from the tee. However, they crowed with joy over Burton's last drive, and it was a mighty blow. He walked and he walked after it down the big green expanse kept free of onlookers, until we began to think he had driven the green. He had driven so near it that he could have scuffled the next one up along the ground, and many a wise and stout-hearted golfer would have done so; but Burton played his normal shot, and pitched beautifully to within four or five yards beyond the hole. "Heavens!" gasped one eminent person beside me as Burton putted, "he's gone too hard." But the eminent person, thank goodness, had mistaken the position of the hole. That putt was never anywhere but stone dead, and, in glorious point of fact, it went in. Hurrah for Burton, for everything and for everybody!

Apart from the splendour of Burton's final round, I think that this Championship will chiefly be remembered for the number of disastrous holes that wrecked the scores of various prominent players. Poor Mr. Storey was qualifying comfortably when he put three balls over the wall at the fourteenth and took 12: I believe Haliburton put two over the wall at the same hole and took 10. Then just think of the major disasters in the Championship itself. There was Locke's 8 at the fourteenth, when he hooked into one of the Beardies, tried too much, and took 2 to get out. He had a wonderful 70 despite this, but it shook him, and he took 7 at that hole in the next round. Barring the Beardies, he might well have won. Then there was Cotton's 6 at the fourteenth and 7 at the Road hole, in his otherwise really gorgeous round of 72. There was poor Pose's 8 at the Road, where he incurred a two-stroke penalty for grounding his

SPLENDOURS AND TRAGEDIES

club on that piece of grass, which by law is part of the hazard—a most regrettable piece of bad luck. Personally, I think that Pose was just about the best golfer, as he was surely the prettiest, in the field, and would have won but for that tragedy. Mr. Bruen, too, was practically put out of the hunt by the Road hole with a 6 in his first round and a 7 in his second. Ultimately, in his fourth, he had a 9 at the Heathery hole, which is as a rule deemed comparatively harmless. Finally—and this is but a casual selection of tragedies—there was the 7 at the fifth which killed Fallon in his last round, and he had started it with a clear lead of all the field.

What conclusions, if any, are to be drawn from these grim and ghastly stories? An obvious one is that poor old St. Andrews is not so easy after all, and not at all likely to go out of business as a championship course. Only two players beat 70 in the qualifying rounds on the Old Course, and no single man could do it when the real thing began. Yet the conditions were very favourable to scoring. What with the watering by a naturally apprehensive Green Committee followed by an all too liberal watering by Providence, the greens were slow and soft, ideally suited to the high pitching approach which the professionals like and play with such precision. Yet the rain had not taken the run out of the ground through the green, and the course was not unduly long—certainly not for the big hitters, who in any case do not worry their heads over a little more length. The wind blew fairly hard once or twice and was doubtless troublesome on the last day, but it was nothing in the least out of the ordinary for the seaside, and there were long spells of almost total calm. Nevertheless, the scores were not particularly low; nothing like so low as the decriers of the Old Course professed to expect. The new tee back at the fourteenth, which once more makes a really superb hole out of it, had something to do with it, but the tee at the Road hole was the same as ever, and with the ground soft there was no insuperable difficulty over a steady second shot and a five. Yet see what fools the Road hole made of the most distinguished! I think the fact is that the players showed as a body the most moderate intelligence in tackling that hole and the other problems which

4 GOLFING BY-PATHS

St. Andrews presents. Doubtless it wants much knowing, but they had played plenty of practice rounds. So often one heard that somebody "did not seem to realise" a danger or a peculiarity of some hole or shot, and I am driven to the conclusion that a great many of the competitors were very poor realisers, better with their clubs than with their heads.

WHAT A MATCH!

I WAS watching Padgham preparing to address himself to a short putt at the thirty-fifth hole of his match with Cotton at Mid-Surrey. If he holed it, and it was scarcely more than a yard in length, the chances were enormously in favour of his winning the match. J. H. Taylor stood looking, motionless and intent, as the referee, and my mind instantly went back to another *News of the World* final, thirty-two years before. J. H. was playing Robson, and on that thirty-fifth green he had a putt, by no means so short, but not very long, to win the match. He took off his cap and mopped his brow, and—he missed it! The green then was different from that of to-day, but I could see the whole scene with extraordinary clearness. Taylor's putt did not matter, for he duly won the match at the last hole, but I fancy Padgham's did matter to the extent of £200.

What a number of great matches this final of the *News of the World* has produced. That one in 1908 was, I think, the first I ever saw, certainly the first I ever reported, and there has scarce been a better. Braid and Ray in 1911 was another most memorable one with Braid six up and nine to play on his own Walton Heath and pulled back and back till he only won on the last green. Then, after a big gap, Sandy Herd *v.* Bloxham in 1926, also at Mid-Surrey, was tremendous, because everybody wanted Herd to accomplish the marvel of winning at the age of fifty-eight. He did win at the thirty-eighth hole, and

BURTON AT THE CORNER OF THE DYKE

Fox Photos Ltd.

COTTON WITH J.H. WATCHING HIM

WHAT A MATCH! 5

such a storm of rain came on at that hole that all those who had gone out to watch it were drenched to the skin by the time they had reached the club-house and the lazy ones had the laugh of us.

Charles Whitcombe and Cotton at Stoke, two years later, I remember vividly from the incredible number of threes that were done on a course so fast that the two-shot holes were reduced to the proverbial "kick and a spit." And then there were Rees and Ernest Whitcombe four years ago, when Rees spurted his way brilliantly home at Oxhey after appearing completely out of the hunt. Those are only a few out of many, but I am inclined to think that not one of them quite equalled this last great battle between Cotton and Padgham, which Cotton won at the thirty-seventh hole.

It had every possible ingredient that goes to make a superlative golfing dish. It was, first of all, essentially a battle. Once upon a time my old friend John Low reprimanded me for writing of some match as a "fight"; he said it was an inappropriate word to use of a friendly game. I bowed to his reproach, but retained, I am afraid, my own views, and if ever there was a real fight this was one. The feeling in the air before it began, the very look of the course, the universal sensation of tenseness and excitement, all made the word "game" altogether too mild. Again, after the first day everybody had been hoping and prophesying that these two would come through to the final, and it is always agreeable when "wishful thinking" is for once justified. There was this additional spice of excitement; everybody felt that if anybody could beat Cotton, Padgham was the man. Cotton had been playing quite superlative golf. In easy conditions, such as do not emphasise small differences of class, he had been annihilating a series of very good golfers one after the other by big margins; so big that one had to go back to the unbeatable days of Harry Vardon at the end of the last century to recall anything quite like it. He was playing so brilliantly that the general impression was that he would in thirty-six holes beat anybody quite comfortably—anybody but Padgham. For that one opponent he would feel the very greatest respect, since in various matches during the last few

B

6 GOLFING BY-PATHS

years Padgham had been a thorn in his side. Here would be no question of going right away from his man with strings of threes; this would be a dog-fight on a glorious scale. Such were, I fancy, the thoughts in most people's minds, and what a noble dog-fight it was! The scores for the two rounds—and these were genuine and not, as often, "approximated" out of all semblance to reality—were exactly equal for the thirty-six holes: Cotton 71 and 72, Padgham 72 and 71. No hole was ever won by more than a single stroke, but I can only recall off-hand one hole where either player was in the happy position of having two for it. Cotton was once or twice two up, Padgham never more than one up.

Considering the obvious tension, I thought the golf very, very good indeed. Those people who do not know much about golf and are surfeited with sixty-sevens done in four-ball matches called the putting appallingly bad. That to my mind was nonsense. True, both parties missed some very short ones, more and shorter than they ought to have missed. On the other hand, Padgham, once he got the rhythm of his putter going, putted magnificently in the second round, and a great deal of Cotton's putting was very good all day; he is an incomparably better putter than in the old days when he used to get, as it were, "locked," and is very, very straight on the hole, so that I thought him unlucky not to hole more than he actually did.

There were too many short ones missed, but we must not forget the excellent ones that were holed. Of these short putts, the one that will be best remembered was that with which I began, Padgham's at the thirty-fifth hole. He had never held the lead after the eighth hole; he had been hanging on for dear life, and now at long last he had only a putt of three feet to hole in order to be almost sure of victory. That is the sort of putt that cannot be forgotten. Nevertheless, I think that in one sense a more important putt was Cotton's on the fifteenth green in the morning; and it was a very short one, not more, I honestly believe, than two feet at most. Having been one down and nearly two down, he had brought the match round till he was two up, and he had this tiny putt to be three up.

Three up is a very different lead from two up; it brings confidence and just the right, precious measure of relaxation. If Cotton had once been three up, a little less grim and more relaxed, I do not believe—though of course these "ifs" are futile—that Padgham could ever have caught him, and he might even have gone right away. As it was, he missed it and the tension was as great as ever. At the second hole in the afternoon he had another putt, not very long and eminently holeable, to be three up, and he did not hole it; that three up never materialised. It was Padgham who seemed to be doing most of the hanging on, in the way of recoveries and fine putts; but at least two most gallant efforts of Cotton's in this direction must not be forgotten. At the fourteenth in the second round, with the match square, Padgham holed in the odd from ten yards, and Cotton, eight yards away, holed in the like for the half. Again at the next hole, with Padgham on the green in two, Cotton was a good way short and laid a long run-up practically dead, having to skirt the very edge of a bunker to do it. Those were two fine bits of fighting, and so was his chip laid a yard from the hole at the thirty-seventh, a chip over a bunker, with very little room "to come and go on," struck with beautiful touch and delicacy. This was so great a match that it was a thousand pities that it could not be halved, but, as somebody had to win, no one can possibly say that the wrong man won it, for Cotton was the outstanding player of the tournament.

THE FOURSOME

BEFORE the *News of the World* there came, also at Mid-Surrey, the foursome between youth and age, Cotton and Compston with a gutty against Braid and Taylor with a rubber-core. What a joy to see a foursome again! That was my first and chief reaction. I had been starved for foursomes ever since the war began, and fell on this one with ravenous

8   GOLFING BY-PATHS

appetite. It was such an unspeakable comfort to see, if one wanted to, every stroke, to know exactly what was happening, and not to be in that state of weary confusion of mind produced by a four-ball match. There seems to me, too, something about a foursome which shows off every man at his best and most characteristic. Mr. Chesterton once wrote of certain unforgettable nights on which "all the numerous personalities unfolded themselves like great tropical flowers. . . . Every man was more himself than he had ever been. . . . Every man was a beautiful caricature of himself." So it seemed to me at Mid-Surrey. Never had Braid's calm been more stately, detached and Olympian. Never had Taylor looked more passionately in earnest than when he studied the line of his partner's putt with intensest gaze before directing him. Never had Cotton appeared more austere, nor Compston more of the buoyant showman. It was an admirable entertainment, and those who left in the middle to watch the rugby match across the way (I was at the moment almost inclined to envy them) missed a finish that was stuffed to bursting with the dramatic virtues.

It is dangerous to trust one's recollection of what happened at least thirty-eight years ago, but I am inclined to think that I never saw better golf played with a gutty than the first nine holes in this match as played by Cotton and Compston. There is, of course, the question of the precise nature of this new "gutty" in inverted commas and how much superior it is to its predecessors in point of resiliency. At any rate, leaving that on one side, those two did play magnificent golf. From the moment that Compston hit his tee shot hole high at the first hole—and 220 yards is "some" drive with a gutty—they swept majestically and faultlessly along, with just one slip at the seventh hole, and their 35 out, with no long putts to help it, would have been very, very good if they had been playing with a rubber-core. Braid and Taylor, with their rubber-core, played very far from badly, and yet they were struggling all the way, and three down at the turn. "There is no standing this"; so said Hazlitt to himself as Neate fell "a mighty ruin" at the end of the first round of his fight with the Gas-man. I confess that I said much the same to myself at this point; and when the Old Gentlemen

THE FOURSOME 9

were still three down with five to play, and some of those five long, flogging holes, I had very faint hope for them. Possibly their adversaries did not remember quite so sternly as they might have done General Briggs's famous remark: "When I am five up I strive to be six up." In any case there is nearly always a tide in the affairs of golfers, and with the long fifteenth hole it turned; Cotton and Compston got mixed up with a tree and lost the hole to a five. That did not seem to matter very much when Compston played a great pitch at the next hole, giving Cotton a holeable putt for four; but the putt was not holed nor the door was locked, and after that everything went one way. I thought that Taylor's putt to win on the last green was one of four feet. He, who could, of course, see far better, was in his account of the match less merciful to himself, for he called it a yard. Whichever it was, I felt pretty sure—and so did all who knew him—that he would hole it, for he has always been most alarming when he has been getting holes back and almost tigerishly unlikely to let off the rash opponent who has let him off. However, he missed it, and perhaps, taking a long view, it was a good thing, for this was no championship, and what better, friendlier end could there be than a half, the same ending as in the similar match at Sandy Lodge?

Have I anything particular to say after this second match that I did not say after the first? Well, I was more than ever impressed by the pitching qualities of the gutty. At Sandy Lodge it was Havers who laid the pitches dead: at Mid-Surrey it was Compston, and when I say dead I mean dead, for the putt had to be given. In both cases it was beautiful pitching, and it looked extraordinarily bold, because we have got used to seeing the rubber-core run a little save only on very soft greens, no matter with how much back spin it is struck. This gutty, however, could be hit right up to the hole and made to fall there lifeless, although the greens were not at all slow and the rubber-core was always inclined to run on. Those time-honoured phrases as to making the ball pitch "like a poached egg" and "cutting the legs from under it" are more literally applicable to the gutty than to its supplanter. Occasionally Cotton and Compston did not seem to appreciate this quite fully enough, for once or twice they were very short with their pitches, notably at the seventeenth hole, where they ought certainly to have become dormy, if Compston had not pitched lamentably short at the foot of the slope. Sometimes one thought that they would have done better to play a more "old-fashioned" shot, lower and with a little run, rather than toss the ball so high in the air; but to say that is perhaps to be hypercritical. As to the matter of length, all that can be said has by now been said. There was really nothing in it, or if there was it was in the gutty men's favour. In this regard the handicap was wonderfully exact, so that it became a straightforward battle, and "honours easy" is the obvious verdict.

THE GOLFER'S LUNCH

I HAVE just finished a dinner so modest, I will not say austere, that even the sternest Minister of Food must needs approve of it. It is therefore, I suppose due to the law of contraries that I am reminded of a letter I received from a friend the other day. He wanted me to write an unashamedly greedy article about lunches at golf clubs in happier days. It is a nostalgic subject and an invidious one, too, for there are so many clubs that have good lunches and I must needs pick out but a few. Still, I will essay it.

Of some of these meals I have a memory which is sentimental rather than gastronomic. Cold beef is, for instance, an excellent thing but not an uncommon one. Yet its name instantly suggests to me only one place, a low dark parlour in the old Crown Inn at Royston, now swept away in the widening of the street. We used to lunch there in prehistoric ages when there was no club-house and only a tin hut for the professional's shop. It was very good cold beef, but when I have said that I have said all; yet it can never be forgotten. Neither for that matter can

THE GOLFER'S LUNCH

some other cold meat that was not good at all, for we called it irreverently "biltong." It was provided in the Aberdovey club-house by dear old Mrs. Evans, on whom be peace, and possibly the memory of it is made radiant by the thought of the Benedictine that always followed it.

And now to more classic ground. Muse teach me to sing of hot collops at Sandwich which I first encountered, *consule* Mr. James, just about this time seven and forty years ago, at my first University match in 1895. I cannot assert that there are no other collops as good, but I am sure that nowhere are there any better. They surely belong to that noble corner of Kent, because, unless I am mistaken, I have also eaten them at Deal. Indeed, in peaceful days I should now be looking forward to eating them at the Halford Hewitt Cup, in that wonderful lunch that begins about 11 a.m. for those who started in the grim dawn and goes on till 4 p.m. for those who began their round a little after noon.

Passing along the coast from Kent into Sussex, we come to a lunch at Rye, which is held in grateful remembrance by all who have eaten it and, since the room is small, have got a chair to sit upon while they did so. It has of late years become rather more varied, orthodox and gorgeous than of old, but its original character remains. The prudent golfer still comes straight into the main room of the club-house even before he has washed and says "Buttered eggs, please, Helen," adding sometimes a demand for sausage. Then by the time he has tidied himself there are the buttered eggs ready smoking on his table; unless, indeed, somebody else has stolen them, for morals in this matter are low. It is a meal with a pleasant suggestion of "high tea," or of a Saturday tea at school after football when Sunday was coming and no unpleasant thoughts of work need obtrude themselves. Something of the same quality of magic belongs to the mixed grill, the sausage, the egg and the piece of bacon at Worlington over which I am conscious of having become lyrical before.

There are certain dishes which are to be met with at many clubs, but seem to belong as of right to a few. To which club, for instance, shall I ascribe fried sole? It seems to me that

there must be two of them in a bracket, Mid-Surrey and Addington. At both it is of a singularly scrumptious quality, and
beyond that I will not go. Fried sole seems by some curious
association of ideas to suggest treacle tart, and here again there
are many competitors, among which I choose Walton Heath.
Rice pudding seems to belong to Mid-Surrey, and in the mind's
eye I see my old friend, Mr. Sidney Fry, devouring it with
cream and strawberry jam—a beatific and now unrealisable
vision. And while I am still near London, I must not forget
Swinley Forest where the lunch awaits us laid out by unseen
hands and we help ourselves in a delightfully cosy and casual
manner.

If I turn my eyes northward I must needs think of potted
shrimps at St. Annes, at Formby and at Hoylake. I put them in
that particular order because it is thus that I have eaten them on
many cheerful tours of the Society in those hospitable regions.
And the blue Cheshire cheese at Hoylake—I must not forget
that, nor a Lancashire cheese which I met at Birkdale, devoting
myself to it so regularly that a kind member of the club was
touched by my devotion and sent me one all to myself. As to
shrimps, by the way, I must put in a good word for those at
St. Andrews and the lunch in that pleasant room in the club-
house looking right up and down the first and last holes. So
many people go back to their hotels for lunch that they are not
fully acquainted with the quality of that at the club; I venture,
after considerable experience, to say that it is second to none.
St. Andrews makes me think of Muirfield and Prestwick, and
of delightful tours in the East and West of Scotland. No
special dish comes to my mind, only a general sense of agreeable
repletion. My friend who suggested this gross topic declared
that at Muirfield he had been allowed to help himself to Kümmel.
It had naturally made a great impression on him. I cannot
honestly say that I remember that, but I do remember having
been helped very generously to it by a number of kind hosts
and especially by my opponents in the forthcoming afternoon
foursome. The Devonshire cream of Westward Ho! the
Cornish pasties of St. Enodoc, the Benedictine of Portmarnock,
the lobster of Littlehampton—they come flocking back to my

HISTORY REPEATS ITSELF 13

mind and I must call a halt, lest I begin to feel that I have made a single and comprehensive feast on them all at once. I am not really so greedy as I may appear, only grateful to many people for many kindnesses and much hospitality. These lunches may be among the things that can never happen again; I rather think they will have to be. If so, they will be pleasant to remember as are many other golfing things which never can happen again. Doubtless we shall bear up and doubtless, also, we shall play our second rounds all the better. There was an old friend of mine who used to exclaim in moments of ecstasy, "It is impossible to exaggerate the pleasures of the table"; but then he never tried to play even one round. I began this catalogue with cold beef and I shall be perfectly happy to end with it.

HISTORY REPEATS ITSELF

I HAVE received a welcome present in the form of a little book on golf, now probably rather rare, which I doubt if I have ever seen before. It is called *Golf and Golfers Past and Present* by the Rev. J. G. McPherson, and was published in 1891. It consists of various papers reprinted from *The National Observer* (previously *The Scots Observer*) under Henley's editorship, and also from *Golf* and other magazines. Dr. McPherson was a highly distinguished amateur golfer at St. Andrews in and before the days of Young Tommy Morris, and I remember well reading some of his articles in *Golf* when I was a boy. I also remember that in those days they aroused in me a faint feeling of irritation, partly because the old gentleman seemed rather pleased with himself and partly because he was so obviously a praiser of past golf at the expense of the present. Now, however, that I have grown less critical with the years and am perhaps rather in the *laudator temporis acti* line of business myself, I have read the Doctor with interest and pleasure.

A good deal of what he says has been said pretty often by this time. The extreme narrowness of St. Andrews when the whins were abundant and the comparative wideness and easiness of the course since they have been hacked away, the difficulty of the old rough putting greens compared with the smooth and perfect ones of more modern times—these things have been dinned into our ears and I will not repeat them. Incidentally, I am modern enough to doubt whether bad greens made golf more interesting, though they doubtless made it more difficult. "There was then," says Dr. McPherson, "a variety of surface which brought out the greater skill. . . . Then, at the Heather hole one had to dodge about and watch the lie of the green, carefully noting any hollow to catch or 'soo-back' to avoid in the gentle stroke; thereby, as old Robbie Paterson used to say, 'wilin' the wether into the hoose.'" That seems to me, if I may irreverently say so, rather like saying that billiards is a more skilful game in a village recreation room than on a championship table. However that may be, it does show, as Dr. McPherson is never weary of pointing out, that Allan Robertson's 79 was a score which it is almost impossible for the player of to-day to appreciate at its proper worth.

One interesting point, as it strikes me in reading this book, is how greatly golfing language has changed. I am ashamed to say that I do not know what a 'soo-back' was, and there are many more instances that could be given. Here, for instance, is the author's description of his own style. "His clubs were upright in a marked degree. There was no spring in the handle of the driver, until within a short distance of the head. The club held very firmly in the left hand, and very easily in the right, was drawn up slowly in an almost vertical plane, until he could distinctly see the head with his left eye; then with gradually increasing velocity, he gave a sharp whiplike stroke with strong pressure of the wrist. This vertical style in his case reduced to a minimum the chances of the ball's deviation to right or left after the stroke. Perhaps no one came near him for continued long 'carries' and 'rocket' strokes." That is rather a mysterious passage. I judge that the Doctor, who was, as is known from other sources, a very fine driver, had an upright swing, which must have been in particularly marked contrast with the sweeping "St. Andrew's swing" of those

HISTORY REPEATS ITSELF

days, but the "whip-like stroke" is a little cryptic, and what was a rocket? I can only guess that it was a stroke that made the ball get up very quickly. And here is another description of one of the Condies which has puzzled me. "His cleek-driving was brilliant; but he adopted the exceptional style of pressing the handle with the upper right arm, without a clear swing." Here I get a picture of a man swinging his club very low and flat so that the shaft of the club hit his arm just below the shoulder at the top of the swing; but my interpretation may be quite wrong. The Doctor seems to me rather obscure, but style is a hard thing to describe and perhaps I could do no better myself.

How history repeats itself! We who are now as old as the Doctor was when he wrote his book make a bitter outcry at the number of clubs with which people think it necessary to play and we are convinced we are right. Dr. McPherson was likewise convinced that golfers used an absurdly large number of clubs fifty years ago. He came from his quiet manse, where there was no golf, to watch a professional tournament at North Berwick, and was inexpressibly shocked at what he saw. He called upon the shade of Allan to witness that golf had gone to the devil. "It was lamentable," he says, "to see the reckless change in the weapons. Each caddy groaned under the weight of seven irons of different shapes, with two or three clubs, whereas old Tom Morris was playing fully better with his two irons." In this sentence "clubs" of course means wooden clubs. Many a caddy of to-day would deem himself very well off indeed if he only "groaned under" nine or ten clubs in all. "Driver, middle-spoon, iron, cleek and putter were all the clubs that the players of old were accustomed to use in their general play; but more than double that number are used now." It was all dreadful, and perhaps most dreadful of all was the fact that most of the competitors had abandoned the wooden putter. Sayers in particular horrified the old gentleman. "On another green Sayers, with semi-circular back, was stretched down and grasping a cleek about a foot-length from the head. . . . We have only to look back to the glorious approaches on the putting green by Willie Park senior and Mr. Gilbert Mitchell Innes, with the wooden putter, to see in contrast the uncertain nips of the lofter or cleek in the modern style of the game."

Poor old gentleman! I become very sorry for him and wish he had never gone to North Berwick for that jaunt to which he had looked forward so eagerly. And here was something worse, if possible, than the discarding of the putter. There was the use by Archie Simpson of "the ugly club called the bulger." The head was so small that the Doctor averred that he would be "afraid of missing with it." Even more degraded was the employment of a horrible thing called a "patent lofter." Here, again, Sayers was the criminal, but he was, according to the Doctor, properly punished. If he had been Allan, or if he had been Tom, he would have played his approach to the Gate hole with his cleek, to pitch and run, but no, he would pitch high in the air and his ball stopped on the face: "for the sake of exhibiting to the spectators the virtues of his patent, he lost the hole and the match." When I read these words I remembered how I had stood watching at the Field hole at Hoylake with Mr. John Ball. A young gentleman had a short approach to play over perfectly flat ground—a clear case as it appeared for a running shot—and he took a mashie-niblick and hit the ball exactly halfway to the hole. Mr. Ball exhibited a malevolent satisfaction almost equal to the Doctor's over the failure of the patent lofter. So it will ever be, and I do not doubt that those who are young now will some day be holding up their hands in horror at the clubs and strokes of their successors and declaring that they "are not golf."

MR. WINKLE

A DELIGHTFUL thing befell me the other day when I was walking in a Gloucestershire lane, and the least I can do is to share it. I came across a young and pretty mamma and her small son, both on bicycles. "Come along, Mr. Winkle," the mother called to the son, who was making rather heavy weather of a slope. "Let's see what Mr. Winkle can do on a bicycle." Then, as they passed on she said, "I'm sure Mr. Pickwick would not have bicycled in those black gaiters of his. He would have thought it undignified."

This was a charming conversation to overhear: here was one small boy, at any rate, being properly brought up. And yet I was a little uneasy because I felt that he was being taught to misunderstand a great and good man's character. I nearly addressed his mamma in some such words as these: "Madam, I congratulate you on a well-educated son, but you must allow me to add that in one respect you are wrong. Mr. Pickwick *would* have bicycled. Don't you remember that the ladies asked him to slide and he answered: 'I should be very happy to afford you any amusement.' No, madam, Mr. Pickwick had no such false notions of dignity and his black gaiters would have gone whirling pleasantly round with the pedals." However, I lacked courage, thinking that I might be deemed impertinent, and the chance was lost for ever.

As the couple disappeared in the distance I reflected how, if *Pickwick* had been written fifty years later, Mr. Winkle would almost certainly have essayed golf, how he might have hit Mr. Tupman a severe blow on some soft portion of his anatomy or broken a window at Manor Farm and frightened the old lady into palpitations of the heart. I likewise reflected how vulgar and tedious such a joke appears if thus badly set down and how it would need the magic of a Dickens to make it entrancing. "The idea of Winkle, the clumsy sportsman," wrote Chesterton, "is in itself quite stale; it is, as he goes on repeating himself, that he becomes original." I suppose it is because we despair of making them original that we have ceased to make the old simple jokes about hitting a fat old gentleman behind or missing the globe or breaking our clubs.

The decadence of the Winkle joke, if I may so term it, does not apply only to golf. I have just been looking at an old scrap book of a hundred years or so ago, one of those books that our ancestors put together with paste and loving care. It is what Jim Pinkerton would have called a "Monster Olio of attractions," a mixture of romantic waterfalls, darkling forests, a fire at the Tower of London, the Allied Sovereigns at breakfast, Abraham and the three angels and Mrs. Bloomer in full costume. There are also a few sporting pictures, and these are one and all comic. The fishermen catch nothing unless it be some foreign body; the horsemen invariably fall off; the shooter kills only a small pig; the one cricketing picture shows a very stout gentleman beginning to run while another gentleman puts down the wicket with the words "Out! So don't fatigue yourself, I beg, sir." Can it be doubted that at a later date that stout gentleman would have been depicted whirling round like a teetotum, having missed the globe?

I remember that the first time I ever met a certain charming lady of my acquaintance she asked me, "Do you often make air shots?" and I felt ashamed of having to answer that I did so but rarely. In fact, considering how small is the ball and how comparatively small the club head, it is surprising that they meet so regularly. I quoted earlier the remark of the Rev. J. G. McPherson when he first saw the squat head of the bulger, namely, that those of the old school would have been afraid of missing with it, and to one accustomed to the long head it was a very natural thought. Are there many famous air shots in history? I can hardly think of any. There was, to be sure, the sad affair of the two Dunns in their often-quoted match against Allan and Tom. Having been four up with eight to play they were all square with two to play and pulled their second under a big boulder. They attacked it with more valour than discretion, for we are told that the iron kept glancing off the stone. That, I suppose, comes under the heading of missing the globe, though it is hardly a perfect example. Then Vardon, I believe, may be said to have missed the globe when he won the American Open Championship at Wheaton in 1900. He attempted a very short putt one-handed and the club head hit the ground and never reached the ball. There is also the story, recorded in the books of reference, of a highly distinguished person though a less distinguished golfer, namely a local mayor, who being invited to open a course with a putt on the home green failed, in the modern jargon, to "contact" the ball.

Apart from the efforts of genuine beginners, I can only

MR. WINKLE

remember in the course of many years to have once seen a complete missing of the globe. It was in a four-ball match at St. Andrews and one of my opponents, quite a good player with a low handicap, had hit a fine tee shot to the fourteenth hole, right down the Elysian fields. The ball lay perfectly, as it should in a place so divinely named; he swung vigorously at it with his brassey and the club-head passed six inches full measure over it. Nobody even sniggered; he addressed the ball again, hit an excellent shot and in the end, I remember, just "snodded us at the burn" by a brilliant four at the seventeenth. I had a delicacy in asking why or how he had committed that sudden eccentricity of genius, and I know no more than perhaps he did himself. It was a real bolt from the blue, one of the most utterly unexpected shots I ever saw.

I can recall another astonishing miss, but I did not see it with my own eyes. It was played a few years since at Deal, in the Halford Hewitt Cup, by a member of my own school team, an eminent golfer and an international. He, too, had a brassey shot to play—at the fifth hole, I think—from a slightly uphill lie, and, by some strange aberration, hit the ground so far behind the ball that the club head bounded over without touching it. He was known by the caddies during the rest of the meeting as "the blighter that hit the air shot," and I doubt if he will ever wholly lose that reputation. And, by the way, what is the precise significance of the phrase "missing the globe," as originally used? Does it mean missing this terrestrial sphere and so striking only the empty air, or was it coined in the mint of some forgotten writer who was a lover of synonyms? Was globe only another word for ball? I remember one brother journalist who, thinking presumably that he had used the word "ball" often enough in one sentence, referred to it as "the article." So perhaps "missing the globe" corresponds to the dear old phrase, "planting the leather between the uprights."

Well, little Mr. Winkle has gone pedalling off into the blue, having inspired these random thoughts, and I am afraid I shall never know his real name. I hope he will continue to be called Mr. Winkle and that he will take to golf and become in time a celebrated player. Surely, the shade of his great original would be pleased, where he walks in his green shooting coat and plaid neckerchief upon the asphodel, to know that his reputation had been redeemed and that his name had become famous all over the world as that of a champion among champions.

A PILGRIMAGE

I HAVE a liking, which I suspect is the sign of feeble-mindedness and sentimentality, for going on pilgrim-ages. It gives me an undeniable thrill to stand on some historic spot and try to conjure up the vanished scene. As I have frequently mentioned before, I say to myself whenever I walk across the cricket ground to the first hole at Royston, "Here the Young Rump Steak punched the head of the Black Diamond." A little while ago Tom Brown's centenary cricket match was played at Rugby, and I wished very much that I could have gone there, as I was kindly asked to do. I do not know many things, but I do know my *Tom Brown's Schooldays*. I would play any Rugbeian at it, and I dearly wanted to see the sacred places where Tom fought Slogger Williams and Old Brooke kicked his goal in the School-house match.

In default of this I went on another pilgrimage to a shrine less well known which I had always wanted to see, not far from where I am now taking refuge. By the kind leave of those living there a friend took me to see the course in Stowell Park where once the young Scotts, who are now rather old Scotts, being in fact my contemporaries, used to play their golf. Here (so I must be imagined murmuring in a reverential manner) the young Osmund was for ever imitating somebody else's swing. Here the slightly younger Denys holed a putt, though not holding his hands, as he does nowadays, upside down; here the infant Michael practised for hours with grim and persistent determination to be subsequently rewarded by many victories;

THE 5TH GREEN AT MID-SURREY
Taylor and Braid v. Cotton and Compston

Sport & General.

FATHER AND SON
Old Tom Morris and Tommy

A PILGRIMAGE

nor did I forget, though alas! I never saw her swing a club, that here, too, played Lady Margaret, who won the first three ladies' championships and then retired with no more worlds to conquer.

It was a heavenly June day, and the park was at its greenest and prettiest, full of sheep and buttercups, beautiful trees (there is a row of noble beeches along the Fosse Way) and grey Cotswold stone walls. Alike in point of summer loveliness and romantic excitement our expedition was an unqualified success, but regarded purely as a golfing pilgrimage it was perhaps just the least bit in the world disappointing. The course is, for the moment, decidedly out of commission; the greens are there, guarded by wire fences, but the only holes on them are made by the rabbits, and the tees appeared monuments of a vanished civilization. We felt a little like explorers in some Nineveh or Herculaneum, wondering which tee led to which green and whether perchance we were walking the holes the wrong way round. We found an old flag with a number on it which gave us a clue, and this we followed up with tolerable success.

One hole in particular gave us a genuine thrill. It was, as we judged it, a long one-shotter across a deep narrow valley and a stone wall to a green carved out of the opposite hillside, such as is sometimes irreverently called a gun-platform. A strong young gentleman would to-day get home with an iron, but as a pilgrim I had to imagine the hole played with a gutty ball, a wooden club and an honest full shot. There was another green which reminded me a little of the Cardinal green at Prestwick as it used to be when the famous wall still stood at the back of it. I imagined one of my youthful heroes trying to take skilful advantage of this back wall and making a slight miscalculation so that the ball bounded clean over the wall and sped far down the hill beyond it, to the unsmotherable delight of his brothers. They must have had wonderfully good fun there, forever dashing out for yet one more nine holes, and I am very glad to have seen in reality the place I had so often pictured to myself. A course that has produced two champions is worth a pilgrimage.

Anybody who has a taste for this form of exploration can

gratify it on almost any course that he visits. Some of the most famous possess ancient greens long since obscured by the hand of Nature, the existence of which is utterly unsuspected by the modern player. I remember, for instance, to have played this sentimental game at Hoylake when, on one of the most blazing of summer days, dear old Jack Morris walked me out to see where had once been the Meols green. He found the spot after some little hesitation, and I have often looked at it since, deep in bents and rough grass, when I have skirted the Telegraph hole and taken a short cut from the Cop to the Briars. For that matter the old Alps and the old Rushes greens, the old Hilbre and the old Far, which seem to me to belong only to yesterday, have now for some years been reverting to a savage state, and many people must have played round Hoylake wholly oblivious of their existence. There is Sandwich, too, where those greens in deep hollows in which men once delighted have given way to plateaux. In particular the old seventeenth is now as Tadmor in the wilderness. It is so overgrown that when I was last there I was hard put to it to identify the place, though it is but a few yards from the eighteenth tee. It had little to recommend it, but there was a certain horrid fun in running up the bank to see what had happened on the farther side. There used always to be one ball lying nearly dead and it was never one's own, although one had played by far the better second of the two; so at least it seems in memory, but one has a way of forgetting one's own flukes.

There is no course on which I feel more utterly confused than Muirfield when I try to find the places where the old holes used to be. I have only to shut my eyes and I can see every one of them clearly and precisely; I can remember exactly the spot from which I played particular shots to some of them more than thirty years ago. Yet when I open my eyes I am hopelessly lost. I do know, or I believe I do, that the seventeenth green was once the old twelfth, guarded by that black-boarded bunker, but where on earth was the thirteenth, with its narrow, frightening tee shot and the little sloping green round the corner? It is now as if it had never been. At Muirfield it is not the jungle-tide of rough that has crept in and obliterated everything; it is rather the removal of a landmark that is so puzzling. The wall on one side of the course has gone, and without that wall, which is part of the picture in my mind, I have lost my old bearings once and for all. Wherever they are, there is something rather sad about these ghosts of old holes, but it is a pleasant, maudlin little sadness that I admit to enjoying.

DRIFT AND DRAW

SOME little while ago I went to see an old friend, a very great golfer, who has for some time past, sad to say, been a sick man and so has seen but little golf for several years. We talked, not about the war, but about golf, and I tried, not very lucidly I fear, to describe to him several of the new good players whom he had not seen. At one point he asked: "What do you think of Padgham?" I said the rather obvious things to the effect that he was very good. To this he answered: "I picked him out when I saw him because he could play them this way," and he made a movement to indicate the ball turning a little from left to right.

This naturally interested me, and in reflecting on it afterwards I came to the conclusion that this power—let us call it power of "drifting" the ball to the right—is one that always evokes the praise of the really good golfer and one for which he looks in appraising another. I remember to have heard Mr. Maxwell say that if he wanted to judge a player he should like to see him play a series of long iron shots up to a green in a strong right-hand wind. This is much to the same effect. I remember, too, and that very vividly, watching Cotton playing his last round in the first championship that he won at Sandwich. After two incredibly brilliant rounds and one extremely good one, he was, to the general anxiety finishing with rather a bad one. One of the mistakes that he was making was that of constantly letting

24 GOLFING BY-PATHS

the ball fade away to the left and not holding it up into the right-hand wind, and it was this in particular that roused the almost frantic feelings of my respected friend J. H. Taylor, who was, if possible, in a greater state of tension than any of us.

There at any rate are three examples, and I could think of more. The ordinary run of mankind is frightened of a ball that turns to the right; that which he envies in his betters is the power of holding the ball into the wind from the left, and his most beatific dream is of being a natural hooker. The really first-class player is apt to take this power for granted and to reserve his observant praise for that rarer being who possesses the converse gift. That there should be this difference is natural enough. To be able to play with a hook is to ordinary mortals a rare and valuable acquirement, and it is small wonder that he sighs for it. It helps him to get the length for which he yearns, and to some extent it renders inconsiderable all the perils that lie on the right hand side of the fairway.

At one period of my life I had a severe spell of slicing. It was with a gutty ball, which made that disease more deadly and uncontrollable, and in those days the man I envied was he who might occasionally hook to glory and the grave but, from the way of hitting that was natural to him, feared no out-of-bounds on the right. I have not—touching wood—been a slicer for a long time now, but I have never got over the horror of it. I still think that up to a certain rung on the golfing ladder this natural hook is, day in and day out, one of great value, but it has its dangers. It may gain so complete a control of the player that he cannot play a shot in any other way; he must always make allowance for his hook; he cannot make the ball stop on the green when the wind is blowing hard from the right; in short, there is one most vulnerable joint in his armour, and it is one that can sometimes be detected among those capable of really brilliant things in conditions that suit them.

Without unduly praising the past at the expense of the present it is permissible to say that there were among golfers of an older generation some who were very, very skilful in this left-to-right shot. Mr. Hilton was a master of it, though he gradually adopted the draw, from right to left, as the foundation of his driving. Yet, as is well known, he once won an amateur championship at Prestwick by going back to his older method at the last moment. That was when the ground was burnt hard as a brick and when a little length more or less did not matter, but what did matter was to keep on the course.

Herd is another who occurs to me, and then there was Harry Vardon, who seemed to be able to do it with no faintest effort. His rather upright swing was, I suppose, naturally adapted to the stroke, and his ball would fly high and straight through a right-hand wind and then fall spent and lifeless, as if it had no other possible course open to it. The same may be said of Duncan, who consciously modelled himself on Vardon and had the same shot in much the same perfection. I am very far from saying that there are not those who can do it just as well to-day. I go no further than to suggest that too much hitting "from inside out" makes the stroke harder to attain.

As I said before, most of us ordinary players are so mortally afraid of unintentional slicing that we are not fond of experimenting in the direction of the deliberately played drift. We feel that we must not let the dormant demon within us have his way to however small an extent, lest, being given an inch, he take an ell. Yet if we try for the shot and bring it off there is nothing that can give keener pleasure. Moreover, there is plenty of that length, which we so much desire, to be gained by letting a left-hand wind have its will, under due control. It is not only the hooker that can get distance. I have intensely enjoyed seeing Mr. Rex Hartley starting the ball out far to the left, so that it comes round and round and back and back to end miles distant down the middle of the course. Mr. Edward Blackwell, too, could use a left-hand wind to a prodigious extent. He could, of course, drive prodigiously in any circumstances, but this always struck me as his supremely natural shot.

Most of us have not quite the courage to try to the extent of our much more limited powers, and part of the reason is, I believe, that we have got it too firmly into our heads that a slice is naturally weak, vicious and contemptible, while a hook is at worst a manly virtue. If we had once been brought up to use the more subtle terms "draw" and "drift" we might have better balanced views. There is a good deal in a name. A "founder" or a "smother" does not sound quite so bad as a "top," but the result is apt to be indistinguishable if we have got a big bunker straight in front of us. A "run up" sounds elegant and accomplished, a "scuffle" fluky and pusillanimous, but it gets there all the same. So let us try to use "drift" and "fade," which are pretty words, suggesting that we do it on purpose, and eschew the hideous "slice" which only suggests, the nethermost hell.

OUT AT ELBOWS

"ELBOWS, Fanny!" Many people must often have wondered why Fanny. "I don't know why Silas and I don't know why Wegg," remarked the owner of that famous name, and I don't know why Fanny was the name given to the little girl or boy, for sex was immaterial, who put elbows on the table at meal times. At any rate it was, and if this infantile solecism was too frequently repeated or if nurse or parent were snappish the offending elbows were cracked on the table by way of rubbing it in. Elbows are in fact ugly, untidy things, which stick out unduly, and golfers who exhibit them to excess are not as a rule graceful (I know at least some of my own faults) and very often ineffective. I have been pondering a little over elbows and it is remarkable how largely they, and especially the right one, have figured in golfing arguments and golfing doctrine.

They have not always been abused. On the contrary the right elbow held almost impossibly high in the air at the top of the swing may be seen in the earliest of illustrated golfing manuals, I think by Mr. Chambers. The golfer in the picture is wearing a bowler hat which scarcely makes him to our modern eyes "the glass of fashion," but it is that right elbow which disqualifies him as "the mould of form." That any good player ever adopted quite so strained and agonised an attitude I can hardly believe. Whether or not the picture was criticised by its contemporaries we cannot now tell, but the real elbow controversy began when Horace Hutchinson wrote the chapter on driving in the "Elementary Instruction" of the Badminton book.

He boldly advocated the elbow well up and away from the body and the illustrations, which were of himself swinging, backed up his advice. He was a good deal, to use his own word, "heckled" about it and modified his views. When, having been originally bred as a sculptor, he made a model of the ideal swinger, he consented to depress the elbow, but later recanted his own recantation and upheld his original opinion to a considerable extent.

By that time another great Westward Ho! golfer had come upon the scene, J. H. Taylor. Everybody saw his right elbow kept as low as it could possibly be and the old theory was held to be once and for all exploded. There are two things to be said about it: I dare say I have said them before. First Horace himself, though his elbow was reasonably high and free from his side, never looked like the Badmintonian parody of his style. Secondly he had been deluded into thinking that he held it so high by the fact that the pictures were drawn not from instantaneous but posed photographs, and anyone who tries to pose at the top of his swing will find that his elbow goes up automatically to support the club.

There is one interesting little point while I am on this subject. We think of Harry Vardon as not only a model of grace in general but specifically with the elbow well down. Yet I have Taylor's word for it that when Vardon first appeared his right elbow went straggling from his side and quite high in the air. It was only later that he remodelled that part of his uniquely rhythmical and lovely swing. Into the whys and wherefores of the whole question I do not propose to go deeply lest I be a bore and be convicted of the atrocious crime of teaching golf into the bargain; but it seems to me that as a rule the high right elbow is a sign of an inadequate turn of the body. When a man pivots freely and fully his elbow goes round and almost of necessity keeps down, as anybody may see by a personal experiment. Finally, I have seen at least one golfer transfigured and improved out of knowledge by learning to conquer that elbow. This was the late George Hannay. I was so much struck by seeing him for the first time in his converted state that I rashly said in print that he had learned not to lift his elbow. I had not in my innocence thought of the *double entendre* but the rude wags of the Stock Exchange did not miss it and confronted him with a picture of himself with his elbow bound to his side and a large whisky and soda just out of reach.

So much for the elbow in driving, and I do not think there is much to be said about it in iron play, but it is otherwise in putting. Again in the Badminton book Horace suggested some crooking of the elbows in describing the "alternative method" of putting which he used so effectively himself. There have been many good putters, who found a help to straightness in some crooking of the left elbow towards the hole, but generally speaking they kept the right one well into their sides. Then there came the sudden flashing of Francis Ouimet into the golfing firmament in 1913. I well remember seeing him for the first time at Garden City in September of that year and being struck at once by the beautiful smoothness of his putting stroke and the originality of his method. He held his putter nearly at the top of the shaft and with his elbows much more crooked and farther away from his body than I had been taught to deem orthodox. It looked awkward at first glance but the result was so good and the clubhead seemed to work so perfectly in a groove that surprise soon gave way to admiration. It was, I fancy, a method that came to him naturally and without study, for he has written somewhere that putting was the one part of the game that he did not practise to any great extent. It remained, as far as I know, peculiar to him until after the war we saw another very fine American golfer, Jesse Guilford. He came also from Massachusetts; he had clearly taken Francis as his model and he putted very nearly if not quite as well. After that it seemed clearly permissible to do what one pleased. To be out at elbows was not necessarily to be in the hole, but at least the two were not incompatible.

What I may call the *furore* for elbows came a little later with the first arrival in this country with the Ryder Cup team of 1929 of that truly remarkable golfer, Leo Diegel. He had, we are told, after many struggles with his putting, retired for several months from the public arena and came back to it with the most extraordinary and deliberately artificial style perhaps ever seen on a putting green. Most of us saw him for the first time at Moortown, where the Ryder Cup match was played, and there we did not know whether to marvel more at his method or its success. He stood with his feet some distance apart; he held his putter at the top of the shaft and his chin appeared almost to be resting upon it; to say that his elbows were crooked betrays the occasional inadequacy of language, for they were contorted to the point of anguish. He kept his wrists entirely stiff and apparently pushed the ball with his shoulders. During the two days of the match he scarcely pushed it anywhere but into the hole. He was palpably full of confidence and radiated happiness. After he and his partner had handsomely won their foursome on the first day I remember seeing him on the practice green outside the Moortown club-house. Some freak of fancy had made him have the shaft of his putter painted a new colour, and there he was holing putt after putt in pure wantonness of joy. He was like a child with a new toy and his inspiration held, for next day he beat Abe Mitchell by 9 and 8, a feat which on *a priori* grounds seemed impossible.

From that moment a wave of "diegeling" spread over the country. Not only those who had seen him putt tried to imitate him, but also hundreds who had only read accounts of him and had to do their best from the written word. The new verb was conjugated everywhere; we were all in a state either of having diegeled or being about to diegel. All new ways of putting, however fanciful, are apt, as we all know, to prosper for a time, and many thought that they had found the secret, only as ever to discover that it was but a will o' the wisp. Nor did Diegel himself, or not at least when I saw him, ever putt so well again as he had at Moortown. He stuck to his method and often with success, but one by one his imitators and their elbows relapsed into their old ways.

30 GOLFING BY-PATHS

Undoubtedly there was something to be said for diegeling. It kept the left wrist firm and many people suffer from constant putting collapses because their left wrists collapse at the moment of striking the ball. On the other hand there is always this to be said against any highly artificial style, that it is apt to fail at a crucial moment. Diegel himself did so fail, and that now and then most noticeably, but then, though a very fine golfer indeed, he was cursed with a highly strung temperament and might have found the supreme crisis too much for him whatever his method. I can recall at least one other eminently successful experiment in point of crooked elbows and that was Henry Cotton's putting when he won his first championship at Sandwich. He looked neither elegant nor comfortable on the greens, in complete contrast to the rest of his game, and all the Solomon Eagles predicted woe, saying that such a style could not last, but it lasted at any rate long enough on that triumphant occasion. How long it endured afterwards I do not know, but I am sure that day in and day out he has been a better and more consistent putter since he abandoned such antics and looked like an ordinary Christian on the green. It was said of Katisha in *The Mikado* that "She has a left elbow which people come miles to see." On the whole it is better to be less conspicuous.

HAROLD HILTON

ONE of the really great figures in golf has passed away with the death of Harold Hilton. He had been hopelessly ill so long and must have suffered so much that one can hardly say that one is sorry he is gone; death to him must have been a true release. But if there can be little sorrow there will always be admiring and affectionate remembrance. It must be a little more than a year ago that I went to see him in the remote Gloucestershire village where he had stayed after leaving Cooden. He was in bed, very ill and helpless, but he was cheerful and courageous; he still smoked one cigarette after another and still liked to talk about golf. We talked in particular of his last round of 75 which brought him in the winner of his second Open Championship at Hoylake in 1897, and I shall always remember the gentle chuckle with which he said: "I began with a three."

There have been greater hitters of a ball than Harold, though very, very few, and they were so simply, I think, because they had greater physical advantages. There have been, in my judgment, none who knew the game as well as he did. Harold knew golf through and through. He was an encyclopædia of names and initials and years, but there are many people who have that sort of memory. He had an exact knowledge of his own game and of how he produced every shot in his large repertory. He had a really astonishing knowledge of other people's golf, not merely of that of the most exciting figures in the game, but of almost everybody with whom he had ever played. He was an instinctive student of method and seemed to have in his head, neatly put away for reference, whole series of pictures of his friends and their various strokes. I very well remember him at a championship at Westward Ho! going out to watch a hole or two played by another famous Hoylake golfer, whom he had not seen for some time, the late Mr. C. E. Dick. After the game he said to him: "Charles, you've lost your iron shot," and proceeded to demonstrate with that most characteristic back-hand gesture of his left hand exactly what he deemed amiss. He was always ready to show anyone, old or young, but in particular the young, how some shot should be played, and this came partly from a natural kindliness of heart, but also from the fact that every golfer's problems were of interest to him.

Harold was, as were the other two members of the great Hoylake trinity, John Ball and Jack Graham, a mighty practiser, and it seems to me entirely appropriate that the first time I ever set eyes upon him he was hard at work playing spoon shots in the "Field" at Hoylake. He was hitting half a dozen balls one after the other and they all seemed to come down within a yard or two of each other and make a little white pattern on the grass. He was amazingly accurate with wooden clubs, more particularly with that spoon of his that served him as a maid-of-all-work. Yet the first sight of him hitting a ball did not convey a notion of accuracy, but rather of a wholehearted flinging himself at the ball. His address to the ball was, to be sure, very careful and precise; he placed his feet and faced his club to the line with great exactness. These preliminaries over he seemed to throw care to the winds, and one had a wild and whirling vision of a little man jumping on his toes and throwing himself and his club after the ball with almost frantic abandon. Yet this was the most deceptive possible appearance, for though he certainly hit for all he was worth, he had a gift of balance such as is given to few. His cap might fall off the back of his head, he might twist his hips and shoulders round in producing the hook which he used so skilfully, but he was always firmly poised, the master of himself and of the ball.

It was his wooden club play that was the most fascinating to watch. For anything in the nature of a long shot he preferred wood to iron, but there was no greater master of the pitching shot, and no one could make the ball bite and stop better than he could. There was an Amateur Championship at Prestwick in 1911, when the ground was keen and hard and sunburnt to a remarkable degree, and he won it because these extraordinary conditions gave scope for his extraordinary skill. He could pitch the ball and stop on to the old "tennis green" court—the sixth—while everyone else went bounding over. He changed almost on the instant from his usual hook to a slight fade and so kept his tee shots on the course, while others hit just too far and ended in the rough. That was by no means the greatest of his wins, and he was then something past his best, but as a victory of acuteness of mind and masterly control it always deserves to be remembered.

Harold was unquestionably at his best as a score player. He won two Open Championships and he very, very nearly won two more. It is rash to talk overmuch about "ifs" and deserts, but I think it almost fair to say that he deserved to win the Open Championship which Harry Vardon won at Prestwick in 1898 with Willie Park a stroke behind. Harold was only two shots behind the winner, and he had taken eight to the Himalayas. Admittedly he committed an error of judgment in taking an iron he had not been using instead of the wooden club with which he could juggle. Yet an eight was too severe a punishment; the Fates dealt cruelly with him. So they did in 1911, another of Vardon's years, when he seemed set for victory in the last round at Sandwich, until an apparently perfect tee shot—and he thought it perfect—was caught in a little jutting piece of bunker invisible from the tee. Of course, the player must know the course; *ignorantia haud excusat*, but again the Fates were hard.

Because he was a supremely good score player let no one think Harold could not play a match. Admittedly there was one man against whom he could not; Freddie Tait, his great amateur rival and contemporary, was one too many for him in single combat. The one went out with the light of battle in his eye, the other nervous and despondent. To be able to produce such an effect on a golfer of Hilton's quality is eloquent of the power of his conqueror; but against any other man Harold was a fine match player; he suffered but he endured. "I could fight pretty well too," he once said to me, "if I could make myself see the humour of it." It was a very astute comment. He had naturally a great sense of humour; every match he watched teemed with sly fun for him as well as with serious interest; but he could not always see the fun—how few of us can!—when he was himself in the throes of a fierce struggle.

I have to write all too hurriedly—for time and printers wait for no man—and this is a very imperfect tribute to one of whom I was very fond and who was, I like to think, a friend of mine. Harold's was in some ways rather a tragic life; he might have fared better if he had applied his very astute mind to other things besides hitting a ball. But if he had weaknesses they were amiable ones, and his many good qualities will be measured by the number of those who will mourn and remember him.

SOME HILTONIANA

WHEN I wrote of the death of Harold Hilton I was conscious of wanting to say many things about him for which there was no space; conscious also that I should have liked time in which to read again his own writings on golf. Since then I have re-read what I take to be the best exposition of his views, namely, his chapter called "Golf: Theoretical and Practical," published in 1912 in *The Royal and Ancient Game of Golf* of which he was one of the editors. It is full of shrewd and interesting arguments on the game, and I propose to take one or two which illustrate peculiarly well his gift for analysis of his fellow golfers.

Of this gift he writes with extreme modesty. "I do not profess to know the weaknesses of other players' games, as one can only guess at them by means of observation, and I have found that the majority of players are not very ready or willing to acknowledge to any decided flaw in their armour, except it be in the case of their putting." But, he says, everybody has certain shots that he plays with confidence and certain others that he approaches with a lack of it. That is a most penetrating truth. We do not tell other people of the shots we are afraid of, partly for fear of boring them, partly from vanity perhaps, but largely because we have a muddle-headed feeling that we are giving valuable information to the enemy, as if a batsman were to tell a bowler the particular ball he dislikes. Yet everybody, I believe, has some strokes that he loves and some that he fears. How many of us, for instance, having toiled out with a wind partly on our backs, at once adverse and slicy, have turned homewards with infinite relief and felt almost arrogantly happy. I am sure I must have quoted Mr. V. A. Pollock's joy in the "Guardbridge wind" at St. Andrews. He always lashed at the ball with a fine dash, but when he was on his homeward way with that wind coming a little from the right, he fairly flung himself at the ball in an ecstasy of confidence. Every man has his own "Guardbridge wind," and its merit is this, that he may not always hit the shot but he always thinks he is going to. To give a small personal instance, I always feel happy if the ball lies a little above me; my swing seems suddenly to become rounder and more comfortable, and though I may make the worst shot in the world I shall still be sure, if I get another such lie, that I am going to make a good one.

Hilton had his own little private weakness in his youthful days, one shot that frightened him till at last he cast out fear by practising. The full iron shot and the wrist shot had no terrors for him, but with the shot between the two he felt, he said, "all at sea." Even when he played it successfully in practice, he would hesitate in a game and take refuge in the wrong shot rather than dare the right one. Still he laboured on till he had conquered it, encouraged by the great mastery of this shot possessed by Mr. John Ball, and in the end he came to think that the power of playing a half-iron shot "represents all the difference between being a first-class player and a second-class player."

To return to my original quotation, that is a shrewd thrust in our tenderest quarters, the saying that we are much more ready to acknowledge a weakness in putting than in anything else. He goes on to amplify his statement thus: "One has great difficulty in coming across any who are ready to admit that their success is in any great degree due to their work on the green, as they seem to think it savours of an admission which casts reflection upon their play in other departments." It is, I think, certainly true that a man is much more ready to admit that he won a particular match by putting than that he is in general a good putter; but there is this to be said: no man, not even the very best, is always a good putter in the sense that some men are always good drivers. We can all putt on some days, and there are days when the greatest cannot find the hole. So there seems a peculiar tempting of Fate in any man saying that he relies on his putting.

Now let me turn for a moment from the idiosyncrasies of other golfers to one that was his own. Those who saw him play or have at least seen photographs will recall how delicately he seemed to finger the club and especially how his right little finger was held off the club altogether. Nearly everything he did had been very carefully thought out, but this peculiarity was not. It arose from his having tried in youth to imitate the overlapping grip of Mr. Laidlay, who was the first great golfer he had watched from outside the boundaries of Hoylake. He found his hands were not big enough nor his fingers strong enough and so gave up the attempt, but his period of imitation remained in the heritage, that his little finger remained in the air and not upon the club. Though he was never himself an overlapper, he was persuaded that this was the best way of holding a club, but not for the reason usually advanced, that it makes the two hands act as one. He had long come to the conclusion that for the swinging of a golf club the human being "has too many fingers on this particular hand." He went on to point out that Mr. Ball, despite his apparent "palm" grip, in fact only used three fingers of his right hand, since "the forefinger of his right hand was pointing out into space, as if it took no interest whatever in the task in hand."

Another little personal point which is interesting is that Harold was not, so to speak, born a great practiser, though I cannot help thinking that he must sooner or later have become one. He was induced to practise by the example of one who has been properly, if retrospectively, canonised as the first Amateur Champion, Mr. A. F. Macfie. We think now of Mr. Macfie as a St. Andrews golfer, for he has lived there many years, but that is to do an injustice to Hoylake. It was at that great golfing school that he graduated, hitting ball after ball away in the dusk so that the caddies, when next morning they found balls that had grown up like mushrooms in the night, knew who had been out on the evening before. Unless in later years it was Mr. Travis, "I do not suppose," Hilton wrote, "that any player living has practised the game of golf so assiduously as Mr. Allan Macfie did in those old days at Hoylake." I imagine he himself must have come within measurable distance, and of modern players Cotton must be a dangerous challenger.

Everyone thinks of Harold Hilton as pre-eminently a wooden

Sport & General.

ON THE ALPS GREEN AT HOYLAKE

Central Press Photos, Ltd.
LEO DIEGEL
In the Ryder Cup Match at Moortown

club player. Probably wooden clubs held the keenest experimental interest for him; it was with them that he played the greatest number of what he called "pranks," but his personal affections never blinded him to realities, a fact that made him a wonderfully impartial judge of a golfer, whether friend or foe. So though the wood amused him or, in modern language, "intrigued" him most, he said this: "I hold a very decided opinion that iron play is far and away the most important department in the playing of the game. . . . The shot up to the hole is the backbone of the game: a failure at it invariably ends in disaster." He thought that the great improvement in golf which had taken place since his early days—particularly among the professionals, for he was, when he wrote, a little depressed about the amateurs—was due to "the development of a certain hard forcing wrist-shot," and this in turn was due more to Harry Vardon than to any other one man. And with that I again come to the end of my space, with the feeling that there is much more to be said about Harold Hilton than I can say. There are just a few people in the world who really know a subject: he knew golf.

"O SWEET, O LOVELY WALL"

YEARS ago it fell to my lot to show a distinguished golf architect over a course for which I had a great affection. When he came to a certain blind hole over a sandhill, the members' pride, he maintained an eloquent silence till we reached the bank of the green. Then he remarked "Take away that thing" and passed grimly on. The thing in question was a low sloping grassy bank. It was hardly deserving of the abusive name of "back wall," but it was in the nature of one, and, despite my eminent friend, I am afraid it is still there.

I have just been reminded of it by reading some observations of Cotton's about a course he had been playing on, in which he professed himself an enemy of back walls. "So are we all, all honourable men," for there really is nothing to be said for them, and very little for their brothers, the side walls. They are generally ugly, they are apt to reduce good and bad approaches to an equality, they tend to outrageous flukes; they are, in short, thoroughly ungolfing things, and yet, having to some extent been brought up among them, I do feel now and then a tenderness for them, and wish I could think of something to be said "for encomium as a change."

Sentiment apart there is really only one thing I can think of, namely, that they repay the man who has the courage to be up with his approaches. It may be said that in such circumstances precious little courage is needed, yet even so we can be miserable cowards. The other day a friend and I were playing on a certain course, and, as we drew near to one hole, we saw a large cow sitting propped against the flag. We were carrying our own clubs, and were too lazy to go forward and drive away the cow, but decided to play firmly at the beast in the certain hope that we should thus both lay our approaches dead. And then what happened? Why, we were both miserably and contemptibly short; we never gave the cow a chance. I should like to think that this was because we were intuitively conscious that laying the ball dead off a cow is "not golf," but it was in fact partly because we were cowards, partly because we feared to make ourselves ridiculous. We thought what fools we should look if the ball bounded over the brute and disappeared into the distance; even as it sometimes did in old days at Prestwick, when a player tried to use the stone wall at the back of the green, and his ball took off at the wrong place.

The fact that there is always such a risk, though often a very small one, makes me believe that some day a great architect, scorning convention, will lay out a great hole having a back wall. It will have to be an exiguous one, only to be attained from exactly the right position, and the use of it must not only necessitate a most accurate shot, but must be attended with grave danger. One of the objections to the average back wall is that no skill is needed. As Locksley remarked, "A child of seven years old might hit yonder target with a headless shaft." But if all my conditions were fulfilled I believe the shot might

"O SWEET, O LOVELY WALL" 39

be a really good one, even though the ghost of Mr. George Glennie were still to call it "Just monkey's tricks." However, I have never seen those conditions fulfilled and I do not expect to.

The walls among which I said I was to some extent brought up are those on the "gun platform" greens often to be found on downland courses. On those long, rolling slopes they are sometimes almost necessary, since without them the ball would roll for ever, but they are both hideous and odious. I am thinking a little of my old friend, Royston, but more particularly of an even older friend, Eastbourne, where I used to play as a boy. I remember one hole there which came into being when the nine holes first became eighteen. It has long, I am sure, disappeared. It was a short hole, having on the left-hand side of the green a rectangular cliff of chalk. Not only did the cliff correct any moderate hook, but even the most outrageously hooked ball which pitched high on the grass above the cliff would come toppling down again, "from Beechy Head," as the local saying went, and end on the green at last. In fact, as long as one did not slice, the hole was more or less fool-proof.

There used to be one hole, having some of these characteristics, on a course of great eminence. This was the old thirteenth, now superseded, at Muirfield. Whether it had the original right to the rather irreverent title of "The Postage Stamp," or whether this belongs to a short hole at Troon, I am not sure. At any rate, at this Muirfield hole it was possible to hit a considerably hooked tee shot, and yet, by a process of toppling and dribbling, to end on the green. It is fair to add that as a rule the ball stopped on the bank above, but I recall one important occasion when it did not.

This was in the Amateur Championship of 1926, when Mr. Andrew Jamieson leapt into fame by beating Mr. Bobby Jones. He already held a winning lead when he came to this thirteenth hole, and hooked his tee shot on to the bank above the green. The crowd stood spellbound watching the ball as it hung hesitating. Then, avoiding all impediments, urged on at its every hop by patriotic Scottish cheers, it sloped slowly on to the green, and the invading champion's last hope was gone.

The kindest of all back walls that I can recollect, though its kindness lasted only for a day, was at Porthcawl. This memory belongs to a Welsh Championship meeting there forty-one years ago, so long ago that I have never satisfactorily identified the hole on subsequent visits. At any rate the hole was cut in some mysterious and magical manner so that almost any ball that ran up the bank at the back of the green did not merely run back dead, it ran in. This is not nearly as big a lie as it sounds. I can assure the reader that numbers of people came into the club-house announcing in an excited manner that they had holed out in two. For a whole day nobody, when he got on or near the green, thought of playing at the hole, he simply played up to the bank behind it. Then on the following day came Nemesis in the shape of a shower of rain, or perhaps only a heavy dew. We all duly tried once more our trick shot off the back wall and we all, to our unspeakable indignation, saw the ball stop at the top and refuse to run back. No doubt it served us right.

In those more unsophisticated days we used to think such a shot rather good fun, and it is still undeniable that the sight of a ball gently running round a slope to end at the hole-side has in it something of prettiness. It is still good fun once in a while, but it is a cloying pleasure; we can easily have too much of it. Since there must still, owing to the nature of much golfing ground, be greens with walls to them, the modern architect has devised a means of reducing their helpfulness. It is that of making a shallow gutter at the foot of the wall. Then the ball, even if it is stopped in its too impetuous course, at least cannot complete the cycle of its nefarious acts by lying dead. That is perfectly just and right; I have not a word to say against it, but I do wish I had laid my ball dead off that cow.

"UNFAIRNESS"

THE Professional Golfers' Association of the United States have lately held their championship tournament, and they have played it without stymies. It appears that there was a committee of eight in charge of the tournament and they decided on their iconoclastic course without a single dissentient. Here is no doubt a piece of news, a subject on which in these hard times the golfing writer should pounce eagerly, but I hail it with no vast enthusiasm. So much has been said, and will probably be said again about stymies; nearly everybody has long since made up his mind one way or the other and is impenetrable to argument. Were I at home indeed I could perhaps find in a drawer various suggestions made by ingenious persons to the modification of the stymie rule, but I am still an evacuated exile and cannot accurately enough remember what these reformers want to do. All I do remember is that there is a good deal to be said for their plans, and that I, being in this matter an irredeemable conservative, was not persuaded by any of them. I am one of those before referred to whom no argument will convince.

This being my frame of mind it may be thought that I am highly indignant over the American P.G.A., but this is not so; I am mildly sorry, but not in the least surprised. American golfers, though they have hitherto faithfully adhered to the rules in this matter, have always, I think, had a dislike to stymies, and this is not to be wondered at. The stymie is admittedly an anomaly; tradition makes people tolerant or even fond of anomalies, but golf in the United States has not a long tradition behind it. Moreover Americans play so many four-ball matches and relatively so few singles, that perhaps a stymie comes to them, when it does come, as a rare shock. If, then, it is natural that American players in general should have no feeling of loyalty towards the stymie, it is particularly natural in the case of their professionals. The professional golfer plays for his living, and to anyone who does so a piece of luck is greatly magnified, since its importance may often be exactly computed in hard cash. Goodness knows that we amateurs are apt to complain bitterly enough of some piece of what we think ill fortune, though by losing us the match it has hurt nothing but our *amour propre*. Our moans would be much more excusable if our pocket and perhaps our standing in our profession had been affected.

So it will be generally found, I think, that professionals attach great importance to what is called "fairness," whether in whole courses or individual holes. They like courses where every shot will be exactly rewarded according to its obvious deserts: they do not like a hole at which a well-struck ball—intrinsically well struck, but not struck quite well enough for that particular shot —can get into a very unpleasant place. In short they prefer a course where they know precisely "what they are in for" and where the man who makes most well-struck shots or fewest ill-struck ones is surest to win. This is no doubt a very natural frame of mind, but it is one which amateurs need not emulate, however much they wish to emulate the professionals' skill. Here again most of us cry out loudly (I know I live in a glass house in this matter) when we are trapped off a good shot or what we please to call one; but afterwards, when we get home and think it over more calmly, we admit that the hole, even though it may have treated us harshly, is an interesting, stimulating and good hole. At any rate we ought to admit it, and the present time, when we play so little golf and take it so little to heart, is one at which we see these matters with clearer eyes, unblurred by personal grievances.

As we see in the mind's eye the holes that have most thrilled us in the playing, how often we remember something that befell us there and seemed at the moment a stroke of utterly undeserved misfortune. It has been pointed out, I think by Mr. Simpson, that all or nearly all of the famous holes of the world have been accused of being unfair. The margin of error at them is in places so small and the risk to be taken so big that

"UNFAIRNESS" 43

there must be occasions on which Fate deals harshly. That is what has made the holes famous and that is why we are always interested to play them. The too scrupulously fair course need not theoretically be lacking in interest, but in fact it often is. I have lately played a little on a course which must in point of fairness be second to none. Greens and fairways are admirable, the rough is of a thoroughly consistent quality and nowhere too fierce; the bunkers and hazards are all clearly to be seen, and are so placed that a well and cleanly struck ball need never go even within dangerous distance of any one of them.

It has suited my kind of golf, if it may be so termed, well enough, because I have had enough to do with trying to hit the ball into the air, and found the ordinary risks quite great enough. But as I have not seen anyone called on to play a shot that could possibly be called unfair, so also I have not seen one that could be called particularly interesting, still less exciting.

Lovers of *The Rose and the Ring* will recall that the Fairy Blackstick wished her royal godchildren "a little misfortune" and that, sure enough, it was very good for them in the end. So there is nothing so good for a hole as a little unfairness. Indeed I doubt if not merely any hole, but any game, is worth playing unless Fate can now and again deal us a blow below the belt.

I said just now that when we recalled great holes we could remember some dreadful disaster that happened there, and so we can, but do we not remember more vividly the times on which we have triumphantly skirted the "unfair" hazard? I think that we do and that memory is on the whole kind to us, letting us remember our hits while our misses grow dim. It seems to be so with stymies. Of course, there are one or two stymies that we cannot wholly forget, because they made so much difference and seemed at the time so senselessly cruel, but for my own part at least I recall much more often those that have been happily overcome. One lofted at a nineteenth hole in the semi-final of a tournament is an abiding joy; the thought of it sends quite a glow through me, or would do so if I did not likewise remember that I was soaked through with cold rain at the time. There is another that might be too bitter if the ultimate end had not been happy. It was in the "last eight" of an Amateur Championship and with that for the hole and the match on the seventeenth green I lofted a stymie bang into the hole. How dramatic a triumph! but that particular course had then particularly devilish tins in the holes, made in an angular shape, so that the ball hit one of the sloping sides and bounced back in my face. I may add that I was not the only sufferer; the very same thing befell somebody else and those tins were abandoned. I must say that if I had not won at the last hole that stymie, even though I laid it myself, would have rankled for ever.

I have been trying to recall any spectacular stymies I have seen and find the garner of my memory unexpectedly empty. I have no doubt, however, about the most dramatic and I think the most skilfully circumvented one. This was on Westward Ho! in 1912, in the famous final between John Ball and Abe Mitchell, on the sixteenth green in the afternoon round. The match was all square and John Ball, being as I suppose, seven or eight feet away, was laid an apparently hopeless stymie. There was no conceivable possibility of pitching it; the only chance—a very slender one as it seemed—was to play the ball at dead strength, so that it might shave past the enemy and then drop in at the side of the hole at its very last gasp. John looked at his opponent for a moment with a smile, half grim, half quizzical, and then proceeded to play the stroke, with a wooden putter as I recall it, to absolute perfection. The ball just got by, just reached the edge of the hole and no more and just toppled in. It would surely be a sad loss if such a shot could never be played again.

ON THE SKY-LINE

IT is always interesting to see our own particular game through external eyes. I do not mean the eyes of those who ask "What on earth can they want with so many sticks?"—though that was growing before the war a not wholly impertinent question; nor those of the kindly, garrulous person in a railway carriage who, seeing his neighbour's clubs in the rack, begins an alarmingly long journey by saying: "I should think golf must be a very interesting game, though I've never played it myself." I mean the eyes of the intelligent observer who is fond of games but has played and seen but little golf. The other day I had this opportunity in a talk with one who is like Professor Dingo, "of European reputation" in his own subject, who is almost passionately interested in some games and has played them not without a modest glory, and has even played a little mild and casual golf. He told me that he had only once seen first-class golf, and this was on the occasion, a disastrous one for us, when the Walker Cup match was played at Sandwich. Then he had spent one whole summer's day in watching.

One thing he said struck me as curious and instructive. It was to the effect that all the players seemed to be playing equally well (a polite and patriotic point of view since our side was sadly beaten) and that to his eye they all looked exactly the same. I supposed he meant that if he had seen them swinging on the sky-line he would not have been able to tell one from the other, and he said that was certainly so; there appeared to him a complete uniformity of posture and movement. Supposing them to be cricketers, I asked, would he have been able to distinguish them at a like distance, and he replied that he certainly would. This interested me because I remembered to have read somewhere a similar statement by the late Canon Edward Lyttelton. He had written that a number of batsmen on the sky-line looked to him entirely distinct in their respective manners of batting while golfers were quite indistinguishable. So there it is, and those of us who are more familiar with golf than cricket must, I think, accept it as a fact. To us the batsmen probably appear by comparison uniform, save that with some of them bat and ball meet more often than with others. The golfers on the other hand have each their almost countless little mannerisms, to say nothing of the broader features of style, which instantly reveal their identities. In short, it is a matter of use and wont, and doubtless the same rule applies equally to other games as well as the two I have cited.

46 GOLFING BY-PATHS

Of course those of us who watch much golf are not perhaps quite so clever and observant as we deem ourselves. We naturally get to know not only the players' styles but their other characteristics and idiosyncrasies and their very clothes. It is with us as with the defenders of Rome in our dear old friend *Horatius*:

> And plainly and more plainly
> Now might the burghers know,
> By port and vest, by horse and crest
> Each war-like Lucumo.

We can tell a long way off him who is "girt with the brand none else may wield," perhaps because we have tried to waggle that brand in our own feeble fingers. When we do not know the champions our eyes are less keen. I was once in like case with my friend at Sandwich. This was in 1913 when, having landed for the first time in the United States, I went straightway to Garden City to watch the Amateur Championship. There were, I think, only three players there whom I had seen before—Walter Travis, Jerome Travers and Chick Evans; even Francis Ouimet, now so old a friend, was then a new one. And for a little while, I must admit, that the other players did look to me very much alike. I soon learnt them apart, but to begin with there seemed to me great similarity; they all, or nearly all, looked very young, they were all in white shirts and white flannel trousers and they all swung the club with much the same long, smooth and leisurely swing.

That is a long time ago now, but I still think, and I fancy many British watchers would agree with me, that there is a greater uniformity of style among good American amateurs than among our own. They have been on the whole more drilled and taught than have ours and have formed themselves on much the same classical models. Of course they all have their characteristics as have ours, and some are particularly obvious; I feel for instance that I could always have distinguished Robert Gardner a long way off. Yet on the whole they have an essentially national method, a smooth, lithe, round

ON THE SKY-LINE
47

swing, easy to identify in a mass, not easy to distinguish in particular instances. It is, I imagine, one of the reasons that they have been so good, that they have aimed at a common model and such an excellent one.

Our own amateurs have had more clearly marked mannerisms. It is probably the effect of advancing years, that the older players seem to me to have been more characteristic than their successors. I feel as if John Ball's perfect rhythm, Harold Hilton's little jump on his toes, the mere waggle of Horace Hutchinson or Robert Maxwell would have allowed of no possible mistake at almost any range of vision. And yet I am not sure. Take our own amateurs just before the war. Could anyone fail to recognise James Bruen? I hardly think so, nor the fine ferocity of Stowe, nor the easy grace of Hector Thomson. Till I am positively blind I shall have no doubt about Harry Bentley putting. To go a little further back could there be any possible question between Tolley and Wethered on the sky-line? I almost feel I could tell the, particular and venemous sound made by Roger's drive among a hundred.

In a general way I suppose that professionals are harder to recognise in the distance than are amateurs, because they have a greater orthodoxy of swing, with fewer mannerisms. Yet having written down that sentence I wonder whether any three golfers could possibly have been more easy to distinguish than were the members of the Triumvirate. The result was in each case equally magnificent and no doubt they obeyed many of the same rules, but no three swings have looked more different, the one from the other. And coming down to their successors of to-day, could one have any doubts? Cotton's left foot would instantly betray him. When I can no longer tell Perry afar off I shall think that my eyes have grown altogether too dim for watching, and so I might go on, with Adams's long swing and Reggie Whitcombe's clipped one, go on for ever and ever.

As we descend in the golfing scale our friends become more and more easy to identify, since they exhibit the grosser and more singular eccentricities. We have no doubt whatever about them, and they have no doubt whatever about us, though in our own case we cannot for the life of us understand what there is so notable or even so laughable in our methods. And yet they tell us with an offensive smile that they would know the things we do with our legs "a mile off" (that is the distance they invariably specify) and we have reluctantly to take their word for it. They must, as it seems to us, be supernaturally clever, and yet in another way they annoy us by their extreme obtuseness. When we have completely changed our swing and are feeling re-born and transfigured they never can see the slightest difference in us. It is true that we have often made such a reformation before, but that was in some trivial detail; this time it is the real thing; like Bottom we are "translated"; we have acquired an entirely new swing, and it is intolerably stupid of them not to perceive it. If one of them were to say to us quite seriously, "I see you've changed your swing," we should fall on his neck with tears of gratitude, but how seldom it happens! I had a friend, no mean golfer, but gifted with a peculiarly awkward and angular swing, who once told me that he had lately been playing just like Miss Wethered, and with great success. The poor fellow was of course suffering from an hallucination; it was positively pathetic and we should never be so absurd as that. Yet it would be very pleasant if some charitable person would one day remark our more modest reformation. Nobody ever does.

CONSOLATIONS OF SHORTNESS

EVERYBODY or nearly everybody must cherish some tender memories of his beginnings in the not too difficult art of bicycling. It seemed for a little while so utterly impossible of acquirement, and then on a sudden the miracle had been accomplished. Almost without the rider knowing it the supporting hand had been removed, and there

CONSOLATIONS OF SHORTNESS

he was careering along by himself, a little unsteadily perhaps, with a tendency to find a hedge or a ditch magnetically attractive, but still the unaided master of his fate. This was so delicious a state of things that in the first flush of enthusiasm he even enjoyed riding against a strong head wind, bowed over his handlebars and purple in the face. That stage soon passed however, and most of us, especially as we grow older, come to the conclusion that bicycling is only enjoyable, indeed only tolerable, when we are bowling along with a kindly breeze behind us.

These reflections come into my head because I have been playing a little golf again after nearly a year's interval, and my pleasure has been greatly enhanced or diminished according to the direction in which the breeze has been blowing. Let it not be thought that I am so utterly lacking in virility that I want to have the wind behind me all the time. That would be dull and enervating. On the particular course on which I have been playing I want to have it always against me going out and with me coming home, and I believe all short drivers would agree with me. It so chances that the holes going out are rather short and those coming home are of a very fine length indeed.

If the wind is as we want it we attain the absolute of poignancy and enjoyment, for we can reach each hole in the proper number of shots; not without effort, not without plenty of wooden club play, not unless we hit the ball as truly as in us lies; *but we can do it*. If the wind is the other way we get to the turn easily enough perhaps and may even call one or two of the holes, as we used to do when we were younger, "a kick and a spit"; but the flog home against the wind is altogether too much for us. It is not merely that it is hard work, but it is unremunerative work. We hit our two best shots at the holes described by courtesy as "two-shot" holes, and we are still a good way short of the green, with a nondescript and not very interesting third shot left to play. Unless we are holing putts we get at best a dreary succession of fives and, say what you will, too many fives "shed a gentle melancholy upon the soul."

50 GOLFING BY-PATHS

There is one hole in particular, the fifteenth; we used to call it "the crater," but only prehistoric persons now remember the name, and the green is a crater no longer. I think it is one of the finest two-shot holes I know anywhere, but for me its beauties are largely gone because I can never reach it in two. The other day a friendly breeze—no more than a breeze, upon my honour—was helping us home and I was for once actually playing the holes as they ought to be played; but when I came to the fifteenth I gave a sad little sigh and said to my opponent: "Ah! if one could but reach this hole in two just once again!" Then—well I must be honest; I did not reach it, but I was only a yard short, tapped the next one up dead and got my legitimate four. It made me for a moment quite pathetically happy. I was reminded of an old friend, long since dead, with whom I once went a Sunday morning's walk at St. Andrews. As we stood on the plateau whence the ball drops gently down on to the second green he remarked: "I wish that just once in my life I had reached this green in two, but I never have." I felt the pathos of his words then and I feel them much more acutely now.

As long as we can reach a hole in the right number of shots with *any* club, then the hole ought to remain for us a good one. It may even be argued that it ought to be better than ever because there is no stroke in the game so splendid and satisfying as a wooden club shot up to the pin. But when we cannot reach it at all then something of the savour goes out of it. That is why the wind can be so kind a friend and can make all the difference between exquisite bliss and resigned despair.

Golfers accept this undeniable shortening of their strokes in different ways according to their temperaments. Some with a gallant fatuity refuse to accept it at all. They constantly walk far past the spot at which their ball has finished and, when their attention is called to it, retrace their steps in great surprise, murmuring that it must have had a bad fall. Similarly they persist in under-clubbing themselves at the short holes, and finish in the bunker in front of the green. Others, on the other hand, become so humble that they are prepared to take a driver at a hundred yards from the green.

"PERSONS ONE WOULD WISH TO HAVE SEEN" 51

I myself have more or less, or so I flatter myself, passed through the first stage and have reached the second. Several times during this brief holiday I have with too much humility over-clubbed myself and seen the ball speeding into trouble on the far side of the green. On the day before mentioned, on which I was playing really quite well, it needed all the arguments of my kind amateur caddie to make me take an iron when I wanted in my modesty to take a brassey. I suppose the truth is that nobody could be so short as in certain moods I believe myself to be. There is something to be said for this frame of mind, beyond the obvious truth that under-clubbing is one of the commonest of all golfing vices. It has made me believe, and in fact I do believe, that I am hitting the ball just a little farther than I was on my last visit.

This reminds me of another old gentleman I once knew who always thought he had got longer every summer till he was over eighty and, when winter came, never could understand how it was that he had lost his length. But I will not admit the likeness because after the deluges of August the grass was rather slow and luxuriant and there was very little run in the ground. So it may just possibly be true!

"OF PERSONS ONE WOULD WISH TO HAVE SEEN"

I HAVE put my title in inverted commas as in duty bound, because it is stolen from the mighty Hazlitt. In one of his essays he describes a discussion between several friends, of whom Charles Lamb was one. Ayrton began it by saying that he supposed that the two first persons one would wish to see were Locke and Isaac Newton, but Lamb would have none of them. They, he said, were not *persons*, but characters, and he himself chose "to encounter on the floor of his apartment in their night-gown and slippers" Sir Thomas Browne and Sidney's friend Fulke Greville. I have often, in my distorted way, translated that discussion into golfing terms for my own amusement and now that, as concerns golf, we must live largely in the past, I take leave to do so on paper. I look down the list of old champions and reflect which of them I would choose to see in all the pride of their youth.

Well, to begin with, whom have I seen? I can go back to Bob Martin who won the first of his two championships in the year I was born, 1876, but I only remember him dimly in the professional's shop at Coldham Common at Cambridge, whither Mr. Linskill had lured him for a while. The earliest champion whom I actually saw play was Willie Fernie, the winner in 1883; him in my boyhood I saw often, and he remains a vision of unsurpassed grace. A little later in the list come two that I might have seen and did not, Willie Park and Hugh Kirkcaldy. Willie Park I did see and speak to, but the extent of my watching his golf was a single long putt laid dead in such a storm of rain at St. Andrews that I could hardly keep my eyes open. Hughie was the Oxford professional when I was at Cambridge and yet my eyes never beheld that long, lovely slashing swing immortalised in the Badminton golf volume under the title "The St. Andrews Swing."

Most of all, however, do I wish that I had watched one who never won the championship, Douglas Rolland. I caught sight of him once when his golfing days were over and he was but a shadow of his former magnificent self, crippled with rheumatism. In his erratic career he was for a while at Rye, but this was before my Rye days; he was at Limpsfield near my old home in Kent, but I had been transplanted. He came to play at Worlington and hit what was then an historic shot, a carry home in two on to the third green against a breeze with a brassey, but that was just before I had gone up to Cambridge. As far as I was concerned he was a will-o'-the-wisp always flitting out of my reach. And he must have been the best fun in the world to see because he was, as far as the long game was concerned, the best of all hitters of the gutty ball. Mr. Blackwell may perhaps have been longer for individual shots, but for consistent long hitting of inconceivable fire and splendour I think all those

HAROLD HILTON AT SANDWICH IN 1914

Central Press Photos, Ltd.

UNORTHODOX BUT EFFECTIVE
Charles Stowe of our winning Walker Cup side

Keystone.

"PERSONS ONE WOULD WISH TO HAVE SEEN" 53

who knew him united in putting Rolland first. Not only was it fun for the onlooker but fun for him. Mr. Colt has often told me how Rolland in an ecstasy of delight over his own shot used to exclaim "Away she sails wi' dash and spray." I know not if this was an original remark or a quotation, and I cannot get at Mr. Colt to ask him, but they are noble words to describe the flight of a great drive.

Most of all should I have liked to see Rolland on that occasion which has become part of the great golfing legend when he had to come to play an exhibition match with Tom Dunn at Tooting Bec. The legend tells how Rolland had been tasting freely of the pleasures of the town and arrived at Tooting clad in his best clothes and a hard-boiled shirt front, and with no clubs. He had apparently started with them but was like the man in the old *Punch* picture, who had not only lost his ticket but had lost the big drum. Whereupon the shirt was crumpled into greater flexibility, some clubs were borrowed, and Rolland beat the record of the course and beat poor Tom Dunn into the middle of the ensuing week. There must have been something heroic and lovable about the man who could do that, and in fact everybody adored Rolland; he had never an enemy but himself. I shall never quite get over the loss of not having seen him.

When I look down the long list of Amateur Champions there are only two that I never saw, Peter Anderson, the St. Andrews student who gallantly and unexpectedly beat Mr. Laidlay at Prestwick in 1893, and A. J. T. Allan, who won at Muirfield four years later. As to the first of them I have no vast curiosity, but Allan is another matter; he is dreadfully "intriguing" and he too seems something of a will-o'-the-wisp. I played first in the championship in 1898, just one year too late, for Allan won in 1897 and died before he could defend his title. Round him likewise legend clusters. We have all heard that he played with no nails in his shoes, that he travelled every day backwards and forwards from Edinburgh and bicycled from Drem to Muirfield. Otherwise he is a man of mystery. I have only once seen a photograph of him and that a palpably "posed" one giving one no notion of his swing.

E

Even among those who knew him opinions differ enormously as to whether his win was a fluke and a flash in the pan, or whether he was destined to be one of the great figures of golf. As I never saw him play I can offer no opinion, but oddly enough I believe I was one of the few people who were not much surprised at his victory. I was an assiduous reader of *Golf* and *The Field* and had often noticed the name of Allan, with those triple and memorable initials, connected with low scores all round Edinburgh. I did not know the courses but it seemed to me that such scores spoke to some extent for themselves, and that this must be a remarkable golfer. So when he won I could almost say to myself "I told you so." Piecing together what little I have since been able to gather about him, I fancy him a player of no astonishing power and no great beauty of style, but easy and accurate, a fine player of the short game and one gifted with a calm so admirable that it almost amounted to casualness. He always sounds to me as if he were the kind of golfer likely to win his way through more championships, and I wish very much that I had seen him.

I have confined these random remarks to those whom I might have seen. They would go on for ever if it were a matter of summoning up some towering shades from the days before I existed. Among them one stands out far before the rest. Young Tommy Morris died the year before I was born. Everything I have ever read or heard of him makes me believe that he was unsurpassable and that no Vardon or Bobby Jones has, taking each on his best day and under the conditions of that day, been greater than he was. The dash and swagger and confidence of him must have been truly glorious. Let me conjure up one scene from the witch's cauldron of the past, and it shall be Tommy doing his 149 for three rounds of the old twelve holes at Prestwick. I ask no better than that.

A GOLFER'S GOLFER

I SUPPOSE that nearly everybody who takes an interest and pleasure in golf, apart from his own personal playing of it, has certain favourite players whose game fascinates him and of whom he thinks unutterable things. We discover in them some flash of genius for hitting the ball, which for us lifts them above their rivals. Those rivals may in point of winning or losing be just as successful as are our favourites, but we are always glad to see X play, and we would scarcely walk across the road to watch Y. We learn by experience that X is not infallible, that he is perhaps very human and liable to err, but we never cease to think of him, perhaps unjustifiably, as in a higher class as a player.

Those who produce this effect on us are, as a rule, what may be called golfers' golfers. Their style and their strokes attract those who are interested in something more than results. There are such people, I think, in all walks of life, novelists' novelists or painters' painters, who make a particular appeal to those of their own craft. In golf an obvious example has been George Duncan, whom his brother professionals watched in preference to any of his contemporaries. His game fascinated everybody, as with its dash and beauty it was bound to do, but it had a peculiar attraction for those who looked below the surface and came not merely to see him gets fours and threes, but to try to analyse and learn.

One of the players who for me held this particular spell was Rex Hartley, of whose early death I have heard with very real regret. He had great personal charm and a quick, restless, amusing intelligence, but I am now writing of him as a player of the game. The highest compliment I can play him is to say that to me he will always be one of the disappointments of golf. His record of successes is a long one—the St. George's Cup, the *Golf Illustrated* Gold Vase twice, three victories in the London Foursomes with his brother Lister, a bronze medal in the Amateur

56 GOLFING BY-PATHS

Championship, a St. Andrews medal with a record score, and even so I have left out plenty. He played for England against Scotland in every year but one between 1926 and 1935, and he played twice in the Walker Cup match. Nevertheless, I say that his record is not nearly so good as the game that was in him, and that given a greater steadiness and patience in point of temperament, he would have been the outstanding amateur of his day, instead of being one of the best who did not always live up to his reputation.

This is only a personal judgment and may seem an excessive one. Possibly it is, because, I admit, Rex's game fascinated me. It was not that he was a pretty player, for I do not think he was, but there was a tremendous dash about him, and he had what would be called in a billiard player great power of cue; he could do things with the ball that most people cannot. He was a masterly player of all kinds of pitching shots, but the strokes of his that I most enjoyed watching were, first of all, any kind of spoon shot hit right up to the green and secondly —I am not sure I ought not to put it first—a full drive with a strong wind blowing on his back and perhaps a little behind. To see the ball start far away to the left and then come gradually back and back to finish miles down the course was to me one of the perfect æsthetic pleasures of golf; and, moreover, he could play that shot as consistently as he did skilfully.

His rather upright take-back of the club lent itself well to both these strokes, and in respect of his spoon shots he owed, I fancy, at least something to Mr. Hilton. He played a good deal at Cooden and when he was a boy he had plenty of opportunities of studying Mr. Hilton there. In some ways their swings were very much unlike. Mr. Hilton's club described on the way back a wider and flatter arc; but in the suspicion of a jump on to the toes in the act of hitting and the glorious abandon of the fling through of the arms, there was in Rex's swing an unmistakable something of the great Hoylake player. His style was so eminently his own that one might have thought that it owed nothing to any model, but if one knew of the early days in which he had sat at the master's feet at Cooden the likeness was plain to see.

The dash and swiftness which was so marked a feature of Rex's strokes up to the green was not notable when he got there. Indeed at one time he had indulged in rather wearisome antics, such as lying prone on his stomach to study the line. Neither was his putting a particularly strong part of his game, though he had his inspired days. I am inclined to think, though my memory may be at fault, that he was a better putter when he first burst upon the golfing world, and that was when he was very young indeed. How young I had rather forgotten until I looked up his record and found that he and his brother first won the London Amateur Foursomes for Chislehurst in 1923. That was when Rex was not much over eighteen, so that, judged by our standards if not by American ones, he was almost an infant phenomenon.

The brothers won again in the following year and thus when Rex went up to Peterhouse at Cambridge in October of 1924, he was already, by comparison with other freshmen, a seasoned veteran and a very well-known player. He stayed up only two years, playing in the University match at Hunstanton in 1925 and Burnham in 1926, beating his man on both occasions in the singles and being captain in his second year, a rare distinction. After he came down and went into business he played plenty of golf, but he always seemed to me to play it, if I may say so, in rather a hurry. He would, for instance, arrive for breakfast at St. Andrews by the night train and then go straight out to play his medal round. So it was also with other competitions. This was no doubt due to the fact that he stuck to his work, but I cannot help feeling that it was also typical of a certain restlessness and impatience of temperament that was not the best possible for his golf. There was something typical, too, about the way he smoked his cigarettes as he played; he seemed to puff them faster than anybody else.

I have tried to write something of Rex Hartley's golf as it appeared to me. Somebody else who saw just as much of it might have quite a different vision. At any rate, I hope it will not be set down to any deliberate partiality if I say that of all the younger players that I have known, hardly any seem to me to have possessed more definitely what may be called a streak of genius. In that respect I shall think of him with another of an older generation, *qui ante diem periit,* Johnny Bramston. I had not seen Rex since the early summer of 1939 and had heard of him working very hard as a Territorial gunner, both before the war and after it began. Then, after a while, I knew that his health had broken down and now comes this sad news. It will make many people sorry, and when the little world of golf comes back to life again after the war it will be the poorer by one noteworthy figure, a little fantastic, eminently characteristic, always to be affectionately remembered.

THE ANÆSTHETIC OF DON'T CARE

IT is an ill wind, but I have found one friend to whom it has blown one tiny little speck of good. He has very much enjoyed his very occasional round of golf, and he has enjoyed it for the thoroughly human reason that he has played far better than he had done for ages. I must quote a few words of his own vivid account of his feelings. He says that he had been getting steadily worse and that every game was "accompanied by oceans of morbid anxieties and worry about it that made it almost better not to play." Since there has been something so infinitely greater to worry about he has played a few rounds "amazingly well for me just because I don't care a hoot how I play." He ends by saying that here is proof how right was the philosopher William James when he laid it down that "The mood of levity, of 'I don't care,' is for this world's ills a sovereign and practical anæsthetic."

There are, no doubt, some happy creatures who never have worried about their golf, and they may find it a little difficult to sympathise, or at any rate to understand. There are many more, however, who will entirely comprehend my friend's sentiments; they will wish they "had half his complaint" and may be encouraged to take out their clubs, which they had moodily put away. I trust that they may find the "Don't care" cure equally effective, but I think it is one to be taken cautiously. Indeed, I am not sure that it is quite happily named. Perhaps there is not much difference, and yet I should prefer to call it the "Don't mind" cure. By whichever name it is known I assume that its supreme merit is that, when once the round is over, the player will not mind how he has played. He will not lie awake wondering what he has been doing wrong or dating his downfall with a horrid clearness of vision from that terrible let-off at the tenth, when, having the hole in his pocket, he went out of bounds or took four putts; he will feel the better for the exercise and forget everything else. It is the fact that he is going to adopt this eminently sensible attitude which has an admirable effect beforehand, and he plays well just because he knows that he won't mind if he doesn't.

At the same time, while he is actually playing he will, of course, mind to a reasonable extent. He may not think too much about how he is going to hit the ball, and that will be all to the good, but he will think about the simple act of hitting it and try his hardest. Moreover, he will enjoy every good shot, not because he fancies that he has found out the secret and so will win the championship or the next monthly medal, not even because it presages another good shot, but simply for its own individual sake, because it gives him pleasure. I labour this point, perhaps, but the expression "Don't care" does not seem to me quite descriptive of this simple and happy frame of mind. We have all been conscious of not caring, sometimes because we are too many holes down, more rarely because we are too many up. In the first case we have felt cross, and in the second bored, and in either case our game has probably suffered. Not caring implies, for me at any rate, not trying, and that is very nearly hopeless. We may think that we are not trying when we feel that we can walk casually up to the ball, put our feet down anywhere, have the minimum of waggle, and give the ball a resounding wallop. On these rare and blissful days we are in fact trying, but we are trying to just the right extent and not too hard. The professional golfer,

60 GOLFING BY-PATHS

with his almost insolent confidence and brevity of address, may look as if he were not trying or caring, but in fact nobody tries harder or cares more, and he knows that, if he ever allows himself to slip even for a moment into a mood of not trying, it will be the worse for his game. There used to be no better lesson in this respect than to play with James Braid in his prime in a friendly foursome round Walton Heath. He took as much pains over every stroke as if he had been playing for a kingdom. He tried and he cared, but he neither tried nor cared too much, and as to minding I am sure the match, once it was over, did not disturb his slumbers.

The fact that my old friend is playing so well has given me much pleasure on his account and also a little on my own, since it has made me remember how well I played myself for a while during the first war. The reason was rather different and perhaps less creditable. To some extent, no doubt, I did not mind how I played, though not minding has never been one of my strong points; but the real reason was that I played so regularly. On almost every single day, for weeks and even months at a time, I would make a short dash on to the Vardar marshes and either played a few holes or hit a few practice shots. The respite was brief, but it was regular, and the club came to feel an extraordinarily familiar thing in the hand. At the same time one could never play too much and so grow tired and stale. Just that blessed little bit of golf became part of the daily routine, and I think that I then came much nearer to the professional's feeling than at any other period of my life. The hitting of the ball became very easy. There was not much time for worrying about the how and the why, and anyhow there was always the next day, on the which the wrong could be righted. There was not, as for the week-end golfer, a whole long six days in which to worry as to what had been wrong on one Saturday, and as to whether the projected cure would be effective on the next. The driver (stolen, I regret to say, or at least "scrounged"), with which I seem in memory to have hit so far and sure, is still in my possession. When I merely look at it now—for it is too sacred to risk—it does not appear particularly well suited to its purpose. Its shaft is bent

JAMES BRUEN, THE INFANT PHENOMENON

REX HARTLEY AT SANDWICH

Central Press Photos Ltd.

Central Press Photos Ltd.

DALE BOURN AT ST. ANNE'S

JAMES BRAID ON HIS OWN HEATH

and rather wobbly, its head inelegant, its grip, made of some kind of tape which was an R.E. store, is elusive and uncomfortable. Yet it was something of a magic wand then; at any rate, I like to think it was, and I "don't care" if in fact it was not.

DALE

CAPTAIN THOMAS ARUNDALE BOURN, known to everyone as Dale, has died on active service, and his name brings back many memories. His loss is sad, but those memories cannot be sad ones; they are rather pleasant, gay, amusing, as he would have liked them to be.

They are of many courses, and in particular perhaps of Rye and Deal. It is at Rye, when we meet again some day, as please heaven we shall for the President's Putter, that his name will be among those of "absent friends" that we of the Society toast at our dinner. It is at Deal that we shall always think of him battling, so light-hearted and yet trying so desperately hard, for the old Carthusians in the Halford Hewitt Cup. These are both essentially cheerful gatherings where, in Dick Swiveller's words, "the wing of friendship does not moult a feather," and it is natural to associate Dale first and foremost with them, because cheerfulness and friendliness and conviviality were of the very essence of him.

As a golfer Dale was always something of a riddle. He could play the most astonishingly eccentric shots; he was not, save in respect of his ever dauntless heart, invariably to be relied on; the observer was sometimes tempted to wonder exactly how good he was and exactly how he had accomplished what he had done. But it is easy to be too fanciful in criticism and it is wiser to judge by results. Mr. Alfred Lyttelton once wrote a sentence—about cricket, not golf—which is always worth bearing in mind. "When" he said, "supremacy is measured, as it ought to be measured, by results in runs, the good hard standard coin and test of cricketing successfulness . . ." Applying that standard, *mutatis mutandis* Dale was a very good golfer indeed; his record is there and you cannot get away from it. He won one English championship and was runner-up in another year; he was runner-up to Mr. Michael Scott—in the Amateur Championship; he won the French Championship and—though not the highest achievement it was the occasion on which I thought he played best—he won the President's Putter. Leaving out various minor victories such as in the London Foursomes, that is a good solid record of successes such as not many of his contemporaries have equalled or even approached.

It was technically that he was sometimes such a puzzle. He looked anything but a good putter; he had a curious little stabbing movement of the club; in certain moods he hardly seemed to take it back at all. And yet there could be no mistake about this, that if a man were wanted to lay a nasty curly one stone dead at a crisis or to hole a five-footer on which everything depended, Dale was the man for the job. Handsome was as handsome did.

On the other hand he looked the easiest and most graceful of swingers in the long game, and it was his long game that periodically let him down. There was some odd little demon of mistiming in that pretty swing which neither he nor his professional advisers could wholly exorcise, though both tried hard, and so ever and anon the ball would go floating away, still easily and gracefully but into fearsome places. Thus his game always seemed to me something of a golfing paradox, weakest in what looked to the casual observer its strongest point and strongest where it seemed weakest.

There was, however, one feature of it as to which nobody could have any doubt; he was full of a fighting spirit that might justly be called heroic, if there did not seem something inappropriate in so solemn a word. He had tremendous sticking power; he never gave up hope; he always rose to the occasion. If he could make gratuitously bad shots he could also make most brilliant ones, and it was in the nature of him to make them when they were wanted. He was the best of foursome partners, as I have good cause to say, since, when I was in a distinctly sere and yellow stage, he pulled me through, for Woking, into the final of the London Foursomes. When we got there I must admit that his supporting arm weakened a little and I spent a good part of the afternoon up to my waist in the Camberley heather: but his play up to that point and the heart-warming, comforting feeling of such a partner is the surviving memory.

He was, from a temperamental point of view, an ideal foursome player and he loved foursomes, especially for the Old Carthusians at Deal. He did not always play well there, but somehow or other when his side was in direst need Dale seemed to bob up at the right moment to play the "counting" stroke. I shall never forget a match I watched between the Carthusians and the Wykehamists, Dale and Middleton on the one side, Kenneth Scott and Micklem on the other.

Even when the Charterhouse pair saved the match and went on to the nineteenth it seemed the forlornest of hopes, because another Winchester pair had looked certain to win; but that other pair did not win, and so all depended on this match, which ended on the twenty-third green. Dale did all manner of Jack-in-the-box recoveries, but I recall one that might have broken, in Andrew Kirkaldy's phrase, the heart of an iron horse. It was the twenty-first hole. The Wykehamists played it like a book—two perfect shots, a pitch and the first putt all round the hole for a four. Not so the Carthusians, for Dale's brassey shot floated away towards the sea shore and ended in a stony, sandy wilderness. Middleton hewed it out but could not do more than reach the deep hollow in front of the green. Dale rightly took some straight-faced club, gave the ball a short, sharp tap up the slope and raced after it like greased lightning. I can see him clearly now. He got to the top in time to see his ball end stone dead. It was one of those typical Dale holes that made him so hard to contend with; he would first seem to give it you with unexpected generosity and then take it back out of your very mouth.

Dale, as it may be inferred, did not take golf or indeed life too seriously. There were occasions, no doubt, when he might have played better if he had gone to bed earlier the night before, but nobody would want him to have been other than he was by nature. Moreover, he had a fine hard power of trying deep down in him somewhere, and of tackling a job conscientiously when he really "got down to it." I am sure that he tried hard at this new job which the war thrust upon him and made a good soldier, as he must inevitably have made a gallant one. He had got pluck, a quality that everyone must long for in his heart, for which there is no substitute.

MY FIRST OPEN

I AM writing at a time of year when in happier days I should have been watching and writing about the Open Championship. The thought naturally brings with it poignant regrets and wonderings. I wonder—and this is common to many people—whether I shall ever watch one again. I wonder —and this is purely personal and selfish—whether some day I shall watch one without having to report it. I have no desire to be cast upon the scrap heap, but the notion of watching an Open just once as an idle spectator with nothing to do is, I admit, a seductive one. Let people believe it or not, the reporting of that last day in particular is no joke, especially if you have two accounts to write and a broadcast or two thrown in. In my ears, as I think of it, is a confused sound of the rushing of crowds, the pattering of rain, the shouting of stewards, and the clicking of typewriters. I see myself, cowering in a shelter, asking imbecile onlookers for information which is never true, staggering back to the club-house for dry clothes, writing on my knee under the lee of a sandhill and having the paper blown out of my hand by a playful wind, looking at the cards pinned up in the Press tent and trying to invent some interesting manner in which the scores may have been arrived at. I long in the depths of my being to be doing it once more, but *it is hard work.*

MY FIRST OPEN

When a friend with nothing to do but relapse into a drink asks me how I "get my stuff off," and whether I post it, I could do anything to him that is sufficiently malignant and has for choice boiling oil in it.

It seems to have become harder work since I first embarked upon it, partly because I have grown older and lamer, partly because championships have grown bigger. My mind goes back with yearning to the first Open that I ever saw and reported, that at Prestwick in 1908. I have forgotten the writing about it, which I took in my comparatively youthful stride, and remember only the fun of it. It seems to me, perhaps inevitably, the pleasantest championship I ever watched. The weather was fine and hot and sunny, the course green and lovely after a deluge of rain on the Saturday before; I stayed with kind friends right on the course, looking out on the Goose-Dubs from my bedroom window. It was ten years since I had first played in an Amateur Championship, but this was my first Open (I never was so rash as to play in it); it was all fresh and exhilarating; I was still rejoicing in a new life and in a new freedom from thraldom of the law. Finally I saw golf played as well as I have ever seen it played since and, as it then appeared, incredibly well, for that was the year in which Braid won with 291, and only once before had the winner's score been under 300.

Apart from the tremendous nature of that score I suppose this could not be called an exciting championship, because Braid was winning easily all the time. Even when he took his famous or infamous eight at the Cardinal in the third round he finished in 77, and his nearest pursuers, already faint and far away, scarcely closed the gap at all; some of them even fell farther behind. Apart from that eight and the general magnificence of the winner I have grown rather hazy and, even though I have just read the account in the *Golf Year Book* of 1909, I do not remember as much as I ought, though certain things do come back.

James started in such a way as to make it perfectly clear that he was going to win. He began with two threes, went out in 33 without the ghost of a slip, and finished in 70. When we came back to the Club, open-mouthed from watching this round, we found that it did not lead the field, for Ernest Gray of Littlehampton had done a still more astonishing 68. Gray was a fine player and on his day really brilliant but, with all possible respect to him, we felt that he was one of those who would "come back to his horses," and in fact that was a sound prophecy, since the next best of his four rounds was 79. Those who were assumed to be Braid's most dangerous competitors, Vardon and Taylor, were already nine strokes behind him after one round; so was Ray, and though Sandy Herd had played very finely he was four behind; Tom Ball ultimately destined to be second, had taken 76. In short, it seemed as the Americans say, "in the bag," and Scottish patriotism rejoiced accordingly. It had still further cause for rejoicing after the second round. This time Braid began quietly 4–4–5, letting a shot slip at the tiny little second hole. After that he went sedately mad with four threes in a row; he was once more out in 33, home in 39, round in 72, and five strokes ahead of all the world.

Looking at the figures, I observe that in this second round he has a three at the twelfth hole, and that brings something back to me; in fact it brings two things, a tremendous brassey shot followed by a long putt, and the only occasion on which I ever saw the sage of Walton so far demean himself as to run. The long since departed stone wall then guarded the twelfth green and ordinary mortals played their seconds short of it and so home with a pitch. This time Braid had hit a very fine tee shot, rather to the left as I see it in my mind's eye, and took a long reconnoitring walk forward. It was then that, having made up his mind, he trotted or ambled gently and with no lack of dignity back to his ball and lashed it home. Oddly enough this desperate feat had, as its immediate reaction, the only serious mistake that he made throughout the four rounds, apart of course from the eight at the Cardinal. He frittered away the spoils of that three by taking a six at the Sea Hedrig. How he did it I do not remember, but accidents can always happen on that fascinating little pocket handkerchief of a green perched among the hill-tops. Immediately after that he got another three, at the Goose-Dubs. No doubt he holed a putt;

MY FIRST OPEN

the number of what may be called middle-length putts which he holed was appalling.

It was next morning in the third round, which is generally deemed the most crucial, that the eight happened, and by this time every earnest student knows how it happened—a second from a not very promising spot into the Cardinal and then two mashie shots, over-bold perhaps and striving for distance, which sent the ball glancing off the boards and out of bounds into the Pow Burn.

Apart from that horrid spectacle, I remember, or I think I remember, two things clearly. The only sign that James was a little shaken came at the fourth hole; he put his second on to the green and took three putts. At the Himalayas came glorious amends, a putt holed for two. I see it a little down-hill and from the right, but I daresay I am wrong; James doubtless recalls it with perfect accuracy. What I remember beyond all question is how we all broke into rapturous clapping. The crisis, in so far as there had been any crisis, was past. He was out in 39, home in 38; he was six strokes in front, and the eight had done no more than keep his pursuers just within sight of him. His last round was a model of confidence and steadiness combined and he beat Tom Ball, who ended with a 74, by eight shots.

The looking back at the scores has perhaps swept me a little off my feet into reminiscence. If I have been tiresome I apologise on the inadequate ground that I have myself enjoyed it. I have felt once more in imagination the Ayrshire sun on my back, climbed with eager steps the Himalayas, sat on the soft dry turf behind the Alps green, and watched Braid moving stately and processional towards inevitable victory.

THE MOST EXCITING

WAR-TIME does not make life any easier for the writer on golf, who is driven back more and more on his own inner resources. I was therefore the more grateful the other day to an old friend who said that he wished I would "dig out" some more of my memories. It happened, too, not long afterwards that another friend asked me what was the most exciting Open Championship I had ever watched, and so it has occurred to me to be shamelessly reminiscent and combine the two suggestions.

In gauging the excitement of a championship a reporter of golf may not agree with the crowd. If he has followed the wrong man, if he has had to be "in two places at once, like a bird," if he has had in his heart the horrid fear lest somebody should win whom he had hardly seen play a stroke, then his personal emotions are likely to make that championship seem more agonising than it was to the carefree spectator. Conversely, when his duty has lain clear before him, so that he was bound to watch the one important couple, then he may under-rate the excitement because his own task was so comparatively tranquil. For instance, there has been nothing more dramatic than Hagen's successful pursuit of Ernest Whitcombe at Hoylake in 1924. I never saw such a round of recoveries as that, or one so full of "ifs." If he had not holed a really stout putt at the tenth, if he had not miraculously got a three at the new Rushes after a deplorable tee shot into a bunker, his last chance would seem to have been gone, but all those "ifs" came off and he won magnificently. It was thrilling, but there was no rival attraction, and I could watch it almost at my ease. Two years before that again, at Sandwich, there was this same Hagen, this time not the pursuer, but heroically pursued by Duncan. I saw plenty of that excitement, for, while Hagen was placidly smoking a cigar and nearly everybody else reposing by the club-house, I had with hideous energy gone out to look for Duncan. Everybody saw him just fail (confound that spoon

THE MAIDEN GREEN AT SANDWICH

Fox Photos, Ltd.

JOHN BALL PLAYING OUT OF WATER AT ST. ANDREWS

THE MOST EXCITING 69

shot which did not drift enough at the last hole!) to tie, but I had also seen him at earlier holes laying incredible seconds within feet of the hole, and just missing the putts. Yet to me the recollection of yet another Sandwich victory of Hagen's, that in 1928, appears more poignant, for a purely personal reason. I could not end my account of the championship until Sarazen, almost the last man out, had finished. The minute I had ended it I had to dash off by car to Deal to broadcast; there would only just be time, and the road might be blocked, and altogether the circumstances were distinctly agitating. Sarazen never looked quite like doing it, but there was excitement and to spare for me.

For the same selfish reasons I dismiss two obvious instances. One in 1914 at Prestwick, with only Vardon and Taylor in the hunt and so no temptation to see anyone else. True, "see" was not the right word, for the Lanarkshire miners meant to see that day, and prevented most other people from doing so. The other instance is that of Bobby Jones and Watrous playing together in very similar circumstances at St. Annes in 1926. And so having named some of those I don't choose, I do unhesitatingly choose 1911 at Sandwich on every possible ground, public and private. With a round to go there were at least eight players, scattered all over the course, each of whom might win, and finally two of them tied. There was excitement, whether for spectator or reporter, and my memories are not merely of seeing the shots but of writing about them as I saw them, sheltering from the wind in some little nook among the hills and trying to prevent my paper from blowing away. There was, too, that year the very particular thrill that Harry Vardon, after suffering a partial eclipse owing to ill health, seemed likely to win again. Harry was, if I remember rightly, in the solicitous hands of his friend, Mr. Browne from Luton, who had invented the Browne-Vardon putter for him and was training him on his own principles. He had only, so we were told, the lightest of meals till the evening—we heard of a mere apple for lunch—and had also been put on a strict ration of pipes. Anyhow, he was playing beautifully; I think I never saw such ideal driving, and till the fourth round at any rate

F

70 GOLFING BY-PATHS

his putting was good enough. The first three rounds were 74, 74, 75; at that point he led the field by three strokes and should he play a good fourth round all would, humanly speaking, be over. Moreover, he was out early, and so had the chance of setting up an unattainable mark for the rest to shoot at. So the excitement had not begun yet; but wait a bit.

It was said at the time that Vardon relaxed his apple-a-day rule before that fourth round and ate a normal lunch, which did not suit him. I do not know whether this was so. There seems something deleterious in lunch before a fourth round at Sandwich, because we heard a great deal about Cotton's when he nearly frittered away his first championship there. In any case Vardon fell off. I saw but little of his round (perhaps I was having my own lunch); I know he missed putts and finished in 80, and now the fat was in the fire. With a round to go the scores had been: Vardon 223, Herd and Taylor 226, Ray, Massy, Braid and Duncan 227, Mr. Hilton 228. Here was richness indeed, and it was clear that the pursuit was anything but hopeless, for Taylor and Herd had to do no better than 77 to tie, and that was a good score in such a wind, but not at all an inconceivably good one. I wish I could remember but I cannot, the order in which those eight were playing. What I do remember most vividly is being in the neighbourhood of the ninth hole and suddenly spying Mr. Hilton coming from the tenth tee, with a few spectators who were obviously wrought up almost to a pitch of frenzy. One of them rushed across to whisper "He's out in 33," and no lightning calculation was needed to see that here might be, nay, ought to be, the winner. Mr. Hilton himself said something to me to the effect that it was such a long time since he had been in the hunt in the last round that he felt rather odd. At any rate, he got two more perfect fours, and then—I have often told the sad story before—hit what looked and what he thought a perfect tee shot away to the left at the twelfth hole. It was just not enough to the left, and the ball was caught in a little jutting bay, invisible from the tee, of the left-hand bunker. He got well out, but he missed a putt and took six; the victorious stride was broken. He struggled on well and might easily

ELEVEN AND THIRTEEN

have won even then but for a bunkered tee shot at the short sixteenth and a consequent five. That made 76, and Harry Vardon, who had been awaiting him for an uncomfortable hour, could breathe again. He had still more anguish over Herd, who, standing on the last tee, wanted a four to win. That meant, in the wind, two very good shots, but a five should be certain. I believe I saw Herd hit his drive, but did not see the hole played out. It seemed to take a long time, as such holes always do, and then came back the sad news, a six. Between all these tremendous events I was scribbling away in my nook and picking up odds and ends of information about Taylor and Braid and Duncan, all of whom had faded out a little, rather, I confess, to my relief. Then came Massy. He too had to do a four, not to win but to tie. Respectfully to emend Lord Macaulay:

> Never, I ween, did golfer
> In such evil case

play a hole more magnificently. A perfect drive left him well within reach, but his ball was cocked up on something of a pinnacle, the last lie that he wanted against the wind. He hit a grand wooden club shot, which ended some dozen yards short of the hole, and laid the long, curly putt stone dead. Everybody knows that Vardon won the tie easily, the gallant Frenchman giving up on the thirty-fifth green, but heaven knows there had been enough excitement.

ELEVEN AND THIRTEEN

THE system of handicapping by giving holes instead of strokes has, I imagine, lapsed into desuetude. Not that it was ever very popular, but match-play competitions were sometimes played under it and it was comparatively common in casual games. I think it must have vanished, because when I consult *The Golfer's Hand Book*, I am told all about handicapping in a "Greensome," in which I have never played, and under the Stapleford system, which I have never attempted to understand, but nothing at all about the ratio which holes ought to bear to strokes. There is here no cause for lamentation, for it was not, I think, a very good plan. Among players who were of something like the same calibre, there was a certain amount to be said for it, but much less when the difference was a wide one. The man who received eight or nine holes start must have felt rather lonely and helpless with never a stroke to help him, with his lead ever decreasing and that tigerish pursuer drawing ever nearer. To be sure if he began brilliantly or his opponent badly he could get a lead that should almost defy pursuit and this was another disadvantage of the plan; human nature being what it is, too much was apt to depend on the first few holes; the receiver of odds was either caught too soon or the chance of catching him became, or at any rate appeared, hopeless. I remember some matches in the old days with adversaries to whom I used to give two or three holes up and capital matches some of them were, but on the whole strokes were much better.

These remarks are prompted by a letter I have just received from a kind correspondent who thinks, and I should guess rightly, that he is the only man who has been eleven up with thirteen to play in an eighteen-hole match and been defeated. The whole story is rather a pleasant one from times more primitive than ours to-day and I will briefly tell it. He was staying at a Scottish course which is famous but difficult of access and entered for a match-play tournament in which one hole was given for every two strokes difference in handicap. His handicap was 12 and in the first round he had to receive six up from a Scottish schoolmaster who was scratch. Scratch indeed was said to do little justice to his powers since it was rumoured that on some other courses he had attained to plus 5. My correspondent was naturally alarmed, but for a while all went quite surprisingly well; the schoolmaster's golf was such as would have shocked his pupils; he lost hole after hole and so it was that he was eleven down with thirteen to play.

ELEVEN AND THIRTEEN

Then came a turn in the tide. The schoolmaster suddenly became as a devil unchained. At the sixth hole he drove straight down the course instead of very crooked in some other direction, put his iron shot on the green and holed his putt for three. He continued to play very well and I suspect that my correspondent, though he does not specifically say so, played but poorly. The holes fell away not, as in the well-known simile, like snow off a dyke, but with the cataclysmic rush of an avalanche. By the time the sixteenth hole had been played the match was all square. Then on the seventeenth tee the schoolmaster made a curious and, in the circumstances, a charitable proposal: he was, he said, tired of golf and wanted a rest; if the match were halved both of them would go on into the next round; let them therefore call it half. He further volunteered the information that he had played so badly at first because he had whisky for lunch, a thing which, as Mr. Pickwick found with orange peel in punch, always disagreed with him. This seems hardly worthy of a Scottish golfer but we may let that pass. They played out the last two holes and the schoolmaster won the match but honourably reported the result as a half. My correspondent, feeling a little uncomfortable in his conscience, told the circumstances to the secretary, who declared that the contract was a valid one so long as it was made before either party had actually won. So both players passed into the second round and what befell them there, whether the schoolmaster won the tournament or whether he again lunched indiscreetly and was beaten, history and my correspondent do not record.

That little story opens up a vista of almost unlimited possibilities in the way of agreement between two players. I have seen two distinguished golfers give each other uncommonly long "short" putts on the home green for a halved hole and match, since neither liked to face it; but that was in an Amateur Championship and they had to face the nineteenth hole. But what of a tournament such as that in which my correspondent and the redoubtable schoolmaster figured? Could each have given the other a full brassey shot for a half at the home hole? Nay, why should they go to so much trouble if they might

74 GOLFING BY-PATHS

have agreed to call it a halved match on the first tee and then played the round for fun? There are to-day but few tournaments in which that kindly rule allowing both players to pass on still exists. I can only think of two, the Jubilee Vase and the Calcutta Cup at St. Andrews. If, and this is admittedly a *reductio ad absurdum*, all the players agreed to halve their matches, the tournament would represent the nearest approach to infinity which the human intellect can conceive. These things are "not done" and probably never will be done. The legislator would have to be called on for some extraordinary measure.

Incidentally no statistician has ever tried to discover whether the rule allowing both players to live and fight another day produces more halved matches than does the relentless system of the nineteenth hole. It has sometimes been suggested that it does, but I doubt if there be any good evidence. It is perfectly true that as soon as one becomes dormy in one of those two St. Andrews competitions, one relaxes very pleasantly, lights a pipe perhaps and feels at charity towards all the world and one's opponent. If he saves the match there is no bitterness, no regret for what might have been. But the very fact that it does not matter and that there is no dread possibility of going to the nineteenth, with ghoulish, gloating friends looking on, has often a sedative and therefore beneficial effect on the leader's play. He does not much care how he plays the last hole and so plays it pretty well and gets the half which is all he needs to win. Circumstances do arise of course, under this system, which make for a halved match. The man who has a putt of six feet, let us say, to win the match and so two for the half is very likely to lay his ball six inches short of the hole; he is not taking any chances, especially on a slippery green. Apart from that, I do not think the statisticians would make any very revealing discoveries.

To revert to the schoolmaster and his bargain it is rather remarkable, or perhaps it isn't considering what creatures of small vanities we are, how much importance we attach to being beaten by only 3 and 2, let us say, instead of 4 and 2. It is wholly absurd, but it is a feeling that is strong in many breasts. I am myself conscious of the weakness and if I were not I should have realised it from an experience of many years ago in an Amateur Championship. I was two up going to the seventeenth and on that green my ball lay six inches from the hole while my adversary having played a similar number of strokes was full fifteen yards away, a long curly down-hill putt, and he therefore gave up the match with the best grace in the world. Someone asked me the result and I unthinkingly replied "Three and one." My opponent's face instantly fell and he protested in an aggrieved tone. I apologised profusely and said that I had made a mistake and that it was of course two and one and he was all smiles again. Doubtless I had been stupid but doubtless also it was odd to mind so very much. That is how we are made, nevertheless, and I recall another instance from a foursome tournament of years ago. I was not this time myself a player. It was a day of pouring rain and all four players were soused to the skin, for there were no mackintosh coats and trousers. One side was dormy five and on the fourteenth green they had two for the hole and three for the half, from some two yards or so. "Will that do?" they asked. The opposite side consulted a moment and replied, "We'll give you a half but not the hole." The offer was gladly accepted and the four splashed home through the rain gushes. Five and four was harmless, but six and four would have been unendurable.

I am conscious of being very desultory, but the schoolmaster's unorthodox behaviour reminds me of another heterodoxy as to which the rules appear to be silent. A golfer, and quite a good golfer too, who is now dead, had, so I was told, an odd habit on his local course. On the day of a monthly medal he would tee up several balls on the first teeing ground and drive them away. When he had hit one to his perfect satisfaction he would declare that now he had begun his round; his partner thereupon drove and off they went. That this was very singular conduct no one will deny, but I do not know exactly what rule he was offending. Certainly it was not Rule 4 for stroke play; he was not "playing on or on to any of the putting greens"; he was not "intentionally playing at any hole of the stipulated round within his reach," for the first hole was far out of anybody's reach. He was, he would have said, merely practising, which was perfectly lawful, and he happened to choose the first teeing ground for the purpose. I am sure there is a flaw in this argument, but exactly where it lies it is not so easy to say. Some behaviour is so palpably absurd that the rule-makers do not contemplate it. No appeal was ever made to the Rules Committee; the habit was regarded as an amiable weakness of an old and respected member, in short as "pretty Fanny's way." As far as I know no one has ever imitated him, which is a good thing, as otherwise the tee might grow congested on medal days.

WRY NECKS

LONG before he died the golfing world was full of John Ball stories; he had become in his lifetime a figure of legend. Now that he is dead golfers have ransacked their memories, fondly to recall something that he said or did, and several of them have told me their stories in letters. Here is one which I like particularly, only a very little one, but it illustrates both his rather stern and conservative outlook on the game and his habit of having sly digs at his adversaries. It comes from an old friend of mine who used to play a good many rounds with Mr. Ball at Harlech in 1913, the year after he had won the last of his eight championships at Westward Ho! This friend can, alas, play golf no longer, but even so he says that he "hesitates to write the fatal word socket." Being in dread of that ghastly affliction not to be named, he had a mashie with an exceedingly wry neck, and, having to play a pitch "over the then formidable sleepered chasm in front of the seventeenth green" took it out of his bag. When he had played the shot Mr. Ball held out his hand for the club, took it, cast one withering glance at it, and handed it back with the words: "That's the sort of club I should like to see barred. If you can't play with the proper tools why not learn?"

WRY NECKS

My friend was afraid of socketing, but he was still more afraid of august disapproval, so he never used the club again and put it away in his locker, where it came to what Mr. Ball would have thought its appropriate end in a club-house fire. Let us hope that his socketing was frightened away for ever, even as Jack Mytton's hiccup was frightened away by his setting fire to his nightgown. I myself feel a moment's retrospective tremor in recalling that I had both a mashie and a mashie-niblick with distorted necks when I played my last game with the great man, at Hoylake in 1924. Perhaps he did not notice, though he had a most observant eye, or perhaps he did not think it right to abuse me, since we were playing in a real match, between the Royal Liverpool and the Society. At any rate I escaped, and I cannot help thinking that he was just a little hard, though doubtless in the most disarming manner, on my poor friend. It is all very well to tell people to learn, but a socketer in the throes of his hideous ailment is past all teaching. Prayer is for the moment his only hope, and a club without a socket is better still. By the way, I have just remembered with great joy that I possess a treasure at home, a club that was once Mr. Ball's *and it has a wry neck*; but I must add that it is no form of pitching club, but a Park's putter, which even the most conservative will permit.

There seems some little unfairness about this. Herbert Pocket (in "Great Expectations") remarked to Pip that "it is indisputable that while you cannot possibly be genteel and bake, you may be as genteel as never was and brew." So you may be a pillar of orthodoxy and an upholder of the "best traditions of the game" and yet have a putter with a crooked neck, but you are, even to-day, a little suspect if the necks of your irons are similarly bent. Here is an inequality which ought to make truly democratic blood boil. It must in fairness be added that this prejudice against "kinks" is not what it once was, although necks have got not less but, if anything, more wry than they used to be. The first clubs, which the late Mr. Frank Fairlie invented for a remedy against the sin of socketing had not in fact bent necks; but they were rather ugly and clumsy in appearance because the head was, so to speak, set in front of the shaft.

George Low of St. Anne's improved on the Fairlie pattern in so far as his iron heads were smaller and neater in appearance. I possessed a cleek of his which, no doubt with an owner's partiality, I thought almost pretty, and, by the way, long before I possessed it I had publicly used something far more unorthodox. I have told before how my Uncle Horace, a distinguished maker of scientific instruments but no golfer, made an aluminium cleek, on the croquet mallet principle, with the shaft running into the middle of the head; further, that, with what Mrs. Gamp would have called "bragian" boldness, I used it in an inter-University match.

This is, however, to meander. It was that admirable golfer, the late Mr. G. F. Smith of Formby, who devised the important alteration to these anti-socket clubs by giving them bent necks. His irons, which I think he made himself—at any rate they were forged under his eye—were extremely tortuous as to the neck and looked rather like corkscrews, with a dash of some gigantic dentist's instruments such as might be seen in a nightmare. They had, however, this great advantage, that the player no longer felt that the head was in front of the shaft; the crook in the neck brought it back to the proper place. Mr. Smith played extremely well with these clubs, and from that moment all crook-necked irons were, I think, made on his principle. They have grown more elegant to-day and less pronouncedly eccentric in aspect, but they are his clubs. *Exegit monumentum.*

The virtue of such clubs lies not so much in preventing us from socketing (I have accomplished that supposedly impossible feat with one of them) as in inducing us to believe that we shall not socket, so that we swing the clubs freely and without fear. A socket is rather like a "boo" in that oldest of golfing stories wherein A challenged B to a match on the terms that just once in the round he might suddenly say "Boo." As is well known, the fatal monosyllable was never uttered; it was sufficient to creep up behind the victim with the air of one *booiturus*, about to boo. Similarly we may, when afflicted, go through a whole round without a single shot hit towards point, but the thought that we can do such things plays the deuce with our mashie shots. Personally I have for some years now given up my old clubs with their crooked necks. So I can, like Mr. Micawber, stand erect before my fellow man and punch his head if he offends me. Nor am I, touching wood, nowadays at all afraid, but should this hubristic remark ever be followed by a severe attack I should have no hesitation in reverting. Whether all is or is not fair in love and war, it certainly is in socketing.

A PREHISTORIC PEEP

A KIND friend has told me in a letter a little story of nearly forty years ago, and I found it so pleasant that I hope others may do so too. As he has written at least one admirable book and ought to write several more, it would be a piece of impertinence for me to paraphrase him; so here it is in his own words: "In the early days of the present century, as Thomas Hardy would say, I went one evening to a restaurant near Piccadilly Circus and, as I sat down, I saw Braid and Vardon at the next table. They had evidently been playing golf, for their bags of clubs were leaning against a vacant chair. There were no hoods in those days and the irons were pushed into the bags with the grips uppermost. I am an indifferent but enthusiastic golfer, and the sight of these great men eating food alongside me was a delightful experience. I felt as I suppose a typist would who found herself sitting beside Greta Garbo in a tea-shop. At another table a young man was sitting with two girls. They were what would now be called 'bright young people,' and they evidently intended their conversation to be audible to everyone in their neighbourhood. Bags of golf clubs were about as common in London as hansom cabs are now, and the young man explained to the girls what the funny things were which they saw leaning against the chair. He said he had played golf when he stayed with friends at North Berwick. He then rose and walked over to the bags and, saying 'Excuse me,' he pulled out an iron. He made me think of the man in the Bible who reached out his hand to steady the

80   GOLFING BY-PATHS

Ark of the Covenant when he thought it was going to fall off
the bullock cart, but no fire came down from heaven to destroy
him. He waggled the club in a knowing way, and then said
to the great ones, 'You know, I don't like this club. There's
something wrong with the balance.' Vardon looked at him
solemnly and shook his head; Braid just gave him a good-
natured smile. Neither of them spoke."

A gentle little story, perhaps, but, if I may respectfully say
so, very well told, so that it brings a picture before the eye.
It is highly characteristic, too, of those two distinguished golfers,
men of unexampled dignity, never given to superfluous conversation. I enjoy my friend's similitudes, and I like his simple
reverence for the truly great. I cannot help wondering whether
the champions of to-day are quite such deities to their admirers.
That they have a larger circle of them there can be no doubt,
but is it quite so reverently an adoring one? It may be that
when golf was more of an esoteric mystery than it is now its
votaries, feeling themselves of the elect, were the more devoted
in consequence. It may be, again—and this is probably nearer
to the prosaic truth—that my friend and I are now a little past
the hero-worshipping age, in that we can still prostrate ourselves in memory before the heroes of our youth, but not quite
so deeply before modern ones. We have become a little too
stiff in the knees for such genuflexions. It is interesting, too,
to be reminded of the days when bags had no hoods. It brings
back the sensation of wet and slimy grips, for, in a real deluge
the rain reached the uttermost parts of the bag. Yet that was
not the worst; the real sorrow of a drowning day, which had
nothing to do with a lack of hoods, was the terrible harm that
could be wrought to a wooden club-head, made, as it used to
be, of soft wood. Its face could be reduced almost to pulp.
After such a day the club-makers were busy putting in leather
faces, but even a leather face could become sodden and horrible.
The life of a cherished club was brief and precarious, and one
never knew when one might be in mourning.

There is one point in my friend's narrative which a little
surprises me, namely the extreme rarity of the sight of a bag
of clubs in London, so late as the twentieth century. I should

A PREHISTORIC PEEP 81

have said that by that time it had ceased to be an extraordinary phenomenon. He is, unless I insult him, fully as old as I am, but I am not sure that he has played golf as long, and moreover he is a Scotsman and so may be inclined to attribute ignorance to the poor English. I am disposed to think that all those who have played golf for a good long time, at any rate in England, believe that the moment of their beginning was also the moment of golf beginning to boom there. I began to play "way back" in the 'eighties, and so I should attribute to some such ante-diluvian period as that the general astonishment caused by the strange spectacle of clubs. In the first *Golfing Annual*, published in 1888, and unique in its red cover as contrasted with its green successors, there is an article supposed to be by a non-golfer. I have always suspected Horace Hutchinson of it, for no better reason than that it dealt with golf at Eastbourne, where he used to play. The writer, whoever he was, describes how he saw a golfer pick up a shell and, rushing up to him, exclaimed: "Ha, my dear sir, I observe you are a conchologist." That kind of joke comes from the days when golf and golf clubs were still new and astonishing in England. Indeed, it seems now to belong to almost as remote an age as that which concho-logists presumably investigate. But between that date and the beginning of this century the game had made vast strides. Beyond doubt there was an era, which lasted a good long time, in which the sight of a bag of clubs served as an introduction between those who were otherwise strangers. It was in the 'nineties—I am sure I have told this story before—that a very good golfer, whom I will simply designate G. E., was in the train bound for Sandwich, with his clubs in the rack. To him enters a friendly gentleman who, seeing the clubs, at once opened fire with "I see you're a golfer. Going to Sandwich, I suppose." "Oh, no," replied G. E., with instant resource; "I've never played the game in my life, I'm only taking the clubs down for a friend." How different are things to-day, when clubs form no such bond. One would no more address their owner than one would say fraternally to a stranger with an umbrella: "Ah, I see you think it's going to rain."

WRITING IT DOWN

IN a golfing dairy which I kept during the first few years of this century there is after the record of one day's play, this entry: "Could not drive. Must learn to keep my —— —— head still." A day or two later there is one more cheerful: "Driving pretty well now." The circumstances have, not unnaturally, vanished from my mind, but the inference is that I did momentarily contrive to keep that qualified head still, or at any rate thought I had done so, which was probably more to the point, since faith is the greatest of golfing gifts. This makes me reflect that, considering how constantly golfers devise new tips which they believe will make new men of them ever afterwards, they seldom or never write them down. They may, to be sure, do so secretly in little locked books kept in the most private of drawers, but as a rule I fancy they do not, believing that, as they have become completely reformed characters, there will be no need.

I wonder if they would benefit by doing so. Now and again perhaps they would, especially if the tip were not some fantastic creation of their own but a piece of advice given them by a good player well acquainted with their game. But the book would be rather sorrowful and ironical reading since it would bring back to mind so many disappointments. Those who know their *Cranford* will recall a pathetic little speech of Miss Matty's. "My father once made us," she said, " keep a diary in two columns; on one side we were to put down in the morning what we thought would be the course and events of the coming day, and at night we were to put down on the other side what really had happened. It would be to some people rather a sad way of telling their lives." So it would be in golf, for these wonderful devices that are to see the very stars out have as a rule swiftly to be abandoned. "All taps is vanities," as Mr. Stiggins once observed, and I am afraid the same is true of all or nearly all tips. Yet now and again the written word might bring back to memory one which had not only helped us once but would do so again. Most of our golfing diseases are chronic and so the same cures, of however temporary a nature, ought to be applicable.

I remember Horace Hutchinson making an interesting remark on this point. At the time when his game was at its best he had from some extraneous cause ceased to play altogether for six or nine months. He believed that he had never played quite so well again, because in that golfless interval he had forgotten some of the tips which had been stored up in his mind during his time of full practice. Whether he was right no man can say, but how curious and interesting a record it would now be for the golfing student, if he had thought of writing down that accumulated experience. That the best of golfers can for a while forget the most obvious and elementary pieces of golfing knowledge is, I think, certain. To keep the hands well up at the top of the swing was a tip of John Ball's and, after he had been knocked out in a championship late in his career, a friend of his tentatively suggested that he had not been following his own advice. "Why didn't you tell me before?" was the answer. "I should have won." I remember, too, J. H. Taylor telling me how he found his driving much shorter than it ought to be; the ball was hit cleanly and flew straight, but it would not go far enough. He went out to commune with his club in private and discovered, so he said, that he had been forgetting to pivot. He had probably been rubbing that rule into his pupils day by day, and had unconsciously been failing to obey it himself. If the great can forget that which is almost a second nature to them, how much more easily can humbler people do so!

At the moment of writing I have played a very little very mild golf after not having been on a real course for hard on two years. The results were at first heart-breaking, but towards the end of my second abbreviated round I began to hit the ball almost decently. Common sense would no doubt say that this was solely because the game had begun to feel less strange, and there may be something in so eminently prosaic a view; but in my present state of comparative happiness I attribute the improvement to two tips. What they are would be of no

84 GOLFING BY-PATHS

interest to anybody and in any case I would not tell lest the virtue should go out of them; but my point is that they were not in the least new; I had often had recourse to them both before with beneficial effects. Yet it had taken me a considerable time of impotent misery before I had thought of either of them. Perhaps if I had had in my pocket a little notebook full of tabulated tips my recovery might have been speedier. Perhaps for that matter it is not really a recovery at all and the two tips will prove to be a fallacious mirage. The next nine holes will show, and I am not too sanguine.

Apart from that entry in a diary with which I began these desultory observations I confess that I have several times made notes of some discovery that appeared of value, but I cannot add that I ever studied them again, partly because they were generally lost and to this day possibly repose in some neglected drawer. Of one thing I feel tolerably sure, that it is not enough for the patient to write down the cure, unless he also writes down details of the disease as well. There are some remedies so invariably applicable, such as "Don't press," that they can seldom do any harm; but a cure for slicing is of little value to him who is in the throes of a quick hook. The diary may record an improvement owing to some dodge or another, but that will scarcely avail if its owner has forgotten what had been the matter with him. A long time ago my father, who lived in a state of equable despair about his golf, had a lesson from a then well-known professional, an excellent teacher, which temporarily restored his driving. For years afterwards, whatever crime he might be committing with whatever club, he used to say: "Let me see. What was it that T told me to do?" and would forthwith try to put the old cure into practice. This pathetic faith in an universal panacea was, alas! seldom if ever justified.

Harry Vardon had a belief, to be found somewhere in his books, that everybody has a putting stance which is for him the ideal and that he who is putting well should make notes of his stance accordingly for future reference. This would presumably have to be done with careful measurements in terms of inches, reinforced perhaps by a diagram. Whether or not

AT ABERDOVEY'S FIRST MEETING IN 1892

In the middle is the Author, winner of the Scratch Medal with 100

ON THE 4TH TEEING GROUND AT GLENEAGLES.

Sport & General.

the belief is sound, such a diagram might have great value as a faith cure, for in putting more than any other department of the game confidence is temporarily more than half, nay, nearly all, the battle. Vardon's theory was, incidentally, opposed to that of one very fine putter, John Low, who held that if a man was hitting the ball cleanly he might even stand with his legs crossed. John was by far the better putter of the two, but I have a notion that for those less gifted Vardon's belief is the better. And yet he was in this respect in his later years a physician who could not heal himself. Perhaps he forgot to try his own remedy.

For the last five years golf may be said to have been a game without a tip. Those who have played it occasionally have done so for air and exercise and pleasant companionship and to distract their minds from sadder and graver matters. Soon we may hope they will be able to play more of it and with a better heart and will take a deep interest in whether they hit the ball or not. Once more they will wonder what they have been doing wrong and will make felicitous discoveries. Once more they will write them down in their diaries or in those secret and hypothetical notebooks. Whether they will be the happier for so doing is an open question. For myself I think they will, but then I have been all my life a tip addict, and these habits are difficult to cast aside.

LONG SWINGS AND SHORT

NOWADAYS on the very few occasions on which I hit a golf ball it is only quite casually. I take some balls in my pocket and an iron masquerading as a walking-stick, and when I see a field free of long grass or cows I say in the manner of Mr. Wemmick: "Halloa! here's a field. Let's have a shot in it." I do not dress up for the purpose in the now orthodox woolly or jumper: I hit these shots just as we used to hit them once, dressed like ordinary, dull, Christian gentlemen in coats. I have been wondering whether I shall

86 GOLFING BY-PATHS

as a consequence play it coated evermore. It was during the other war that I first played in a woolly, not because I wanted to, but because a military tunic was altogether too constricting for the purpose. As a result of that too easy-going woolly, or so I imagined, I fell into a bad habit of slicing. As soon as ever I was demobilised I put on a reasonably tight coat again, and behold! the slice disappeared as if by magic. What am I going to do now when, after many struggles, I have more or less learnt to play in a woolly?

I am still, as a true blue Tory, a little prejudiced against it. It has something of an undignified and unduly curtailed air as worn by the elderly and the plump. As I survey myself in a glass before setting out I am inclined to address my image as Mr. Pickwick did Mr. Tupman before the fancy dress breakfast: "You don't mean to say, Mr. Tupman, that it is your intention to put yourself into a green velvet jacket with a two-inch tail?" However, it is admittedly of no interest to anyone but myself what I wear and the coat has long since been doomed ever since the invading hosts from America first appeared, looking so lithe, lissom and comfortable in their jumpers. Already we had been flirting with a greater freedom, with coats of stockinet and coats made, if I remember their title aright, with "pivot sleeves." Then the tide of jumpers came flooding in and it was all over in no time.

One rather curious little reflection on the subject does occur to me. Is it not odd that to-day when our golfers are so much freer than they were of any impeding garment, they swing the club a much shorter distance than they did when they were comparatively speaking tied up? I pick my words with some care; I do not say that they swing less freely than of old, for they do not; but they swing much shorter. An era of tight coats and long swings has been followed, rather paradoxically as it would appear, by one of those loose woollies and short swings. It used once to be said that the gutty ball needed a much fuller swing to get the most out of it than does the rubber-core. I am inclined to think that there is no foundation for this statement. If the modern player, brought up on a rubber-core, ever hits a gutty ball he does so with his natural

LONG SWINGS AND SHORT 87

swing, and there is certainly no lack of power to be detected. That theory will not do, and yet there is no question that men did on the average have longer swings than they do now. Our memories, if we are old enough, as well as our old photographs, tell us so. The man with a comparatively curtailed swing was once the exception among good players. Andrew Kirkaldy's swing, for instance, was deemed short, and it looked like a half-swing beside the long slashing typical St. Andrews swing of his brother Hugh. It would not be deemed anything out of the way now. There has clearly been a definite change of method, and I am perfectly prepared to believe that the modern. players have discovered at once a surer and more effective one. I think, however, there is one definite reason for the change which is not generally appreciated.

If any reader of a theoretical turn of mine will look again at the *Elementary Instruction* in the Badminton book, he will find the words: "When the club, in the course of its swing away from the ball, is beginning to rise from the ground, and is reaching the horizontal with its head pointing to the player's right, it should be allowed to turn naturally in the right hand until it is resting upon the web between the forefinger and thumb." If that reader will then try for himself this method of letting the club "flop" if I may so term it, at the top of the swing, he will find that the head of his club has probably gone a good deal farther than usual. Then if he will look at any professional of his acquaintance he will see that the club is not allowed to turn or "flop" to even the slightest extent in the right hand. It stays exactly where it has always been, gripped between the right forefinger and thumb.

I am convinced that here is at least one reason for the general and apparent shortening of swings. When Mr. Hutchinson wrote in the Badminton, men held the club with what is now called the "old-fashioned palm grip," and that letting the club rest upon the web at the base of the thumb came naturally to those using such a grip. I am not for a moment contending that he described the then current mode inaccurately. What I do say is that as soon as the finger grip, and in particular the overlapping grip, became the fashion the old method departed and with it the old advice applicable to it. I remember to have talked to Mr. Hutchinson about it once and he was hard to convince. He scarcely believed, I think, that players had come to hold the club immovable in their right hand; but there can be no question that they now do so; nor is there any question that with this method the swing is naturally shortened. One player in the old way comes into my head whom I hardly dare call modern since he is a little older even than I am; but he is modern by Badminton standards. This is Sherlock. He has always had a "two-handed" grip, and I remember his once telling that he felt as if his swing "could not finish itself out properly" unless the club enjoyed some liberty in his right hand.

Here is another illustration of my belief, not, I hope, without interest. The late Mr. Frank Woolley was a very fine golfer in the Midlands, who played for England before the last war and had, owing to illness, an all too short career. When I first knew him he was a schoolboy with a typical schoolboy's long "head over heels" swing. When after some years' interval I met him again he had the shortest swing I ever saw in a first-class player. I asked him the reason for this metamorphosis and he said that it had come to him quite unconsciously from the time when he had adopted the overlapping grip. No doubt he had let the club "flop" before and with the change of grip came this most noteworthy shortening of his swing. In his particular case the change was exceptional, almost exaggerated in extent, but I am convinced that his was the right explanation, the more so as I experienced the same thing, in a much less marked degree, in my own case. I am afraid I may have been labouring a small point, one which may seem a dull one to those who are bored with technique; but I like a little theory myself sometimes and I hope a few others may like it too. After all it is pleasant to be reminded of the days when we wanted passionately to know "what we were doing wrong," and to look forward to happier days when we may do so again. Air and exercise are very well in their way, but golfing man cannot live by them alone.

A GAME OF CHOOSING

THERE are few people so modest that they have not some little accomplishment which they like now and again to show off. Mine is a particularly tiresome one, tiresome, that is, to other people, though full of intense pleasure to its owner. It consists in reeling off certain lists of names of very doubtful interest to anybody but myself. They are a miscellaneous lot, and among them are the five members of the Cabal, the Knights Challengers in the *two* tournaments in "Ivanhoe" (any schoolboy can do one), the first four wranglers in Frank Fairlegh's year, and the Cambridge eleven of 1878. The Seven Bishops I have, alas! forgotten, and I always come to grief over Mrs. Nickleby's lovers. As regards golf, my one little trick is, I am convinced, rare, but may strike the modern golfer as singularly futile. It is the list of the eight courses in England, in their correct order, over which Mr. Horace Hutchinson halved his great match against that mythical opponent, James Macpherson. Hoylake, Westward Ho!, Bembridge, Wimbledon, Blackheath, Felixstowe, Yarmouth, Alnmouth. There they are, without looking at the book (though, to be sure, I have often looked at it at other times), on my honour as a gentleman.

That list is, I maintain, interesting, though my remembering it may not be so. Mr. Hutchinson wrote his most attractive little story just over fifty years ago, and the eight courses figuring in it were chosen as representing "the main golfing greens" in England at that time. It may be that Wimbledon and Blackheath gained their places not on their intrinsic qualities but in order that London and inland golf should be represented. Even so, they were not grossly undeserving; the eight, taken as a whole, were representative, and it is interesting to compare the list with one that might be made nowadays. The game of choosing is an amusing one to play, and every golfer will play it differently. I am going to try, but I announce beforehand that I do not propose to adhere too slavishly to sheer merit. All my courses will be good, but now and again I may cheat a little, either on territorial grounds or in favour of one that I particularly love at the expense of another which, by the strictest canons, would generally be deemed better. So if anybody disagrees, and everybody of necessity must, it will not be worth his while to be cross with me. As a final declaration before starting, I mean to choose two inland courses because there were two in the original list; and now for it!

I am afraid that a clean sweep must straightway be made of six out of the old eight. It is obvious that Hoylake and Westward Ho! stay in; it is equally obvious that no one of the others is good enough. The original pilgrimage began at Hoylake, and then came the long journey to North Devon. By all means let us begin at Hoylake again, but before we go so far south, is there not another course near at hand? Formby and Hall Road and Birkdale and St. Annes cannot all be left out, but there is only room for one, and my one shall be Formby. I do not say dogmatically that it is the best, but it is an old friend (I remember it before all those fir trees had clothed the sandhills) and wonderfully good and charming. In it shall go, at any rate, and we shall have had two days of divine shrimps before flying elsewhere. Even now we are not quite ready for Westward Ho! I have to consider two inland courses, and if one of them is in the north now is the time to visit it. After mature thought but with little ultimate hesitation I am going to choose Ganton, a noble spot and the sea-sidiest of all inland courses. So from Lancashire to Yorkshire before at last we start for Devon, and I suppose there is no one with the hardihood to deny Westward Ho! its place. If we want golf in the most perfect, natural country of sandhills we get it there. If we want dour, flat golf, where the game looks easy and is in fact "aye fechtin' against ye," we get it with a vengeance in those long, deceitfully open holes at the beginning and end of the course. If we want Devonshire cream we can have it, even as James Macpherson did, and it will not, as in his case "get jolted into bad lies inside of us," because there is no longer a jolty, bumpy drive to the Pebble Ridge.

A GAME OF CHOOSING 91

When we are in the west there is an obvious temptation towards Saunton and Burnham, but it must be ruthlessly put aside; there simply is not room, for we have half our eight already, there is another inland course to come, and we must end in that richest golfing corner of Kent. Let us take the inland course next, and now, without the least shadow of doubt, I head for Suffolk and the nine precious holes at Worlington. "What!" exclaims some hypothetical reader, "no London courses, no Sunningdale?" "Certainly not," I reply. Sunningdale is a charming spot and a good course, and is generally regarded as the metropolis of inland golf, but it cannot get in here. "Well, then," says the reader, "what of Walton Heath?" There he has, I admit, touched me nearly. That is a great course, but so, as all who know it will admit, is Worlington, and its solitude and its line of fir trees are very near to my heart. The only question which will admit of discussion is where we go next, and, since we are in the east and Norfolk comes next to Suffolk, I am going to vote for Brancaster. I may be cheating a little, as I said I should, but Horace and James Macpherson finished up with three east coast courses, and surely we must have just one in their place. Besides, I love Brancaster. It is a very good course, make no mistake about that; it is lonely and peaceful, and it has another endearing quality which I mention with diffidence. It looks so terrifying that, when we find ourselves not utterly crushed by those terrors, we gain an agreeable belief that we are better players than in fact we are. That is exceedingly soothing.

Now we must make straight for Kent, and already we are in a quandary: we are seriously embarrassed with riches. Only two places remain, and here, when we alight at Sandwich, are three famous links cheek by jowl—St. George's, Prince's and Deal. It is like a game of musical chairs. "And how about Rye?" interposes that hypothetical reader; "do you mean to say you are going to leave Rye out, after all the stuff you have written about it and the wind roaring in the Dormy House chimney?" It is really a very awkward situation, and I must take refuge in saying that with only eight courses it would never do to have four of them in one corner of England. St.

George's *must* go in on every ground, historical or sentimental, theoretical or practical. To leave it out is inconceivable and, that being so, I think Prince's must go. It has every beauty and virtue, but it is not St. George's; and now there is one place left, and either Deal or Rye is to occupy it. Deal has tremendous claims, because it is a tremendous course, in sheer stern golfing quality perhaps the greatest of these four; but then Rye is quite adorable and, moreover, as that confounded reader reminds me, has lately gone up in the world in point of severity, by the making of those new holes in the country over the sand-hills. I can see nothing for it but cowardice; I shall toss up, and nobody will know which course has won the toss. There we are, at any rate, with our seven courses and one place in abeyance. It would very likely have been a slightly different list if there had been no need to go inland, and if we had not felt bound by some little geographical obligations. Still, a tour of those eight would be extremely pleasant; it is not a bad list. "Which I meantersay," as Joe Gargery observed, "that what I say I meantersay and stand or fall by."

FAVOURITES

SOME time ago I came to the conclusion that there was nothing like boldly proclaiming one's wants. One day I happened to write that sausages were hard to come by and a kind soldier sent me some (scrumptious!) all the way from Africa in a tin. Another day I referred in a more or less impersonal way to the growing shortage of golf balls and a distinguished poet, who had given up the game, sent me his remaining few. I was much touched, but also a little ashamed, and resolved never to do it again. And yet I have, quite innocently this time, broken my vow, and again have found my good Samaritan. I once wrote an article suggesting a game of guessing the favourite courses of eminent players as given in the *Who's Who* of the *Golfer's Handbook*. I added that it would

FAVOURITES

93

be interesting to know which courses obtained most votes but that assuredly I should embark on no such statistical task.

It is hardly to be believed, but a kind friend having had a cold which put him to bed—blessings on his snuffles and sneezes—has actually carried out this formidable piece of research. Not only that, but he also investigated and tabulated the favourite shots of the great as set out in the same place. It has not killed him, for his cold is much better, and with the profoundest gratitude to him I propose to inflict some of his results upon the reader. I ought to add that his labours are not quite up to date, since he has during the last few years lived chiefly abroad and his only edition of the valuable book is now more than ten years old. However, golfing taste has probably not so very much altered in that time; I at any rate have found him interesting and I hope some other people may too.

And so here goes. The distinguished players included in my friend's edition named between them 105 courses and he has extracted all those courses which received ten or more votes. These are they: St. Andrews 81; Sunningdale, Prestwick and St. George's, Sandwich, 35 each; Portmarnock 30; Gleneagles 25; Hoylake and Westward Ho! 24; Princes, Sandwich 23; Troon 21; Deal 16; Muirfield 12; St. Annes, North Berwick and Formby 11; Walton Heath 10. What a judgment on James Braid for refusing to set down his favourite course! He would certainly have named Walton Heath as one of them and then by his vote it would have joined the other three bracketed immediately above it. It is a sad business and yet I fear his withers will remain unwrung.

It would be easy to comment on that list at almost any length but I will refrain and leave it to speak mainly for itself. I am glad that St. Andrews comes out so easily at the top of the list and it makes me think better of my fellow men. It doubtless owes something to prestige and tradition but its majority is so great that it cannot be explained away. Then it is interesting to find that out of the leading courses only three are inland. Sunningdale comes first of these and is indeed second in popularity only to St. Andrews. Here again I may respectfully say that prestige has something to do with it. Sunningdale was the first inland course to become really famous and it has ever since been unofficially regarded as the premier inland course. It is a charming place and a very good course, but that it so far excels some of its peers I cannot think. Nearly everybody has seen Sunningdale but there are a great many golfers who have not seen Portmarnock and therefore could not give it a vote. So I think its high place on the list is a striking piece of testimony to its great qualities. There are one or two features in that list that puzzle me and even make me rather cross. How in the world anyone can rank Gleneagles above Hoylake and Westward Ho!—well, well. I will not pursue this invidious question, but turn to the rest of my Samaritan's statistics as to favourite shots.

In this matter there must be some little ambiguity. For instance a large number of people simply, and rather lazily, put down "iron," which may mean any one of a variety of strokes. Few are so admirably precise as my old friend, Mr. Willis Mackenzie, who, as I observe in my edition, specifies a run up with a mashie. I like that because I too am fond of the shot, which I call a "scuffle" and have always thought it heterodox to play it with a mashie rather than an iron. That is by the way, however; the iron must benefit by the vagueness of its devotees and it naturally comes very high up on the list, but not as I should have expected at the top. It is the mashie that comes first with 75 votes and the iron next with 62. It is true that by a little, perhaps legitimate, manœuvring the iron might be brought to the top, since no fewer than 28 players vote for the mid or medium iron; 5 vote for the three-quarter iron; 3 specify the No. 3, 5 the "push iron" and 2 the jigger. With these various allies the iron comfortably beats the mashie.

After those two rivals comes the mashie-niblick with 45 adherents, beating the driver by a short head, two votes. Next, and I am very glad to see it so high in these comparatively degenerate days, comes that fine old club the cleek with 25 faithful suffrages. Whether it would have so many to-day I do not know but in my own more recent edition I found several of great distinction—John Ball, Arnaud Massy and among the younger men Ernest Whitcombe. The cleek,

FAVOURITES

rather to my surprise, beats or did beat the spoon by two votes. One player, by the way, was so very nice, almost to the point of priggishness, as to particularise the three-quarter spoon shot The spoon is closely followed by the brassey which gets 20 votes. I should have expected it to have more, but perhaps the great drive so far nowadays that they seldom need that noble club. In my edition it had some illustrious supporters of the older school, in particular two now gone, Harold Hilton and Sandy Herd. I imagine that it would often be the ladies' choice since they have more need of it than the stronger male animal, and extremely skilful and accurate they are with it. It is, I observe, Miss Cecil Leitch's choice.

Three heroes give the niblick as their favourite, though whether they think of it as a pitching instrument or love the full-blooded thump out of a bunker I cannot tell. It may be they were moved to set it down by a rather weak-minded sense of humour, such as is occasionally exhibited in the original *Who's Who*. Finally the putter gets twelve votes and I think that is notably to its credit, for there must be many who would have liked to put it down but were deterred by the fear of a frightful Nemesis. Putting is so horribly elusive an art, even among unquestionably fine putters, that it needs a bold man to say he is fond of it. My friend has gone to the trouble of setting out for me the names of these twelve who were not to be intimidated and I have studied the roll with interest. Doubtless they are all good putters, but as to some of them I was not peculiarly aware of it. Three of them, however, need have no fear of proclaiming their allegiance—Mrs. Percy, Eustace Storey and Jack White. Mrs. Percy earned, I believe, the sobriquet of "One putt," and the two men are two of the doughtiest and most trustworthy as they are also two of the most studious putters I know.

I shall always think that *the* best putter I ever did see was Jerome Travers and I looked him up at once in my book, only to find, a little disappointingly, that he plumps for the "Full iron." Well, that is only showing proper gratitude, for there was a time when his wooden clubs so utterly betrayed him that he had to play his full iron from the tee and I saw him win a championship when so doing. I am afraid that my own favourite is to-day an iron shot in a field when there is nobody to see me and a nice hot sun on my back to limber me up. But that is another and altogether too painful and egotistical a story. Meanwhile my best thanks to my good Samaritan who has saved me the trouble that I should never have taken. If he catches another cold I hope he will remember me.

A PUTTING CHALLENGE

A FRIEND, speaking in awe-stricken praise of E. V. Lucas's facility, once declared that he could, if need be, write about a match-box. E. V., hearing of this, said he must see what he could do about it, and thereupon, allowing himself some legitimate licence, produced a peculiarly charming and Lucasian little essay. I am in no mind to derogate from the achievement, but at the same time he might have been set a much harder task; a match-box, with its easy transition to matches and so to light in general, was almost easy, what our airmen call, as I understand, "a piece of cake." The author himself thought lightly of it and would doubtless have agreed with Uncle Pumblechook in "Great Expectations," who averred (I write away from my books) that there were plenty of subjects, if you could put salt on their tails.

In a general way that may be true, but there have been moments of late when I have felt inclined to deny its truth as to golfing subjects. The other day I was bemoaning myself to a friend, alleging with a perhaps unmanly touch of self-pity that subjects were very hard indeed to find, when you hardly ever played golf yourself and seldom even saw a course and there were no matches between illustrious persons to watch. As he did not seem much impressed I said to him with a challenge in my voice: "Well, if you think it so simple perhaps you will suggest a subject for me." He pondered for some moments, dragging the depths of his powerful mind, and then looking up brightly, as if he had thought of something really original,

A PUTTING CHALLENGE

exclaimed: "What about putting?" I did not trouble to answer the poor man. It would have been vain to tell him that thousands and thousands of articles had been written about putting, and that I had written hundreds and hundreds of them myself. He was clearly past praying for, but when we had parted I began to wonder whether after all I might not pick up the gauntlet he had unwittingly thrown down. It would be a brave thing to do, and perhaps there might be some aspects of putting that had escaped any considerable amount of attention. In short, like E.V. but alas! without his gifts I decided to see what I could do about it.

Here then is one question about putting to which I have never heard a satisfactory answer. We have all, even the meanest of us, some days on which we putt not merely steadily but brilliantly, in the sense that we hole a number of putts that could not possibly be called short and a few of which are almost outrageously long. What I want to know is why those days never coincide with those other and more frequent ones when we are playing with commendable accuracy up to the green. I assume it as axiomatic that this is so and I think most people will agree. I am not talking of champions, but I think it is relatively true of them also. The days on which the long putts go flying in are those when they are rendered necessary by previous errors; scintillation on the green is a corollary to eccentricity on the way there. It would almost seem that the consciousness of our need spurs us on to hole long putts, but that explanation will hardly serve; long putts travel too clearly on the wings of chance and it is not in the power of the will, even when goaded by despair, to make them go in. I rather incline to the belief that the goddess who rules over golf, though she can often be so spiteful, is yet in this matter kindly and gives us a long putt or two to console us for the miseries we are suffering on other parts of the course.

I do not go so far as to assert that when we are driving and approaching really well our putting will be really bad. That would be putting the case too high, but in such circumstances it never attains more than a highly respectable two-putts-to-a-green standard and very seldom that. Just as the golfing goddess never allows us to do all our good holes at once—if she did we might go round in an average of threes—so she holds that a little misfortune is good for us on the green lest we grow arrogant and hubristic. Therefore she balances our good driving by exceedingly moderate putting. I recall a talk with George Duncan, in which he applied this theory of what I may call averages, not to a player's single round but to his whole game. He supposed a young golfer who came rapidly to the front chiefly by means of his brilliant putting. If, he went on to say, that young man gradually improved the rest of his game so as to live up to his new position in life, so surely would his putting fall away and become no more than "average." He gave as an example his old foursome partner, Charles Mayo. Those whose memories go tolerably far back will remember that Mayo burst on the world as pre-eminently a putter. His driving was at first rather short; both off the tee and through the green he was decidedly "average"; but he made up for any deficiencies by holing a great many putts. The rest of his game quickly improved; he became a very good golfer indeed and, as will be recalled, he and Duncan challenged Vardon and Braid and were not too severely beaten. By that time this mysterious law of averages had come to apply to Mayo's putting; he remained a good putter but was no longer in any way a brilliant one. There was something no doubt in Duncan's theory, but I hardly think it was applicable to some of the great American players, who added diabolical putting to the most accomplished play up to the green.

Another point is that we are all more superstitious (that is the best word I can think of) about putting than about other parts of the game. We are convinced that in this particular respect the Fates will, after a period of granting us their favours, turn malignantly and rend us. When we are driving really well, each fresh tee shot struck well and cleanly down the middle of the course adds to our confidence. We become more and more convinced that we are going to hit the next one and, unless indeed we are led astray into an orgy of pressing, we generally do hit it. It is otherwise with putting. Up to a certain point indeed success begets confidence and confidence

A PUTTING CHALLENGE 99

leads to success; one putt holed makes another more likely. But this can hardly, as in the case of driving, go on for a whole day or even a whole round. After a while, even to a good putter upon his good day there comes the inhibiting thought that he has had his ration, that the Fates will not allow him to go on holing those essentially "nasty" ones of five or six feet, to say nothing of the long ones. Once that horrid notion has come into his head it is terribly difficult to exorcise, and he will cease to strike the ball with the same insolent freedom. His putting need not collapse altogether; indeed, if he is an habitually good putter with a sound method there is no reason why it should; but it will become for the rest of the round just "average."

Of course it is possible to think of people whose putting has been not merely average, not merely very good, but positively sparkling right through several days of a tournament. The two instances that come to my mind are both of great American amateurs; Walter Travis in our Amateur Championship at Sandwich in 1904 and Jerry Travers in the American Amateur at Garden City in 1913. Day after day each of those two not only made, humanly speaking, no mistake on the green but holed an unconscionable number of long and longish putts from beginning to end of the championship. No doubt many more examples might be given, and it seems to me in recollection that James Braid putted with a persistent brilliancy right through the Open at Prestwick in 1908.

I said a little way back that long putts travel on the wings of chance, and so, when they are our opponent's, they appear to do, but the statement is not really quite accurate. Granted that there is some luck about the holing of long putts, they are not the scandalous flukes that we sometimes bitterly call them. When we ourselves have one of those rare and heavenly days when "everything" goes in, we are conscious of hitting the ball unusually true and unusually clean; the ball leaves the club with a delicious click too seldom granted to us. When there is a question of an inch one way or the other there must be luck, but the ball does not even look as if it were going in save on the days when we are hitting it truly. The fine putter's long putts do not always go in, but they are generally pretty straight on the hole and look at least as if they might go in. How different from the long putts of the rest of us! Except on our red-letter days they are palpably anything from a foot to a yard off the line, and that almost from the moment they leave the club.

BACK TO MACEDON

IN the war before last, as it may now mercifully be called, I played my golf on the Vardar marshes in Macedonia, and perhaps I may be allowed to hark back to it for a moment. It was the one bright spot in an otherwise drab existence, so that, at a safe distance, I like looking back on it: it *was* good fun. I played altogether on seven courses in that accursed and interesting country. I saw an eighth, and at the time I wished I hadn't. It consisted almost entirely of nullahs full of bully beef tins, and I wrote a possibly offensive article about it and its players in *The Times*. A nurse, presumably enamoured of one of the players, resented the article and insisted on the return of a particularly attractive spoon which, through an intermediary, I had borrowed from her. Of some of the seven I can only recollect the names and assuredly could not now spell them. The one that I loved as the child of my own brain was near the base at Dudular, and though I did lay it out I will assert that it was far from a bad one. The turf in winter—and golf was a winter game—was, for playing through the green, perfect, for it had an encouraging bristle in it, never met elsewhere, which made the ball sit up. It might have been too bristly for perfect greens, but that did not matter, as we had no greens. The course was too near a road along which passed the Commander-in-Chief; he would have been "wery fierce" if he had seen soldiers making putting greens, and very possibly he would have been right. So we just cut a hole, and got into it with lofting irons as best we could. We envied

A TYPICAL SUNNINGDALE VIEW
The 4th Green with the 5th and 6th Holes in the distance

Sport & General.

GEORGE DUNCAN PUTTING

Sport & General.

BACK TO MACEDON 101

rather bitterly a friendly course at a hospital for Serbians near by. They had beautiful greens; but then nobody could see what they were at. In winter, when the fiend of malaria was dormant, there was, so we malignantly said, one medical officer for each patient. At nine o'clock the M.O. looked at his patient; at half a minute past he heard what his temperature was; at one minute past he told the sister to carry on, and then, for the rest of the day, there was the golf course. No wonder they had good greens.

Our ground was flat with some gentle undulations—just what it ought to be—and our hazards, though few, were of a most orthodox description; a road and a railway that St. Andrews would not have despised, some patches of rushes, and a water hazard that guarded one flank of the course. St. Andrews would certainly have despised, though old Tooting Bec would not, our only "artificial" hazards, tall perpendicular ramparts for the sheltering of sheep from the wind. We had sixteen holes, playing one of them twice from different angles, and this one was on the best natural "island" green I ever saw; quite small, slightly saucer-shaped, but with the ground falling away on every side into marshy troubles. That made two admirable short holes, and there was another very pretty one on a peninsula jutting out into the water. There was one two-shotter, which I recollect with parental pride as making full use of both road and railway. First we drove over the railway, cutting off as big a chunk as we dared, to find ourselves in a narrow strath with the railway on our left and the road on our right, and a second shot to be struck straight and true between the pair. There was another hole which many people might think dull. Some misguided people think the Dowie hole at Hoylake dull, and a great man who ought to have known better said that it looked like a hole you might find on Clapham Common. If there were many such on Clapham Common I would never ask to play anywhere else. At any rate my hole was made in pious imitation. It was a "long one-shotter" needing a wooden club. The tee was close to the railway, which was on the player's left, thus corresponding to the out-of-bounds at the Dowie; so was the green. There was nothing else at all, but

H

GOLFING BY-PATHS

then, except for the patch of rushes, there used to be not much else at the Dowie, and many think that that hole has been not at all improved by the bunkers on the right. At any rate, mine was a very hard hole to play; not hard to get a four at, or perhaps a three with a run-up and a putt, but an extraordinarily hard one at which to attain artistic perfection. To hit a full shot dead straight on to that green, skirting the railway for the whole flight of the ball, was a desperate task: one tried as a rule to bring it in with a hook from the right, or sometimes, greatly daring, to hit the ball out over the railway and let it drift back into safety at the end of its flight. Either of these was a feat to bring satisfaction and to spare: to hit it dead straight was too much altogether, and indeed to hit the ball dead straight when you *must*—it is easy enough when you needn't—is one of the hardest things in all golf.

There was another hole, a long two-shotter, which also depended for its very considerable merit on a hazard, this time of water and marsh, which lay close to the line on the left for the whole length of the hole. Now when I look back on the course I wonder if I used my position as architect dishonestly and laid out the holes to suit myself, who am, on the whole, less afraid of a hook than a slice. It certainly appears that in the holes I have tried to describe the terror lurked always on the left. Ought we perhaps to have played the course the other way round? One notable architect of my acquaintance, Sir Guy Campbell, boldly turned a course round the other way at Bexhill, going out by the right instead of the left, making things nastier for the slicer and making the course generally better and more interesting. However, I do not think that that would have done for Dudular, and I am not going to let my conscience prick me severely at this time of day. Anyhow, ours was a course *sui generis*. No other that I know of had sixteen holes instead of eighteen: certainly no other had "flags" consisting of large rocks painted white and placed at a stated distance behind the holes. All other kinds of guide, except a sheep's skull and a helmet with a hole in it, were instantly stolen by the otherwise amiable inhabitants. No other had as its features "horses, dead, one," to use Ordnance language (it was only temporary, thank heaven), or dogs, wolfish, in considerable numbers, who hung on our flanks with the most disagreeable expression of countenance imaginable and would not allow of any protracted waggling. There was also the little gipsy girl who used to beg by the tee to the water-hole jump, who would not be silenced, and was the excuse for some bad shots. Likewise there was the shepherd, strongly scented with garlic, who would come and show us with a pathetic gesture his watch that had stopped, saying "Johnnie" in a tone that would have melted a heart of stone. Sometimes he would also bring us a lost ball he had retrieved and receive not pence but leptas "in his unwashen palm." Yes, it was very good fun, the more so as hardly anything else was fun at all. Besides—perhaps it is only a pleasant delusion—I think that because I was in such good practice, I wasted on that course some of the best golf that in my humble way I ever played. It has long since, I believe, been a "real" course now, with a brick club-house, the home of the Salonica G.C., and doubtless eighteen holes, all new and all different from mine. It can never be mine again.

> 'Twas my first-born, and O how I prized it!
> My darling, my treasure, my own!
> This brain and none other devised it—
> And now it has flown.

A CHOLEUSE PLAYS GOLF

IT happens now and again that people give up golf for years and then take to it again, feeling like so many Rip Van Winkles who have awakened to a new world of far-flying balls and steel-shafted clubs. I have just heard of a case of this kind. Chivalry forbids that I should state the precise tale of ungolfing years which preceded the great awakening, because the golfer in question is a lady; but she will not, I am

104 GOLFING BY-PATHS

sure, resent the statement that the number is considerable. She is, in fact, a cousin of mine, and my last recollection of her as a golfer is of a little girl in a blue holland frock and a red woolly cap. To-day she is an eminent person in the service of the State, and the call of duty has swept her away from London to "somewhere in England," where there is an admirable golf course. I may add, that it is a seaside course where I have played in many and pleasant matches; but beyond that I must not go. I rather envied her for being there, and felt that the natural advantages of the place were wasted on her. The State, I thought, had better have sent me there, though, to be sure, I have no notion of what use I could have been. However, I received a letter the other day in which I read to my surprise : "I am thinking of playing golf!! and have in fact bought some second-hand clubs from a colleague." I am delighted to hear it, and can only hope the colleague has not taken advantage of her inexperience and done her in her eminent eye.

I shall be anxious to know how much she remembers of her ancient golf, and when I say golf I should more accurately say "chole," for it was that venerable Belgian game that we played in my father's garden and a bit of a field beyond. The principles of the game are simple and are familiar to those who know the historical chapter in the Badminton volume. There are two goals, a considerable distance apart; I believe a church door is a popular goal in Belgium. Our goals were, at one end the space between two trees which really did make goal-posts, and at the other a small triangle of grass, guarded by a bank of laurel bushes and a tin hut containing bicycles. The players divide into two sides and engage in a spirited bidding match after the manner of Bridge. This bidding is as to the number of innings in which they will back themselves to reach one of the two goals, and an innings, according to our rules, consisted of two consecutive strokes. After each innings the other side has its turn, technically known as a *décholade*, in which they endeavour to hit the ball as far as possible away from the goal, or, better still, into the most abominably bad lie within reach. When I add that on our course there was a wood-shed and a slimy green pond, it will be understood that the *décholeur*, if sufficiently venomous and accurate, could do the deadliest damage. There were four players, and so two aside, in our games, three little girls and I—a good deal older and, I may not immodestly add, more skilful. I was handicapped by having to play with a left-handed iron, but even with that weapon I was relatively a long hitter, and I have a guilty recollection that my side generally won.

We played that game, as it seems to me in memory, for hours together with unflagging enthusiasm. I have never in my life played it on any other course, but it was certainly a noble pursuit on that one, and it has one valuable element in which golf is deficient. You can do your enemy actual positive harm; you can attack him by something more than mere propaganda; you can fall on his ball and put it into a wood-shed, from which it is the devil and all to get out; you can hit it hard on the top with the back of the club, thereby driving it straight down into the soft ground, but that is a dangerous form of *décholade* and not recommended. At any rate, you can do something directly to that enemy which is malignant and revengeful in the highest degree, and there was, as I recollect, no law of etiquette forbidding you to express your joy when you had succeeded. Golf is a polite game, in which it is not the thing to stand over a man in a bunker and count his strokes, but chole knows no law against standing over an enemy in a wood-shed with every possible demonstration of delight. And supposing by some miracle that the enemy just got the ball out in their next innings, it was the best fun in the world to put it back all among the faggots, with the succeeding *décholade*. In short, it was a fine, hostile game.

No doubt my Miss Van Winkle will find substantial differences between golf as played at ——-on-Sea, and the chole of yester-year. She will not find the ghost of a wood-shed nor, I think, any ponds, though I did once hole a niblick shot out of casual water there. She will have to mind her manners about gloating over people when they get into bunkers, and putting will be an entirely new art to her, because, of course, we had none. Neither, on the other hand, had we, save on the tee, anything but the worst possible lies. A rough, wild bit of garden, a tussocky bit of field, gravel walks and flower beds—those were in fact the only lies we had; so if she retains her ancient skill, nothing in the way of trouble ought to appal her. Sand she may not like, but the velvety smoothness of the fairways will be a joyous revelation. I am confident that she will make rapid progress, if only her clubs are suitable, but I gravely mistrust that colleague. Have they, I wonder, ancient, twisted wooden shafts and heads with pulpy leather faces? Are they at all like the bundles, tied with string, of second-hand clubs sometimes to be seen exposed in moderately tempting array outside a pawnbroker's? Not, of course, that one might not light on a perfect gem of a club wasting its sweetness in some such place. Indeed, I have thought that one might find the one club in the world that would be a magician's wand by attending sales of unclaimed property by railway companies. Still, I should like to know a little more of the colleague's reason for selling the clubs. Is he or she merely tired of the game, or has some princely tip from a rich uncle made it possible to buy a new set? Do these discarded ones constitute a set, or are they only a miscellaneous job lot? Finally, is the putter made of gun-metal, with an overhanging face, such as is, for some inscrutable reason, always provided for those who putt on municipal courses in public parks? If it is, then, in the words of Praed:

My own Araminta, say no.

Meanwhile, I am seriously contemplating sending a little ladies' golfing literature as an offering. She might begin with Miss Hezlet and so work through Miss Leitch and Miss Wethered down to Miss Barton. The books are all on my shelves—but no! one who began in childhood must have retained a natural flowing, easy swing, and needs no such dangerous learning. There is nothing like a thorough grounding in a wood-shed.

A MATCH IN ITALY

A LITTLE while ago I was able through the letter from a friend in the Low Countries to give some account of golf on the course at Waterloo, untouched by the Hun and still in admirable condition. Now two other friends of mine in Italy have been playing near Florence and one of them has kindly given me a minute account of their round of nine holes. I hasten to pass it on to a wider public, with such proper reticence as must be observed and without giving any clue to their respective identities. I will call the writer of the letter R and his opponent T which will convey nothing of value to the enemy.

This course is at Uglino some five miles from Florence and I think it must be a very good one since the two players enjoyed it immensely despite certain superficial disadvantages. The view, I gather, is lovely and R describes the course as "extraordinarily well laid out." He adds it is not unlike Wentworth, with a touch of St. Cloud and Chiberta " to make it continental," which certainly sounds an attractive mixture. Its condition was not that of Waterloo, for it had apparently been left to itself for two years and the greens "varied in length from four inches to bare patches." In some cases the holes had worn rather too large, a most comforting and flattering state of things as I know from my own experiences of Greek golf in the first war. In other cases by way of compensation they were so overgrown with grass that there was, as I judge, barely room to get into them. The fairways had suffered to some extent from various military exercises. The players' equipment was on a modest scale, two borrowed sets of clubs and three balls. One of these bore a famous name but was of 1929 vintage which by now must be losing some of its quality. The other two would normally "have been given to the dog" before they reached their then condition, but beggars must not be choosers.

And now for the match, which is really quite exciting, and I will say at once, lest any reader finds it too much for his nerve,

108   GOLFING BY-PATHS

that the ending is a happy one. I had also better say before-hand that both R and T are good players, a fact which might otherwise not be guessed from their delusive scores. The first hole was one which, had I been reporting it, I should have scented as having a far-reaching effect on the match. It was about 430 yards long and began cheerfully from a high tee. T however began poorly by topping his ball fifty yards into a heap of stones among some trees. R being in a generous mood after having ballooned his ball quite straight a full 150 yards said that T might lift and drop under the inadequate penalty of half a stroke. What a lesson to us all to stamp on our adversary's head when we have the chance! R justified his own confidence by reaching the green in three but he took four putts with a mashie niblick and T won the hole in 6½ against 7.

At the second the match was squared because T picked up (no details given), but the third "like the far hole at Wimbledon coming back up the hill" he did in five and so was one up again. The fourth, a one-shotter of some 180 yards, was another that the reporter might pick out as crucial. Both played superb tee shots and ended about four yards from the hole. T took three putts. "Aha," exclaims my hypothetical reader, "then R squared the match again." The assumption is premature; for R took four putts and became two down. However he won the next, a long hole, in a perfectly played five, and the short sixth was halved in what he calls a glorious four. The adjective may seem excessive to those who sit at home at ease, but all things are relative.

At the end of the seventh the match was square again; R won it as he says, "easing up," for T, who seems to have been rather too soon discouraged, retired after topping five wooden club shots consecutively without approaching the green. That is all square with two to play and the spectators begin to hold their breath. The eighth was a short hole, and R having the honour had bright visions of being dormy as he saw his ball soaring straight for the pin. Owing to some miscalculation, however, the ball pitched 40 yards over it and the lesson was not lost on T, who took a cautious No. 7, reached the green and won the hole.

A MATCH IN ITALY 109

So R was now "dormy one down." I copy out his own deplorable expression, but he ought to know better, even though he has been some time away from the game. At any rate both he and his enemy hit good tee shots straight down the course. R had to play the odd and topped his iron shot straight along the ground but also straight down the middle of the fairway. It was not a good shot but it was good enough, for T in an exuberant moment took a wooden club; the ball "hit a tree middle stump" and was never seen again. So there was the happiest of all endings, a halved match. I cannot attempt to give T's score as he twice picked up and once lost his ball. The data as to R's are more definite but there are one or two gaps and I never did approve of "approximate" scoring; I will therefore leave it alone, merely remarking that the match is the thing and that no true golfer thinks too much of his figures on such an occasion.

If the story has any dramatic quality, as I venture to hope it has, the credit is all R's, for I have but slightly expanded the information which he managed to crowd within the limits of a single air letter. When I first read that letter I felt a pathetic yearning to be reporting golf matches again. His letter also made me reflect what a much better chance of being picturesque the golf reporter would have if only he were set to report, I will not say bad golfers, but good golfers when they are a little out of practice. What the reporter wants for the successful plying of his craft is incident, and those nine holes at Uglino were rich in incident. With champions in full practice there is a lamentable lack of it in any real sense of the word and one has to call a shot rather too much on the left of the fairway a "hook" in sheer desperation. But with balls bounding off trees and burying themselves in stones there is no need for such dishonesty or for padding in the shape of descriptions of style. Facts, as Mr. Gradgrind, I think, remarked, are what we want, and those nine holes were essentially factual.

Many, many years ago I remember being hard up for a subject when the time for an article drew near. So I walked out with two friends of mine at Ashdown Forest in the hopes of finding one. I did not have long to wait. Nothing of interest happened at the first hole, but those who know the second will understand that here my hopes were high. What with a drive uphill over a country of chalk and deep ruts with some heather beyond, another belt of heather farther on, a stream guarding the green, and the green itself full of alarming slopes and borrows, there is ample scope. So when, after many breathless adventures one of them had won the hole in eight, I was able to say good-bye to them with my warmest thanks and make for my desk, having almost more material than I knew how to deal with.

This epic combat of Uglino had one quality very important to the reporter. How can he arouse any sympathy in the reader's breast if one player is not making a gallant uphill fight of it? Well, here was R at one time two down, then squaring the match, then having the cup dashed from his lips at the eighth and finally saving himself by that master stroke of the straight, topped iron shot. There is by the way one thing he forgot to tell me. I do not know which of the two players used that single ball of superior vintage or whether, in a truly sporting spirit, they used it alternately. It must have made some difference.

PAST DAYS IN THE SUN

I READ somewhere a symposium, if it may be so termed, of various readers as to the things for which in their innermost hearts they most yearned, the things they looked forward to after the war. Only two of these pathetic wishes can I remember. One was for crumpets to be eaten before a blazing fire, and that awakened beautiful buttery memories. The other was for a small villa at Bordighera, and when I read that I exclaimed: "Ah, thou hast touched me nearly." Not that I precisely want a villa but I should dread-

PAST DAYS IN THE SUN

fully like to play a little golf once more on those lovely, easy-going, sunshiny Riviera courses.

It chanced, too, that the day of my reading was of an icy description with a wind demanding a minimum of two pairs of mittens, a day on which one would have liked to wear a shawl as did the traveller on Pickwickian coaches. Suppose, just suppose, that one could have leaped into a train, a Blue Train, and after a few hours of delicious expectation woken up to see golden islands set in a "perfumed sea." The only thing I could do was to sit down, very close to the fire, and dream of my two visits to the Côte d'Azure and its courses and two to the Côte d'Argent, to Biarritz and St. Jean de Luz and particularly to Pau.

I loved the golf then, but I think I should love it more now when I long for sun on my stiff back to limber it up, and prefer holes that are not too long on courses that do not profess to be "a fine test of golf." One judges golf by a different standard in that country, and olive trees, umbrella pines and sunshine give an air of enchantment to courses that amid frost and fog and mud at home one might scornfully set down as suburban mud-heaps with steeplechase bunkers. There are some that are definitely good, apart from their heavenly surroundings, but one does not necessarily love them the best. The warmest corner in my heart is beyond all question reserved for Coste-belle for the reason that I saw it first, and nothing in all four visits came up to the first morning there, a little sleepy after the train, in a garden of palm trees filled with all the drowsy hummings and buzzings of a summer day.

On my first visit one drove to the Costebelle course, which was comparatively long and plain sailing; on my second there was a new course, a good deal shorter, to which one loafed gently on foot from the hotel garden. The earlier was the better, the later the lazier, and I cannot now recall a single hole on either, but I have only got to think of them to feel drenched in sunshine of a magical quality. There was Hyéres too, close by, where the hazards consisted largely of hurdles, but there was one hole that far transcended the rest where one played down an avenue of lovely silvery trees. I do not know that even that was a very good hole, but seen in retrospect it appears to have come out of a fairy story.

On both my Riviera trips we went from Costebelle to Cannes, which I suppose I ought to have liked better but did not in fact like nearly so well. It was too urban and smart for my taste. The golf was unquestionably good. At least part of Napoule is good, with a resemblance to the New Zealand course at Byfleet. And all Mougins is good with its charming fir trees and its touch of nightly frost to keep the greens fresh and verdant. It was wonderfully pretty and peaceful there too and I am not ungrateful, but my heart goes out more to a course now no more, Sospel, near Mentone. We drove there and a most horrific drive it was over a slippery mountain road of hairpin bends, where the big car had to make two bites at the cherry over every bend, and there always seemed to be a gap in the stone wall exactly where we were backing towards the precipice. In compensation we had a divine omelette for lunch when we got there. Cancelling these things one again another, Sospel was entirely fascinating with its little town of bright houses, pink and blue and white, and the River Bévéra rushing swiftly down the middle of the valley. The holes were good holes, too, the best, I thought, in the Riviera. Alas! that there came, as I am told, first a railway and then a big hotel, and finally the course, I know not why, vanished.

The Nice course at Cagnes with really good greens, a rare excellence in that baking sunshine, and groves of olive trees, was thoroughly pleasant if unexciting. La Turbie, high above Monte Carlo, was rather a matter of *dejeuner* and the most wonderful view in the world than of golf. Of Valescure, near San Raphael, on the other hand, I entertain very tender memories. The golf was still in the making and there was, as I recall, a good deal of red mud, but the umbrella pines made up deficiencies; so did the drive back to Fréius towards evening, a drive through the woods behind two little ponies whose hoofs made scarcely a sound on the road of thick white dust. We had some time to wait for a train at Fréius and sat in lonely contemplation in the Roman theatre. So quiet and lonely was it that I was tempted to play an iron shot from a patch of

PAST DAYS IN THE SUN

113

grass amid the stone seats. Perhaps, I thought, nobody had ever played an iron shot in a Roman theatre since the world first rotated. Thank Heaven I overcame that odious instinct of the tripper and refrained.

The Riviera has rather run away with me and that is unfair to the Côte d'Argent, because if I had to choose one of these places for a holiday of mild golf I feel pretty sure I should choose Pau. Chiberta was only in the making and Biarritz I found rather disappointing, though there is to be sure some good fun by the cliffs and the sea. Nivelle was somewhat muddy, though it had a gorgeous view, and it also had then the great Arnaud Massy, who told one, with many chuckles, of the innumerable francs he had won from too enterprising Spanish visitors in the summer. Hendaye was pleasant and had one hole never to be forgotten, guarded by a deep chasm with the waves boiling and foaming at the bottom of it; an ingenious booby trap of a hole since, if one played a mashie shot from the tee one could carry the chasm comfortably enough with the second shot, whereas a full drive from the tee left so great a carry that one had to play humbly round.

All these were courses to be placidly grateful for, but Pau possessed some quality of real golf that they lacked. It was not too crowded and one could play more or less when one liked; but that was only one small thing among the many that made up its charm. It had a fine ancient dignity of its own and that of right, since Pau is one of the oldest golf clubs in the world. When Hoylake and Westward Ho! were not, Pau was; the club was founded in 1856, and tradition hung palpably round it. Here was no course made by some enterprising speculator or hotel-keeper to attract the visitor. Here was a golf club for gentlemen to play golf at their leisure.

Moreover the course, at first perhaps a little flat and disappointing, grew on one. There was a subtle interest in the holes not at first perceived; they wanted more playing than was apparent. Some of them, where they drew near the rapid river Gave, could be both exciting and alarming. The only criticism one felt inclined to make was that the greens could have been made worthier of the rest of the course. There is plenty of rain at Pau; there was no question of the greens being over-baked and something, one felt, might have been done about it. In fact I believe it was done after my last stay there and perhaps I am giving vent to murmurs long since out of date. Anyhow, it was a jolly, friendly, tranquil place to play golf. Willingly would I hit a considerable number of balls into the Gave in order to hear the small caddies cry in unfeeling exultation, as they are whirled irretrievably away: "A Bayonne! A Bayonne!"

THE ALLIES

I HAVE been reintroduced to a rare form of golf which may be recommended to golfers conscious of being agitated, incompetent, out of practice and generally out of conceit with themselves and their game. I had played it once before with one whose golfing nerves had attained such a pitch that they could not endure an opponent of flesh and blood. His particular motive was, I think, that he had putting "staggers" in an extreme form and feared that a hard-hearted enemy would make him hole out the short ones. So he proposed that he and I should match our better ball against Par. I think, but I am not quite sure, that he took his strokes to help him. That which I do clearly recollect was his generosity in the matter of those short putts. As soon as his ball was within four feet of the hole or even further he hastily knocked it away; nor did his liberality stop there, for he wanted to knock mine away too at similar distances and I felt a delicacy in protesting. The not unnatural result was that we did pretty well and Par suffered a reverse at our hands.

My reintroduction to this game was owing to a kind and considerate friend. Being himself in good practice and knowing that I was lame and stiff and had played only two rounds of

THE ALLIES

nine holes apiece in two years he suggested that we should play not as foes but as allies. We were to combine not against Par but against Bogey, and I must add that, the course being long and the wind high, I could see very little difference between the two. The Colonel was a most fierce and active young officer and gave away very few chances. I was well content to agree to his proposal and we had an entertaining if not, from a merely sordid point of view, a successful game. I will not go into exact figures, but Bogey had the best of it. My partner began by playing extremely well and carried on the fight single-handed with dash and courage. After a while he lapsed a little; I then had several chances of coming to his aid, either by holing a shortish putt or by putting a chip dead from the edge of the green. Alas! I consistently refused to accept them, becoming more and more overwhelmed with shame and contrition as they slipped, one by one, away, and did little or nothing to justify my existence. I had moreover—some excuse is permissible—a beast of a wooden club of an odious and toy-like lightness, borrowed from somebody else. In that respect the game was a failure, but my partner was very forgiving and as soon as the worst of my stiffness has worn off we are to try again, when I hope to be better armed and more useful.

There are some perhaps rather obvious things to be said for this game. It does away with any undue spirit of hostility and promotes one of fellowship and friendliness. Instead of wishing the other man in the bunker, as the mildest player must some-times do, we wish him whole-heartedly on the green. If his long putt appears certain to go in and then turns off at the last moment the tears that we shed are no longer those of the crocodile; we make no mental reservations when he calls gods and men to witness that a malignant plantain had turned off a perfectly struck ball. In short we enjoy all the pleasures of partnership, as we also must endure with such fortitude as we can that fear of "letting the other fellow down" which makes foursomes for some people a misery, but it not quite so para-lysing in a four-ball match. The well-worn tactics of a four-ball should be followed just as if there were a human opponent

116 GOLFING BY-PATHS

the partners solemnly discussing which is to lay his putt dead for four while the other goes for his three, and so on. This is perhaps harder to do than in a real match, for there is a tendency to go out selfishly for a dangerous carry and let Bogey go to the devil. It is tempting to take excessive risks just as it is in playing cards for love or for a negligible stake; but the more seriously it can be taken the better game it will be.

It is a game of the kind which is good to play with children, and my play was on this occasion childish enough in all conscience. I still gratefully recollect how, when I was a small boy at Felixstowe my father, having finished his round, would take me out with him after tea. We played a solitary foursome, not a four-ball, but we did not play against Bogey, who had not then come into existence, but sternly counted our score for nine holes in a medal round. It was when I was very young indeed and I think my best unaided score for the nine holes was then 70. We reckoned our score by an average of sixes and once, to the best of my belief, we accomplished a 53. One under sixes—that was a proud moment. I may have been one or two under sixes when I played with my kind friend, but sad to say I was not proud of it.

I have so far left anonymous the scene of this singular game. It was at the Gog-Magog course, generally known as the Gogs, near Cambridge. I used in the earlier part of its career to know it most intimately and indeed I think I must have been one of the first who ever struck a ball on its then stony and chalky surface; but save for a single round—and that was some years ago—I had not seen it for ages and it was interesting to go back. From that last visit I had carried away the impression of wonderfully good greens and a course altogether in admirable condition, and this impression is now if possible strengthened. I had imagined, and indeed rather hoped, that the ground would be burnt hard and dry, so that my poor little "shotties" would run as far as might be; but I found everything verdant, the ground at its summer best, neither too hard nor too soft, and the greens no more than pleasantly and reasonably fast. In short, except for my play, it was "all wery capital."

I am not going to describe the changes in the course as I used

PLENTY OF TROUBLE
On the links of the Royal Lytham and St. Anne's Club

THE WINNER ALMOST HOME

R. A. Whitcombe's brassey shot to the 17th at St. George's in 1938

THE ALLIES   117

to know it, for that would be both uninteresting and unintelligible; but there is one point perhaps of some little interest, since it is of more general application. Those who knew the Gogs in earlier days will recall a certain bareness and bleakness. There was still the great and noble stretch of view, and a very small hill can make a very big view in Cambridgeshire. Incidentally, a young gentleman playing there for the first time the other day, after contemplating the prospect, pointed at the imposing tower of the new University Library and asked: "And what is that water tower?" What a good thing Sir Giles Scott was not there to hear him! That is, however, an irreverent digression. There was, as I said, an unquestionable bareness about the course; it looked too much like one huge undulating field, and this, though it might not affect the quality of the holes, had a depressing effect upon the spirits. It has now been wonderfully changed by little spinneys and copses, chiefly, as I remember, of fir trees, which are dotted here and there. The player may well become involved in them if he goes crooked, and there is one particular little wood which must tempt the long driver to a mighty carry every time he stands on the third tee. I could see Mr. Tolley in my mind's eye lashing out at it. But that is but a secondary point. The real object, which seems to me to have been very skilfully accomplished, was the breaking up of the landscape's monotony.

I mention this not merely in praise of a particular course, but because everybody knows other courses which in their youth lack landmarks, and by this barren and featureless quality induce a feeling of melancholy. It must need some courage and vision to set out on a scheme of planting in what looks at first so vast a wilderness, and when they are planted the poor little trees seem, to begin with, paltry and artificial. But it is worth while to take a longer view and that which was once a dull field takes on in course of time almost a sylvan air.

THE SECRET OF STYLE

ON one wall of my room there are six bookshelves ranged one above the other, and all those books deal with a subject, the game of golf. There must be in all nearly a hundred of them. They were once magnificently tidied and put away there by a kind young lady, and have ever since kept themselves to themselves, while Dickens and murders and other agreeable subjects live separate lives on other walls. Looking through those shelves lately I read with a sudden shock the title "Some Secrets of Style." For a moment I thought that here was a golf book I did not know; then I realised that I had fallen into the same error as that kind young lady must have done when she thought that such a title could in my house mean only one thing. This book by Mr. Henry Bett—and a most excellent one it is—deals in fact with style in writing. I took it out and began to read it again, and then it occurred to me that much that the author had to say about literary style could probably be applied, with a few changes, to golfing style. Of course, the comparison must not be pressed too far, but, subject to that limitation, here goes.

First of all, my author points out that there is a difference between a style and style. Every golfer has a style—that is, a golfing manner of his own; it is easily recognisable in the case of most of us as a bad one. On the other hand, all great golfers. "however widely their styles differ, possess in common the attribute of style." We are then given a definition of style in writing which will do sufficiently well for golf: Lowell has said that it is "like the grace of perfect breeding, which makes itself felt by the skill with which it effaces itself, and masters us at last with a sense of indefinable completeness." Neither all great writers nor all great golfers possess it in the same degree. There are writers "whose powers of thought are greater than their powers of expression"; there are some who have by comparison ordinary things to say but can express them admirably;

THE SECRET OF STYLE 119

there are some who possess both powers in the highest degree. Golfers can similarly be do divided. Harry Vardon, Mr. John Ball, Mr. Bobby Jones, George Duncan—here are four who could do the greatest things in the most perfect style. What they did and how they did it were equally interesting and entrancing. On the other hand, take Ralph Guldahl, who won the American Open Championship two years running, beyond doubt a magnificent player. In some degree, of course, he has style, but not in the greatest. Here is not the "grace which makes itself felt by the skill with which it effaces itself." We are interested, even overpowered, by what he does, but we have no great æsthetic pleasure in observing how he does it. Neither had we in seeing how Walter Hagen did it. He was a most fascinating player, but that was on account of the man himself and not his style. Sometimes, of course, a golfer can charm us by his style in one part of the game and not another. It is great fun to see the present Open Champion, Burton, hit his drives; there is glorious power, but there is not beauty of style, perhaps—to be technical—because of his rather unorthodox right elbow. When, however, he comes to the shorter iron shots there is plenty of grace, and the smoothness of his stroke on the green represents style in the highest degree.

Of course, we do not all admire the same style, whether in writing or golf. Some, for instance, are all for simplicity and naturalness in writing and do not care for any style that appears mannered or artificial or elaborate. Others have no such feeling, and so it is in golf. Take two recent champions, Cotton and Reggie Whitcombe. There is a lovely smoothness and ease about Cotton, an immense power with absurdly small effort, and yet a great many people do not care about him purely as a stylist, because they find traces of artificiality. These will be all for Whitcombe—and he certainly is a jolly player to watch—because his swing is the perfect example of the caddie's swing brought to maturity, utterly natural and with no apparent trace of thought. You pay your money and you take your choice, but there is just one thing to be said, and it may be applied also to writers. Stevenson is an enchanting writer, but he would perhaps be even more so if he had never

GOLFING BY-PATHS

told us how he toiled at it and in his youth "played the sedulous ape." Similarly, Cotton has never made any secret of the fact that he was not, in his own opinion, a natural golfer and that he has worked almost incredibly at the game. Therefore in both these cases we are prepared to find signs of artifice, and I wonder whether, if we had not been told, we should have been clever enough to find them for ourselves.

To return to Mr. Bett, he points out the great importance of the first and last words in a sentence, and quotes Ben Jonson as saying: "Our composition must be more accurate in the beginning and end than in the midst, for through the midst the stream bears us." Is this true and, if so, how true of golf? Well, we certainly enjoy the beautifully free, upright and confident address of some golfers, and I can think of no better example than George Duncan. So also we enjoy the other end of the swing, the follow-through, which can be a thing of supreme beauty, as was Vardon's in his prime. So far so good, perhaps, but there is another interesting remark of Mr. Bett's which I cannot quite reconcile with golf. He rightly says that the beginning of a book is important, and that many more people would read Scott were it not for his introductory pages. "Ivanhoe," he says, ought obviously to begin, not with disquisitions on Normans and Saxons, but with the vigorous words of Gurth the Swineherd: "The curse of Saint Withold upon these infernal porkers!" Now in golf there are some long introductions which, far from being tedious, are a joy. Sandy Herd would be nothing without his waggle. For the most part the quick player is most attractive, but against that waggle I will hear no word. It is full of style, and, indeed, I think that the brief, colourless American waggle which has superseded the flamboyant Scottish one means a loss in style.

Finally, for it would be easy to go on for ever, I turn to the chapter on "Movement and Rhythm," and this time I think that literature and golf will have definitely to take their separate roads. Rhythm is essential in both, but Mr. Bett says that in literary style nothing is more fatal than monotony. He cites. Hazlitt not only as affording an example of unmonotonous prose, but as pointing out that "smooth, equable uniformity"

was a grave defect in the eighteenth century Addisonian styles
Now when we come to golf, is it not just that "smooth, equable
uniformity" that we admire in our heroes? I think it is, and
that if a man swung now slowly and gently, now fiercely and
fast—sometimes, as it were, in conversational mood and sometimes at a high pitch of eloquence—we should not deem his
swing a model of style. When I see in my mind's eye Mr.
John Ball, who has and always will have for me the loveliest
of all styles, smoothness and uniformity are the two obvious
qualities that I admire, though there is, of course, an unique
grace as well. That is the secret of style for which there is no
name.

OFF THE SOCKET

I AM always losing letters. I put them away in my coat
pocket (not before I have answered them, for I am a
good answerer) and there they lie rotting and forlorn.
Ultimately they emerge yellow with age, and as I look at them
I wonder drearily why on earth I ever kept them. A distinguished painter of the past, when he wanted money, used
periodically to conduct sovereign-hunts through the pockets
of all his trousers and often, I am told, with success. That is
just what I have been doing through all my coat pockets, but
the wanted letter has not turned up. It was from an old friend
a good golfer, who told me a terrible story of socketing, so
terrible that but for the fact that it had a happy ending, he could
hardly have borne to set it down. Even as it is I don't think
I could have passed it on if it had not been war-time, when
golfers do not take their diseases too seriously. The more
mention of this dread ailment is apt, as scolding nurses say to
nursery-maids, to "put things in the child's head," and I should
have been sorry to have some reader's suddenly induced socketing on my conscience.

Anyhow, here the story is, and if it is not quite accurate my
friend must forgive me; I hope I have the gist of it. He was

playing admirably, and after he had played his second shot to the home hole at Sandwich he had not only the handicap prize but the scratch medal metaphorically in his pocket. He was, I think, a little short of the green and to the left, with a perfectly simple shot to play and a five for the asking. He hit the ball off the socket into one of the bunkers to the right of the green. Thence he socketed again into a bunker at the back of it, and thence again to more or less the point whence he had started, having made an almost circular tour of the putting green. He still had two to tie and—here comes the happy ending—he laid a skilful run-up dead and so duly tied for the scratch medal with an eminent person. Happier ending still, he beat the eminent person in the play-off.

That a player at the top of his game can on a sudden become apparently insane and do such things shows what a truly devastating complaint socketing is. There is nothing else in golf in the least like it. It attacks without warning and is no respecter of persons. Truly did Sir Walter Simpson write: "When the adept's driving leaves him for a season, it does not do so entirely. It is otherwise with approaching. A medal winner unable to hit with any part except the socket of his iron is no uncommon phenomenon." Indeed I think the disease attacks the high rather than the low. Perhaps I was wrong in saying it attacked without warning, for as a rule there are two or three shots hit perceptibly near the heel of the club which precede the ultimate tragedy. Often, however, they pass unnoticed, since the man who is striking the ball rather near but yet not too near the socket may be playing his mashie with particular efficiency.

Beyond question there is no other form of golfing error which gives such an utter feeling of impotence, such a fatalistic certainly of ruin. Once in the throes of an attack the player feels as one hypnotised; he is in the grip of some baleful magician and it seems useless to struggle. Moreover even when he has been mercifully restored to golfing health the possibility of a relapse will suggest itself and that at the most crucial moment. Fancy, for instance, playing a nineteenth hole at Prestwick with the wall and the railway line on the right. Fancy having only to pitch on the green to win the match, and then being suddenly beset with "What if I socket!" The nineteenth hole at Hoylake (I know all about that) might furnish an equally dreadful situation, and every reader can doubtless imagine plenty of other holes to suit his own taste.

The obvious safeguard is to take a socketless club, but even that is not an absolute protection. I am not—touching wood—often afflicted, but the last time I was it was with a club having no socket. I had taken it out into a meadow to play a few idle shots without the slightest fear or anxiety, and before I could realise it heaven's worst curse had fallen upon me. The ball sped away to cover-point and almost to point in as bewitched and inevitable a manner as if my club had been all socket instead of having none. What is more, I retired, driven in by darkness, baffled and uncured. On thinking it over calmly I came to the conclusion that I had too many clothes on—it was a bitterly cold day—and that this had been the cause; I had been so cramped as to be unable to swing the club. Whether or not this diagnosis was correct I cannot say, but next day when I went out less cumbered about with woollies the ball and the middle of the club once more met and I was miraculously healed.

Despite such dire possibilities a socketless club can be a great comfort. I still remember clearly an agitating and, for me, important moment in the President's Putter at Rye. My opponent and I were all square with one to play and he had got into serious trouble under the railings by the road on the left. I was safely on the top with several strokes to spare and only an attack of socketing could defeat me. Though I could not possibly reach the green with it I took my socketless mashie and attained my haven on a cowardly instalment system. There are those who always carry a left-handed club in case of accidents, and it is on record that Bob Kirk once won a big match at Westward Ho! by doing so. This may be carrying forethought rather too far, but it would be wise always to have a socketless iron in the bag. You never can tell.

Considering that this is a fault from which the greatest are not exempt. it is odd that I cannot think of many historic socketers, but with one notable exception I cannot. That exception is Mr. Jerome Travers when he won the American

Amateur Championship at Garden City in 1913. As I recollect the disease only attacked him with one particular club but that a particularly crucial one, the mashie niblick. Round after round he hit at least a couple of shots off the socket and lost a couple of holes by them. Every day after lunch he went out to wrestle with the demon and at last he exorcised it. Considering that in that same tournament he dared not take a wooden club from the tee for fear of outrageous hooking he must be regarded as the most severely afflicted man who ever won a championship. Only a great player and a great putter with a great heart inside him could possible have done it.

It will be observed that in writing of this affliction I have not attempted to suggest any suitable treatment. It might endanger my amateur status if I did—not that it is now of any great value to me—for I might be held to be teaching golf. I have, however, a better reason than that, namely that I know no cure which can be guaranteed effective. Various distinguished professionals have tackled the subject and their view generally seems to be that socketing comes from too much use of the right hand. Doubtless they are right, and yet I remember one distinguished amateur, the late Mr. Charles Hutchings, who used to preach an apparently opposite cure with the greatest confidence and conviction. "Rip it right through," he used to say, "with the right hand." It only shows you, doesn't it? I remember to have tried Mr. Hutchings's cure and found it effective against the first mild threatenings of an attack. My impression is that the value of his prescription lay not in the right hand, but rather in the words "Rip it right through." They made the patient hit out at the ball and not stop the club in abject terror as he came to it. However, that is only a guess; I don't know, and I think the victim must just worry out a cure for himself. That remark can hardly come under the head of teaching, and if any of my former colleagues on the Championship Committee read this article, as is exceedingly unlikely, I trust they will not be too hard on me.

MY FIRST AMATEUR

I HAVE written about my first Open. Now to make what Mr. Peggotty would call a "merrygorounder" of it, I think I must say something of my first Amateur, even though I have to go back to the dark ages of 1898. The other day I received a very kind letter from a reader who said he had been much interested in my account of Braid's win at Prestwick in 1908, though he himself was only five years old at the time. He added that he was rather less interested when I went back into the last century. Well, he may be grateful to know that I cannot find my old green *Golfing Annual* which deals with 1898; so I shall spare him some details and give only a few general impressions. He is a Scotsman and so perhaps he will be the more forgiving since the hero of my tale will, I fancy, turn out to be that very great Scottish golfer, Freddie Tait.

Apart from its more prehistoric character this story must differ a little from my previous one. To Prestwick I went solely to watch the doings of others. In 1898 I had not yet taken to the bad habit of reporting; I went to Hoylake to play myself, and it was for me a great occasion, for it was not only my baptism of fire in the way of championships, but the first time I had seen many of the great ones of the earth. John Low was the only one I knew well. I had had a glimpse of Horace Hutchinson at Eastbourne, and Mure Fergusson at Sandwich; I had reverentially spoken a word or two to Freddie Tait at Woking and had actually played a round with Jimmy Robb at St. Andrews, but all the others, and in particular the Hoylake triumvirate, John Ball, Harold Hilton and Jack Graham, were entirely new. Fortune arranged for me the perfect opening scene. I was in the upstairs room in the clubhouse, hill-gazing "with a wild surmise" on the view of Hoylake which has so often disappointed the eager pilgrim. There, practising in the Field, was the great Hilton himself, then the reigning Open Champion, and dressed just as I had seen him in many photographs, with his white shoes and check coat and

126 GOLFING BY-PATHS

with his small cap on the back of his head. He was practising spoon shots and that so accurately—I have said this before— that the balls looked as if they were a clump of mushrooms suddenly grown in the night. It was a great moment.

Let me get myself out of the way as quickly as possible, and it did not take very long in fact. In the first round I drew a bye. In the second I played a Scottish golfer, Mr. Burns, whom I have never had the pleasure of seeing again from that day to this, and won by 5 and 4. In the third I vanished, having created what was then a record, though for me a disastrous one. My opponent was Herbert Farrar, a good Hoylake player whom I had encountered before in Wales. We went to the twenty-fourth hole, where I succumbed. If I had won I should have had a quarter of an hour or so for lunch before meeting John Ball; so the result of our match was of purely academic interest. I did not think so at the time, and when an urbane young man with a pencil found me lunchless, exhausted and depressed in the dressing-room and said: "Mr. Darwin, I believe you represent the Banking and Insurance Golf Club," my reply was not so polite as I now think it ought to be to a reporter. At any rate that was the end of me, and after that I watched hard.

As I have said, Freddie Tait not only won that championship but was by far its most dramatic figure. There were two Freddie Taits. There was the one who had swept through the championship of two years before at Sandwich, having the hardest part of the draw, encountering one famous player after another and knocking their heads off, murdering Harold Hilton in the final. That one could play beautiful faultless golf, making none of his traditional recoveries because none was needed. The other Freddie could be extraordinarily erratic for so great a player, in need of all the recoveries in his bag, and it was this one who was chiefly on view at Hoylake. His long game was all awry, and though his swing looked as graceful and easy as usual, the ball went to very odd places, and only a real genius for getting out of them, together with some of that fortune that favours the brave, pulled him through.

As I remember it now, everything in the championship

MY FIRST AMATEUR 127

seemed to be working up to a grand climax, the meeting of Tait and Hilton in, I think, the fourth or fifth round. From the start it was clear that they were foredoomed to meet. All Hoylake and all Liverpool hoped that now, when Harold was Open Champion and on his own course, he would not only win the Amateur at last but would conquer once and for all the weakness which always beset him when he had to face his Scottish rival. He was playing well, he had won his early matches with ease, and the crowd poured out to see the match and did not, I fancy, do its hero much good by many preliminary pats on the back, which were meant to be encouraging.

Harold looked uneasy and Freddie full of confidence. I remember seeing him practising at the putting holes inside the chains and white posts in front of the club-house. A friend asked after his game and he replied cheerfully: "All right except this part of it, and that'll be all right by the afternoon." So it was, for not only did he put away his eccentric mood in the long game but his putting seems in the recollection to have been devastating. Neither began very well, but Harold putted dreadfully on the second green and lost a hole which he looked as if he were going to win. At the fourth, The Cop, Freddie holed a good putt to be two up and all was over. Only one other shot do I recall, a long putt which Freddie holed on the Briars green. I can see him thrusting forward his right foot in a most characteristic movement, just as the ball is going in. The match ended at the Rushes, the thirteenth, and it was a sad procession that took its way back to the club. A perky little Cockney golfer, long since dead, with a "quiff" of hair, who looked like a drawing of Phil May's, said to the defeated champion: "Well, Harold, I don't think you ever will win this championship." As an example of sympathetic tact, the remark left something to be desired.

In that match Freddie Tait had played his proper game, and so he did, I believe, in the final against Mure Fergusson, but that I did not see. On the other hand, he had some desperate adventures before reaching the final. Charles Hutchings took him to the nineteenth by holing a putt all across the last green, and at that nineteenth Freddie pulled his drive into the rough, only to recover with a tremendous wooden club shot and win in a four. Jack Graham took him to the last green and ought, according to patriotic Hoylake opinion, to have beaten him comfortably, if he could have holed some infantile putts. The shortest of all Jack missed on the home green, and walking in the evening across the links I saw a number of little caddies practising it. No doubt they had shortened it, for it had shrunk to a foot at most. As to the semi-final against John Low, I was a passionate partisan of John's and so perhaps a prejudiced witness; but it certainly seemed to me that Freddie had the gods on his side. Two wooden club shots laid practically dead, one of them on the twenty-first hole, however magnificently courageous, did appear "a bit thick," and so did a putt of seven yards or so rattled in across the twentieth green. Harold Hilton always said that for once Freddie was almost in despair and hit that putt without caring. I wonder. At any rate, he was the only golfer I ever saw who could have won a championship while making the mistakes he did. It was a terrific achievement.

I find I have said nothing of John Ball, and the plain fact is that I remember little about him in that championship, except that Robb beat him in the last eight. I recall him so vividly on so many other occasions at Hoylake but this time he has faded. I have tried rubbing an old crook-necked putter of his which I possess, as Aladdin rubbed the wonderful lamp, but even that magic will not bring him back.

THE SEVENTEENTH HOLE

THAT which comes very near, but not quite at the end possesses in golf some peculiarly nerve-racking quality. The end is in sight, but there is yet one more river to cross, in which the golfer may come to abysmal grief. The third round in the Open Championship is always said to be the most testing; the semi-final in the Amateur used traditionally to produce mistakes of an agonising quality. So it is the last hole but one, the seventeenth, which has on many courses the

THE SEVENTEENTH HOLE 129

most sinister reputation, and it is on that hole that architects lay out treasures of fiendish skill. Some years ago Mr. Tom Simpson and Mr. Newton Wethered in their architectural book chose the ideal golf course, and it is noteworthy that, having surveyed all courses "from China to Peru," they included in their select eighteen no fewer than four seventeenths.

Their four came from St. Andrews, Prestwick, Walton Heath and Saunton respectively, and it was to the Saunton hole that they gave the highest honour by allotting it the penultimate place on their ideal course. Unless my wits have, in Mr. Peggotty's phrase, gone birds'-nesting, that hole has now become the sixteenth at Saunton, and this fate has certainly, to my eternal regret, befallen the grand old seventeenth at Walton Heath. It is true that the seventeenth at Prestwick, the famous Alps, was chosen on the principle that to play eighteen magnificent holes in a row was more than human nature could endure. So they decided to have "one thoroughly bad but amusing hole for the sake of variety and a brief interval of mental tranquillity," and paid the Alps this equivocal compliment. Certainly the hole has a blind second over a high hill and a hidden bunker beyond it on to a green of too acute slopes. It may be a bad one; but when I recall how in a championship I have waited, chafing to play my second, while my caddie points out the particular post on the hill-top over which I am to play, I cannot, however hard I try, connect the hole with any sort of "mental tranquillity."

Of course no seventeenth hole, though essentially mild, can produce peace of mind, not even when we are dormy two and the other fellow is in a bunker; but the greater the seventeenth the greater the anguish. What then are the peculiar qualities of the greatest? They must demand skilful play, with but a small margin of error; they must hold possibilities of dire calamity, and they should, I more doubtfully suggest, contain a slight, very slight but still perceptible, element of luck. Their characters vary, according as we think of them in match or medal play. The Road hole at St. Andrews, for instance, is at its greatest and most terrible in score play. There is always a chance of disaster there, disaster ridiculous as well as ruinous.

130 GOLFING BY-PATHS

It is one of the few holes in the world at which it is possible to putt into a bunker. I do not think we are much more agitated by it in a match than by other penultimate holes. It is when we have a card in our pocket that it becomes beyond question the most unnerving hole in the world. As we tee our ball we are in one sense nearer than on other courses to a happy ending, because the last hole will be comparatively speaking child's play. Nothing but the burn or a slice into Rusack's will then prevent our doing a good score. But the very fact that safety is so near makes the ordeal of this one remaining danger the more terrible.

I ventured to say that there should be just a little luck about a seventeenth. Even when we have played the shot as we intended, we should have doubts which cannot wholly be set at rest till we have reached the green and seen with our own eyes. Two seventeenth holes come to my mind, which I have often both watched and played in trying circumstances; that at Deal, inevitably suggesting desperate finishes in the Halford Hewitt Cup, and that at Worplesden full of memories of the Mixed Foursomes. I do not know that either is a very great one, and the Deal hole is perhaps too much on the lucky side, but they have this in common, that we are always hopeful that our ball has run round to the pin and fearful lest it has run clean over the green. I need scarcely add that with regard to our adversary's ball our hopes and fears change places. This happy result is produced in both cases by an upward slope in front of a rather narrow plateau green and a moderately Gadarene descent behind it.

One word I must here put in for a seventeenth, now long since passed away, which was, in the words before quoted, "thoroughly bad but amusing." This was the old one at Aberdovey which had been christened, though the name soon became obsolete, "The Crochan." The drive was a dramatic but easy one from a high tee; the length was, sure enough, "thoroughly bad," being that of a drive and a chip, and the chip was an entirely blind one into a hollow. In an ordinary game it was but mildly amusing, from the fact that the ball was apt to run round the bank and lie dead; but in a serious

THE SEVENTEENTH HOLE 131

finish it was almost blood-curdling. Apart from the fact that you might fluff the chip into a sandbank, you always fancied that the enemy's ball would lie dead, whereas your own, contrary to all the laws of fairness, would run through the green and sit impishly on the top of the bank. In short, you never could tell, and, however bad the hole, it did then produce the right and horrible sensation in the pit of the stomach.

Nearly all good courses have good seventeenth holes. There are exceptions, and at Rye, otherwise so noble a course, we have never quite succeeded, but it is an exception to prove the rule. Nearly all are good, but not all have the supremely poignant quality. At Sandwich, for instance, the hole is really a fine one, but at that particular point in the course it lacks something, something which the old seventeenth in the punchbowl did possess, for all its obvious faults. At Muirfield the seventeenth is long, testing, difficult, but somehow not of the first water; neither to my mind is (or must I say was?) that at Prince's. Some courses—Ganton, Swinley, Aldeburgh are three of them—have short holes at the last but one, and they can be sufficiently destructive, but I do not think that this is the ideal position for a one-shot hole. A seventeenth which deserves a good word is on a course not usually regarded as dramatic, Mid-Surrey. The seventeenth there, with its accurate tee shot between bunkers and its big second up to the long narrow green having a drop on either side, may not have beauty, but it has every other requisite. I shall always remember with a thrill Padgham's glorious long iron shot straight past the pin in his final of the *News of the World* against Cotton in the first year of the War. And then he took three putts !

I have kept to the last the seventeenth which I think is just about the best of all. It is no reproach to Mr. Simpson and Mr. Wethered that they did not put it in their eclectic eighteen, because it did not then exist in its present form. This is the Royal at Hoylake. It used to be a fault of that most exacting links that the seventeenth was both dull and easy. Then the reformers carried the green farther on, and now of all holes in the world this one perhaps best justifies the hackneyed similitudes of the devil and the deep sea and Scylla and Charybdis.

132 GOLFING BY-PATHS

On the one side is the hard high road—out of bounds; on the other a deep bunker, and very strait is the way between them. It is true that the hole can be played to some extent in instalments, and that is perhaps a weakness, but to play the right shot there and bang the ball right home is to touch the stars. Hagen's second in the Championship of 1924, when he wanted two fours to beat Ernest Whitcombe—a full-blooded iron shot past the pin—will never fade from the memories of those who saw it. It was a wonderful shot to the seventeenth; an even more wonderful one to the seventy-first.

"A CONGENIAL ACCOMPANIMENT"

IS golf a help to productive thought in other and more serious directions ? I should have rather thought not. Indeed it is generally held to be one of the merits of the game, especially in such times as these, that it temporarily and completely abstracts the mind from all earthly affairs and shuts the player up in a little world of his own, wherein there is nothing to think of but the hitting of the ball. It may, however, be otherwise in the case of more fertile and powerful intellects, and a passage which a kind correspondent has sent me tends to this view. It is from the account of Mozart in the *Oxford Companion to Music*, and probably some readers, less ignorant of music than I am, know it already. At any rate I will make bold to set it out at length.

" Ball games, particularly billiards and bowls, were greatly to his liking. There is little doubt that he pursued these games not merely for their own sakes but because he found in the movement and control of a rolling ball a congenial accompaniment to the movement within his own copious and productive mind. Instances are recorded of his stopping in the middle of a game to make notes, or of his humming, as he played, a theme which was later found in his works. Moreover, he was particularly fond of playing billiards alone, keeping his note-book

JEROME TRAVERS WITH HIS FAITHFUL DRIVING IRON

AN UNCROWNED KING, JACK GRAHAM

Sport & General.

"A CONGENIAL ACCOMPANIMENT" 133

handy—though the notes he made were always the briefest indication of an idea, for he did his actual composing in his head. The ever-flowing rhythms in his mind induced him incessantly to tap his fob, a table, a chair-back or anything to hand, and there is no doubt that he spent some of his most fruitful hours alone at the billiard table."

What an engaging picture that is! I am glad that it is of Mozart because he is the one among the mighty names of music that I am in some small degree able to appreciate. I like to think that had golf been available he would have spared some affection for that too and would have found inspiration in it. He might, if the suggestion be not a profane one, have been at times a trying opponent, had he stopped too often in the middle of a game, so that the other party had to call to those behind " Will you please come through—my partner is composing." Again that habit of humming might have exasperated an irritable adversary attempting to concentrate his mind on a crucial putt.

No doubt allowances would be made for the eccentricities of so great a genius, but even so I fancy that he would have found most fecund and enjoyable the hours that he spent alone with a club and a few balls. That is the time, I think, at any rate for those who make no claim to genius, when the loveliest images spring into the golfer's mind. Set him alone on a wide stretch of the links, where there is no rough to make him hunt for lost balls and no other tiresome players to shout an angry " Fore " at him, and he tastes some of the intensest joys of living. Let the time be that of evening drawing in, when the rest of the world is at tea and a light or two begin to shine out in the club-house windows, and he may enjoy mute ecstasies in which he feels capable of composing almost anything.

I am sure my correspondent has drunk deep of this romantic cup of lonely practising, for he says that one of his happiest dreams is of a strip of close-cut turf 400 yds. long by 80 wide, along the whole length of which there runs a desk " at comfortable standing height with a plentiful supply of paper laid along it." Thus whenever the *genius loci* dowered him with a particularly felicitous fancy or telling phrase he could throw down his club and commit his inspiration to paper and then

K

back again to his task of curing that confounded slice. He reminds me a little—I am perhaps irreverent—of Mr. Jingle's account of his behaviour during the revolution of July when he combined Mars and Apollo, the field-piece and the lyre: "Present! think I was; fired a musket—fired with an idea—rushed into wine-shop—wrote it down—back again—whiz, bang—another idea—wine-shop again—pen and ink—back again—cut and slash—noble time, Sir." This turning from one to another like a man playing on a pair of kettledrums, might be a little confusing at first, but I am delighted to pass on his notion to other golfers and writers.

I cannot say that I have ever tried it myself, but I can cite somebody who has combined not two but three arts in much the same manner. This is an old friend of mine, distinguished in several walks of life and not least as a golfer, a creature of restless versatility and having, like Mozart, a "copious and productive mind." His three combined amusements were dry-fly fishing, landscape painting and golfing. Fishing was the main object of his expedition and to that he would apply himself first and with becoming seriousness. If the conditions were unfavourable and the fish seemed indisposed to yield to his blandishments, he had his easel handy and would devote himself for a while to the art of Constable. When he grew tired of that he had yet another resource in the form of a brassey, a bag of balls and a small boy. He drove the balls down the meadow; the small boy stationed in the deep field retrieved them and he drove them again until such time as the fish might be more amenable or the paint brush called him back once more. Thus he went far towards the practical building of my correspondent's castle in Spain, and I respectfully commend his example. I wonder, now I come to think of it, why he did not also play the fiddle, for that is yet another art in which he is, I understand, expert, but perhaps the fish would not have liked it. The fiddle brings me naturally back to Mozart. My correspondent mentions a picture which I seem dimly to remember having seen myself. It represents the musician leaning over a billiard-table with a far-away look in his eyes; the cue and balls lie abandoned on the table, while immediately in front of him is a music score. It would be pleasant to know whether he hummed as he made a cannon and that "ever flowing rhythm in his mind" communicated a rhythmical quality to his stroke. I feel sure it would have helped him if he had played golf; the swinging in time to a tune is a well-recognised cure for a swing that has become too fast and jerky and has palpably lost all rhythm. A waltz is generally recommended and I have myself found the *Merry Widow* of considerable assistance. Better still in my experience is the hymn tune *Happy birds that sing and fly*, which has, I believe—though I am sadly ignorant in such matters—all the requisite elements of a waltz.

I can still see in the mind's eye a green hill on a certain course where I first discovered the efficacy of this particular tune. Ball after ball sang through the air and flew like the very happiest of birds far into the valley below. As is the case with all the other cures I ever heard of, I soon overdid it, and my tiresome body began all too palpably to sway to the dreamy measure of my humming, but it was an ecstatic moment while it lasted. Moreover I believe this is one of the cures that can, so to speak, be put away in cold storage and be usefully brought out again when needed. The patient must be particularly careful not to overdose himself but resolutely stop as soon as he feels better. Then it will still be effective in his next attack. *Happy birds that*—I feel almost irresistibly moved to go out on to the lawn for a little swinging, but fortunately it is raining and so I must refrain.

BATTLES LONG AGO

IN search of some soothing and easy-going literature, I lately took down from the shelf Dr. Tulloch's "Life of Tom Morris" and opened the book at random. It opened at the great foursome tournament—I think the first open amateur tournament ever held—which took place at St. Andrews in

136 GOLFING BY-PATHS

1857. The prize of a silver claret jug was won by an English club, Blackheath, but with two good Scotsmen as its representatives, Mr. George Glennie and Lieutenant James Campbell Stewart of Fasnacloich, who thus made Blackheath, in the proud language of the club minutes, "the champion golf club of the world." Captain Stewart, as he afterwards became, was obviously a mighty golfer, for he habitually had the temerity to play Allan Robertson on level terms, and four years before this tournament he had won the autumn medal with a score of 90, nine strokes better than the medal winner had ever done before. Now, however, his golf was to be sadly interrupted, for in 1858 he was ordered to India with his regiment, the 72nd Highlanders, and it was then that old Mr. Sutherland was to give vent to one of those sayings of his which showed the profound seriousness of his outlook on golf. "It is a shame," he said, "of a man with such golfing powers to go out to India."

The little matter of the preposition is worthy of notice. It was not a shame *for* such a man to have to go at the bidding of an unsympathetic War Office; it was a shame *of* him to go. We gather that in Mr. Sutherland's opinion he ought, rather than obey so outrageous an order to have given up soldiering and stayed on the links. At any rate, the old gentleman must have had this consolation that the Indian Mutiny was a thing of the past and his young favourite was not going into any deadly peril. His pleasant remark set me thinking how little, so far as we know, the wars of the old days affected golf. Did our soldiers in the Napoleonic era, or our Volunteers, when the Volunteer movement began about the middle of the last century, perform any of their evolutions upon Blackheath, to the mingled admiration and annoyance of the golfers? There was no mention of them in the club papers, if they did, nor could I find anything about any war in those extracts from the minutes of the most famous Scottish clubs, given in Mr. Clark's well-known book, "Golf, A Royal and Ancient Game." War, it seemed, was not allowed in those days to interfere with sporting activities. Think of October 5th, 1805, a little more than a fortnight before Trafalgar. Nelson was writing home: "Should

BATTLES LONG AGO

they come out I should immediately bring them to battle, but though I should not doubt of spoiling any voyage they may attempt yet I hope for the arrival of the ships from England, that as any enemy's fleet they may be annihilated." Possibly the Lords of the Admiralty were interested in the question of reinforcements, but everybody else, including the Duke of Clarence, afterwards King William IV, was vastly more interested in going to Hailsham in Sussex to see the Game Chicken beat Gully. Nine years later, Wellington with 40,000 men was making a stand in Spain against the 60,000 of Marmont, but the really exciting thing was that a negro called Molineaux had had the hardihood to challenge Tom Cribb, and Mr. Pierce Egan was very anxious to know "whether Old England should still retain her proud characteristic of conquering."

However, this was nothing to do with golf, and I had drawn blank until I suddenly thought of Mr. Cameron Robbie's excellent "Chronicle of the Royal Burgess Golfing Society of Edinburgh, 1735–1935," published three years ago. Surely, as I remembered, there was something there to the point, and so there is. Till they moved to Musselburgh in 1877 (their headquarters is now, of course, at Barnton) the Burgess had played from their earliest days on Bruntsfield links. They had no lease of it, but kept a jealous eye on their rights as golfers, whatever these precisely may have been, and were something of a thorn in the side of the magistrates and city fathers of Edinburgh. At various times they had caused to be prohibited the making of a racecourse, the opening of quarries, the beating of carpets, the training of horses, the playing of shinty, the holding of Hallow Fair and, above all, the drilling of troops, since all these things were bad for the links and interfered with the golfers. To be sure, soldiers had been occasionally permitted, from the days when an army had paraded there to march to the disastrous battle of Flodden. Presumably patriotism overrrode golf in Napoleonic days, for several volunteer infantry battalions, raised in Edinburgh, were trained on the links. The line, however, must be drawn somewhere. In 1798 a young lawyer called Walter Scott, who all his life burned with martial ardour, was Quartermaster of the Royal Edinburgh Light Dragoons

GOLFING BY-PATHS

and applied to the magistrates for leave for the drilling of that corps at Bruntsfield. This was too much; infantry were all very well, but cavalry would ruin the course; the Society protested, and the future author of "Waverley" was rebuffed. Fourteen years later the "Military," unspecified, were drilling there, and a certain rough-rider proceeded to exercise some of the officers' horses on the links. He declared that chargers must become used to seeing soldiers at exercise, and was very rude to the Society's officer who told him to go away. This time there was an action in the Sheriff's Court and an interdict was granted, but at the same time it was suggested that the Society should see a certain colonel and come to some amicable arrangement. The rough-rider was told to be more civil, and I suppose the colonel promised not to gallop over the greens.

How different are things to-day, when the war comes rightly first and golf nowhere. It is odd to look back even to the time of the South African War and remember how little, comparatively speaking, it interfered with normal game-playing life. The Championship, of course, went on just as usual. Certainly, there was something of sadness and flatness about the Amateur Championship of 1900, for Freddie Tait had been killed at Koodoosberg in February and his loss was felt with the keenest sorrow throughout the golfing world. There was another big gap, though happily not a lasting one, because John Ball was in South Africa with his yeomanry. Of course, other good golfers fell in that war, and others who came back were away for a time; but, save for those two, I cannot recall the absence of any really conspicuous figures. Golf and golf championships represented "Business as usual," as we may hope they will do again some day. Having written that sentence, I turned back again for a little peace, to that life of Old Tom, and came across the name of that fine old golfer, Mr. William Doleman. He went on playing golf, and playing it well, till he was a really old man, and I well remember, as must many others, to have played in a championship in which he took part. He was a link with a very far-away war, because he was born in 1838, went to sea as a boy, and sailed out of Sebastopol under Russian gunfire in 1854. The picture of him in that championship at Sandwich is

FOSSILS OF THE PAST

very clear before my eyes, in particular that of him taking some ancient form of field glass to study the distant green. Not that it was very far distant, because he could not then hit very far, but he hit very straight, and his opponent, a big hitter, was nearly frightened out of his wits, before he ultimately won, by the malicious mirth of his watching friends. That opponent was a contemporary of my own; and so I might have played a man who escaped from Sebastopol. "What a rum thing time is!"

FOSSILS OF THE PAST

ONE of the Sherlock Holmes stories—"The Adventure of the Blue Carbuncle" unless I am mistaken—begins with Holmes studying an ancient hat which has accidentally come into his possession, and deducing from it that the owner has considerable intellectual development and that his wife has ceased to love him. I feel a little like Holmes at this moment as, without his intellectual development, I sit poring over three old clubs, one wooden and two iron, the latter long since encrusted with red rust. They live in the house which has lately given me kindly refuge, and have lived there so long that their story is "lost evermo' "; nobody knows who bought them or whence they came. They are not really so very old, since the brassey is of the socket and not the "skeered" variety, a fact which gives some clue, while one of the iron clubs is unquestionably a mashie and there was a time—I remember it myself—when mashies did not exist. Nevertheless in their present derelict condition they seem to belong to a prehistoric age.

As to the brassey, at any rate, Sherlockian gifts are not needed to deduce that the owner was no judge of a club, since this is, on the whole, the worst club I ever saw. It is at once very light and as stiff as a ramrod; waggle it as you may, there is no vestige of that spring which Old Tom so poetically termed the "music" in the shaft. The head, which is exceedingly small, not that this is a damning fault in itself, is so put on that the heel projects horribly. It has "slice" written all over it, and the grip is on a par with the rest of it, for it is of odiously slimy leather which slips out of the hand. It has obviously had plenty of wear, but there are no marks on the face from which any deduction of value can be made. I give it up.

The two iron clubs are more interesting, not perhaps from a detective point of view, but as historical objects. One of them for instance I find decidedly "intriguing" because it is hard to identify. A modern iron bears its name and number; its exact place in club society is clear for all men to see; but what is this? It is hardly a cleek, for it is too lofted; it is hardly an iron, at any rate, after the fashion of to-day, for it is too shallow in the face. Perhaps in its youthful prime it was called an "approaching cleek," and the happy owner, when he bore it all glittering from the shop, thought he would lay all his run-up shots dead ever afterwards. The mashie is just a mashie, though with a face smaller and less deep than is now the mode. Both have fat leather grips with plenty of black padding underneath, and I think I am justified in deducing that the owner did not use the overlapping grip.

One other tentative deduction I may make from these clubs, namely that the owner had rather a forcing style, since both shafts are bent into a hoop. That old phrase comes naturally back to me, and yet it is a long time since I saw shafts so bent, for those of steel remain as a rule rigidly and unbendingly correct. There used to be something fascinating in such a shaft, especially in a driving iron. The bend rather reduced the loft on the face and conduced to the hitting of a ball that bored its way well through the wind. I remember a certain driving iron of my own which I once stole—well, well, I must not grow sentimentally reminiscent. Enough that there was a certain tortuous charm about such shafts; but it was a day of wrath, a dreadful day, when the shaft at last broke as break it must. The head developed an incompatibility of temper with the new and straight shaft with which it was mated; it seemed to pine away, missing its old companion, and too often became useless ever afterwards.

FOSSILS OF THE PAST 141

All three of these ancient fossils are beyond doubt shockingly bad clubs, and yet I find myself growing rather fond of them, when I take them surreptitiously out of the umbrella-stand and waggle them in the front hall; they remind me of certain old clubs of my own. In these days of steel shafts and rustless heads everybody's clubs are both good to feel and comely in aspect, and my own are, I believe, just as good as anybody else's, but in the pre-steel days I was one of those always deemed by their friends to have bad clubs. I liked them but nobody else did and I grew well accustomed to somebody picking one of them up, giving it a contemptuous glance and returning it with the words: "Well, how the devil you can play with a thing like that I can't imagine." There was always something definitely ramshackle and disreputable about their appearance. Sometimes I had shortened their shafts in my own amateurish way with some kitchen implement, and, if the binding of the grip became loose I would remedy it with a tin-tack. The worthiest of clubs is not likely to look its best after such treatment.

Those, however, were extreme cases, and apart from such rough and ready doctoring my clubs would insist on looking shabby. I recall one in particular which was in my bag and moreover did not undistinguished service on the one occasion when I had the honour of playing in the Walker Cup. It was an aged spoon which I was using for my shots through the green. There was very little paint left on the head, so that the patches of grey appeared through the yellow; all symptoms of varnish had long departed; the leather of the grip was rapidly disintegrating, and that blessed binding had come loose again so that a piece of string depended and whistled through the air as I swung. Mr. Fownes and I had as our referee Mr. Ward, a good golfer and in his day a very famous player at baseball. For the first six holes he spoke never a word, but at the seventh, I think it was, I made rather a good shot with my disreputable friend. "May I look at that club?" said Mr. Ward, and having gazed at it for some time he handed it back with the words: "If anybody were to tell you that club had been played with in an international match you wouldn't believe him."

GOLFING BY-PATHS

It was during that American tour that my clubs became perceptibly more down-at-heel and out-at-elbows, if such terms are applicable to clubs, than ever before. The free-born American caddie neither tees your ball nor cleans your clubs, and all the members of a golf club pay, or in those days did pay, a certain subscription to have them cleaned in the professional's shop. That was an excellent plan for those who played regularly on the same course, but when one was visiting a series of courses one grew a little tired of paying to have one's irons cleaned and then departing before this had been done. So I resolved to let them, so to speak, return to Nature, and in time they attained a fine rich black colour not wholly unbecoming. But that they lacked smartness I am not prepared to deny.

There are those who keep or used to keep their iron-heads black on principle, though exactly what principle I am not certain. Mr. Herbert Fowler used to do so and so did Mr. Robert Harris. The remark is attributed to Young Tommy Morris that the amateur too often took his eye off the ball because the shining head of the iron attracted that errant eye in the back swing. I can claim for myself no particular principle except that of saving trouble. And yet there is one eminently sound argument for black clubs. Water wears away a stone, or, if I may be allowed a quotation from Ovid (I have just found it in a dictionary), "*Consumitur annulus usu.*" If a ring is worn thin by mere use, how much more is an iron-head worn thin by the vigorous sandpapering of generations of caddies? Many a good putting cleek has grown "tinny" by cleaning and having had to be reinforced by metal on the back, has lost something of its magic. That is the great advantage of rustless steel. The club-heads merely need wiping and retain at once their weight and their perpetually youthful bloom.

My three old clubs have set me dreaming all sorts of pleasant, ancient dreams, and the least I can do out of gratitude is to give them an airing and to play a shot with them. Unfortunately I have not that indispensable requisite, a ball, but there is a kind lady in the house who is believed to possess one. Perhaps if I promised to play nothing but running shots up and down the lawn and not in the direction of the River Cam which flows beside it, she would lend me that ball. I think I shall be very brave and ask her.

ON THROWING CLUBS

A FRIEND of mine once gave up smoking for six years, cut it off with a sudden bang on the advice of a doctor whom he now, perhaps ungratefully, alleges to have been a fool. Then just as suddenly he took it up again, not from any urgent craving, but because he felt that he was becoming too virtuous and too censorious as to the weaknesses of others. That is, however, only incidental to the real point, namely, that, having always been a rather good player of the. short game, he became during his time of abstinence a much better one; he not only putted extremely well, but even developed a habit of holing his chips, a habit which, since abandoning virtue, he has lost. This is depressing news for those who smoke, and I can only cheer them by quoting a converse example The late Mr. Walter Travis, whose fame as a putter was monumental, once gave up both smoke and alcohol for some time before a tournament. The result was, in his own words: "I found that while it made no difference in my long game, my work on the green was simply childish—I couldn't putt at all." That was a good thing for history, since the legend of Mr. Travis would have lost its picturesque qualities without his black cigar. I remember once to have given up smoking for some while and my golf was rather good, but my temper was horrid, worse than usual. Yet it was the kind of bad temper that is not wholly unsuccessful. There is one kind of anger in which we throw our club away, forbid the caddie to fetch it, abandon hope, and cease to try. There is another kind in which, if we hurl our club, we at once pick it carefully up again and settle down to a cold, bitter hatred of our adversary and a determination not to give in. From the point of view

144   GOLFING BY-PATHS

of decent manners and of being fit to play with, there is no
distinction between the two, and I am very far indeed from
defending either. All I say, as a mere matter of observation,
is that it was the second kind which abstinence from tobacco
produced in me, and that if I was a more unpleasant golfer
even than before, I was a more determined one.

This matter of losing the temper hardly plays, I think, the
part in golf that it once did. Where are the truly great losers
of their tempers? Their fires are now with the snows of yester-
year. The man who prayed to heaven to consume the links;
the man who threw his clubs into the sea and then was nearly
drowned in rescuing them: the man who laid his bag on the
railway line and saw the contents reduced to spillikins—these
are now hacking furious divots out of asphodel and have not
left their peers. I hope and believe that I am right in saying
that it is now a good many years since I threw a club myself.
I will not say that I have not dropped, merely dropped, my
putter on the green, but I have not cast it from me. Nor,
indeed, do I remember seeing any of my acquaintances do such
a thing save one, and that is some time ago. He, moreover,
showed so nice a sense of the dramatic as to make himself more
lovable than ever. It was on the fourth green at Sandwich
which stands "high in the stainless eminence of air." He
twirled round and round like a demented hammer-thrower and
then sent his putter spinning far into the depths beneath. When
Mr. Bobby Jones burst on the world as an infant prodigy he had
a tendency to throw clubs, and, since he was sure to come to
greatness, he might have restored an ancient fashion. In Mr.
Keeler's "Boy's Life of Bobby Jones" there is a pleasant account
of the fourteen years old's first championship match against Mr.
Eb Byers, then comparatively a veteran. "With the perfectly
natural reactions carried over from early childhood, Bobby
followed a badly missed stroke by throwing the club after the
ball as far as he could. Mr. Byers did the same thing. Players
in the match directly behind them said later that it looked like
a juggling act on the stage. At the twelfth hole Mr. Byers
hurled a club over a hedge and out of the golf course, and would
not allow his caddie to go after it. This caused Bobby to explain

that he had defeated his opponent because Mr. Byers ran out of clubs first." That was a noteworthy beginning, and Bobby might have become the supreme club-thrower as well as the supreme golfer. We might all be throwing ours in humble imitation. Alas! he gave it all up and became outwardly at least a man of ice, so that this relief for our pent-up feelings is no longer permissible.

The other day, in reading an account of his course written some fifty years ago by an enthusiastic secretary, I found that he expected everyone to pay tribute to the magnificence of his bunkers by getting cross. "If you do not lose your temper you will find yourself between the first and second bunkers in three or four strokes": "The neophyte will be playing sandboy and losing his temper out of sight of his friends," and so on. I do not think a modern secretary would write thus, but then it was the regular thing, the stock joke. The golfer, especially if he was a colonel or a retired Indian, must lose his temper in order to live up to his character. To-day, of course, he would be said to come from Poona. He must also use the most terrific language: swear horribly, as we are told in history our troops did in the Low Countries. In short, he had to be an anticipation of that delightful person, Colonel Blimp. Now profanity has largely gone out of fashion with club-throwing, which is no doubt all to the good. I suppose, though one would hardly think so from its present condition, that the world is becoming more civilised.

One thing there was, perhaps, to be said from a golfing point of view for the club-throwers: that they were not self-conscious. They gave rein to their natural instincts. The same friend with whom I began these desultory remarks told me of a shrewd little Scottish caddie. He was carrying for a very good player before an important tournament, and was asked whether his employer would win. He replied that he did not think he could, because whenever he made a good shot he looked round as if to see what people thought of it. That was a very astute boy, and his judgment proved perfectly sound. If we dance in a frenzy, call upon heaven and cast away our clubs, we are prob- ably not thinking, or, at any rate, not caring much about what

146 GOLFING BY-PATHS

other people think. There are golfers in the world—I could suggest one or two—who would, to my mind, have been more successful if they had once in a while become openly furious instead of secretly unhappy. Nevertheless, as I said before, I am not defending these outbreaks and do not want any golfer to give up smoking that his temper may be worse.

A HOYLAKE FRIEND

ALL sorts of Hoylake memories came flooding back into my mind when I read with sorrow of the death of a very old friend of mine, a member of one of the great Hoylake golfing families, Allan Graham. I had known Allan since 1903, when he first played for Oxford; then a very tall, thin freshman with a mop of red hair, and entirely silent; I dare say he was appraising us all astutely enough, but he appeared in those days almost speechless with shyness. I used to meet him more or less regularly from that time onwards: on the northern tours of the Society: at meetings of the Championship Committee, and in particular at Hoylake Championships, where he and Mrs. Graham kept a hospitably open house almost directly behind the home green. To see him again was always one of the many pleasures of returning to that great home of golf, and he had a kindly flavour of his own, gentle and yet very shrewd, a particular twinkle which will be missed by all who knew him.

Allan was a good golfer in all the best senses of the word. As a player of the game he was technically rather mysterious and inscrutable. He was a natural ball-game player, with a fine eye and wrist, having won the Public Schools rackets for Marlborough and played that game for Oxford: he had been brought up at Hoylake with such great models before his eyes as John Ball, Harold Hilton and his own brother Jack. These advantages were hardly at first sight apparent in the wide straddle and the rather straggling swing, which were entirely his own; he seemed to have borrowed nothing from his incomparable brother. He could on his bad days play very erratically, and I remember his once boasting to me ("boast" is, to be sure, the wrong word for one so gentle and modest) that before the Hoylake course was altered, he had been out of bounds off every tee but one of the whole eighteen. Hoylake is a links with a great deal of out-of-bounds, and such an achievement is more possible there than anywhere else. The one hole was obviously the old Rushes, but I find it hard to imagine how he accomplished the feat at one or two others. At any rate that was, I am pretty sure, what he said.

So he could be wild; but he could also be uncommonly good and, as everyone knows, he reached the final of the Championship at Hoylake in 1921. Moreover, four years later at Westward Ho!, where there were but comparatively few Scotsmen, Allan stepped into the breach for the Scottish side against England and gallantly won his match. Later again, only quite a few years ago, if memory serves, he suddenly emerged to win the tournament of the Hittite Golfing Society for the John Ball Putter, and that takes a lot of winning. In fact he was an adversary not to be underrated, and was always apt to be dangerous, for he was a magnificent putter and possessed a capital temperament. I always used to think that if Jack could have added to all his other gifts Allan's putting and Allan's fine serenity, which sometimes seemed almost sleepiness, then he would indeed have been invincible.

Nobody can remember Allan's putting without also remembering the club he did it with, a curious, battered, shallow-faced weapon with a head of gunmetal, which I used to call his brazen serpent. It was not beautiful, but it was in fact a good and beautifully balanced club and it is noteworthy that at an open championship a few years ago, Gene Sarazen borrowed it and putted extremely well with it. Allan, as far as I know, was never tempted to use anything else, and he was one of those lucky people to whom putting came easily, so that they do not trouble their heads overmuch about it. He stood up and hit the ball naturally, comfortably, smoothly, and there was one thing very noteworthy in his method, namely, that he followed right through and in certain moods would finish

148 GOLFING BY-PATHS

a long putt almost as he might have finished a drive, with his club over his left shoulder. It was with this deadly instrument of singular aspect that he putted Bobby Jones to his death in 1921, to the tune of 6 and 5. *A propos* of that tremendous victory I remember his telling me about his round on the afternoon of the same day against Charles Hezlet. Allan was rather amused at himself than otherwise, and never took the game too seriously; he thought he had sufficiently served his country by beating the great Bobby; he had a good lunch and went out again in an entirely care-free spirit. He again played very well, but without thinking too much about it, and after a while suddenly asked his caddie how the game stood. The caddie said that he was (I think) two up with five to play. "Oh, well," said Allan, "then we'd better go on and win"; which he accordingly did. To be able to look on these solemn occasions with so placid and humorous an eye was a great gift and made of him a delightful companion, partner or opponent, one who will be remembered with affection by all who knew him.

To think of him is naturally, as I said, to think of Hoylake, especially of its golfing families. Among them the Grahams hold a high place, for apart from Jack, Miss Molly Graham won the Ladies' Championship at Aberdovey in 1901, and young John, of another generation, has added to its honours, winning Hoylake medals, helping the Marlburians to win the Halford Hewitt Cup at Deal, and being chosen to play in the Walker Cup trials in 1938. Incidentally it always seemed a little bitter that Jack should so often have aided Scotland against England, for if ever there was an English golfer by upbringing he was one. However, Scottish patriotism is very properly high and, whatever Jack might have done himself, I think old Mr. Graham, his father, would never have recovered from the blow if a son of his had helped the ancient enemy. Golf seems to run in families at Hoylake. I am not old enough to have seen John Ball's father play in the days when that illustrious man was "Mr. John Ball tertius"; but he was good enough to be one up with two to play against Mr. Horace Hutchinson in the Championship at Hoylake in 1887. Then there is "Mr. John Ball (2)" as he was always set down, still alive and well and a

Sport & General.

GOING TO THE ROAD HOLE AT ST. ANDREWS

Sport & General.

A TYPICAL BOBBY FINISH

very good golfer at Leasowe. Moreover, I fancy that Tom Ball and Frank Ball, those two fine professional players, were, though distantly, of the same clan. Harold Hilton's brother Reggie, though of course overshadowed, was a good golfer, and then there have been Crowthers and Duns, Farrars and Dinns, and I am probably leaving out some whom I ought to put in.

We, who played against them regularly on the Society tours, had good cause to know and fear these scions of Hoylake. Some of them played little save on their home green and were not well known away from it, but there they were always formidable. Naturally with such a course at their doors, and heroic examples to spur their ambition, the boys of Hoylake took to golf, and I have always felt a little envious of those who have had such an education. Perhaps it is altogether fanciful, but I sometimes think that "The Field" must have been a definite help to them. There, within a stone's throw of the club house and cut off on all sides by "cops" from the course, is the perfect practising ground, where the studious youth might watch Mr. Hilton playing spoon shots, where perhaps the great man in the kindness of his heart might in his turn watch the boy and pass him a hint. However that may be, Hoylake has always been the mother and nurse of good golfers, one more of whom we must now miss.

PAR TO WIN

I WHILED away an idle hour the other day by dipping and diving into my old copies of the *The Golfing Annual*. My reading was accompanied by various emotions. There was envy at the thought of a half-crown green fee a week for visitors. Golf was a cheap game then, at least at one club. There was astonishment at the contrast between past and present on reading of a hole three hundred and ninety yards long which had once been reached in two by the Open Champion but cost most people six rather than five. There was

L

150   GOLFING BY-PATHS

admiration mingled with awe at the description of a hole on a Midland course which I take leave to set down: "A good and sporting hole," wrote the honorary secretary, "is the eighth or Cabbage Garden, the drive being on the racecourse rails, a sliced second going into the cabbages, a foozled approach into the gorse fence short of the green, a pulled shot over the wall and on to the road, the far side of the green being lined with gravel pits." In our modern idiom, some hole!

All these were pleasant, but that which most gratified me was the discovery of a single sentence in the account of Mr. John Ball in the Open Championship at Prestwick in 1890, and here it is. "When he reached the fourteenth disc it transpired that he had only to negotiate the four remaining holes in twenty to win." If the beauty of journalism consists of using language such as nobody could by any possibility employ in ordinary talk, then that sentence may be considered a journalistic gem. Nobody ever called a hole a disc; nobody ever talked of anything transpiring outside the pages of a newspaper, and nobody has ever negotiated a hole whether in four or fourteen. When Macaulay attacked the wretched Mr. Robert Montgomery, he said of one of his flights: "I take this to be on the whole the worst similitude in the world." Well, in its own line my sentence has claims to be considered the worst in the world. I am proud of it accordingly.

Lest there be any reader unversed in history I may add that Mr. Ball won that Championship at Prestwick. He "negotiated" the four last "discs" in 5, 4, 5, 4—a perfect model of careful steadiness. I was too young to be there, but I fancy I can see him doing it; taking perhaps a cleek from the fifteenth tee and so lying safely at the top of the slope and short of the greedy bunkers on either hand, giving the dreaded Alps bunker no chance at the seventeenth and playing safely away to the left at the Home hole. Terrible things can happen at the Loop at Prestwick, but twenty strokes for the four allowed him a reasonable margin and there cannot have been much doubt. Enviable is the championship winner who thus has a stroke or two put by against a rainy day. The common lot is to need par or better than par for the last few holes in order to win,

PAR TO WIN

and of those so circumstanced how few have succeeded, how many have just failed. Truly fortunate is the early starter who sets up a target at which the others must aim.

This train of thought tends naturally towards memories of the comparatively few who, knowing that they have not a stroke to spare and can afford nothing less than perfection, have yet achieved their task. The classical example in all the books comes also from Prestwick (the old twelve-hole course), where in 1878 (I believe I have mentioned it elsewhere in this book) Jamie Anderson had to finish in par for the last four holes—5, 4, 3, 5—and actually holed them in 3, 4, 1, 5. Leaving such ancient if romantic history on one side, I think of one obvious and most glorious example which I saw with my own eyes, that of Francis Ouimet at Brookline in 1913. With four holes to play in the last round of the American Open Championship, par was not good enough for him; he needed one under par, and that not to win but to tie with Ray and Vardon. The first of the four, the fifteenth, called, as I remember it, for a drive and an iron, and he pushed his iron shot out to the right. If he could not get his par there it was, humanly speaking, the end of him, and he laid his chip stone dead. The sixteenth was a one-shotter and he got a steady, orthodox three. Both the next two holes were good fours and he must get one of them in three. He played as nearly as may be a perfect approach to the seventeenth, but he was six or seven yards past the hole— a downhill putt with a considerable borrow—and down it went slap into the middle. The home hole needed a drive and a long iron off muddy, rain-soaked turf over a formidable bunker. He was over the bunker but a little short; he ran up well but he was by no means dead, four feet away at the least. He walked up to the ball, neither hurrying nor putting off the evil day, and it went in without a quiver.

Taking all the circumstances into consideration, I am prepared to abide by that as the greatest finish in all golfing history. Of course, there are plenty of other great ones, and two more come into my head, both on the part of American golfers. The first is that of Jerry Travers in the American Open Championship at Baltusrol in 1915, and, by the way, it is a wonderful thing

152 GOLFING BY-PATHS

that in the four years from 1913 to 1916 this championship was won three times by an amateur; one of the things that can scarcely happen again. With five holes to play he knew that he had to do exactly the par figures to beat the leader, Macnamara, by a single shot. The fourteenth at Baltusrol has an "island" green, a real island surrounded by water, on to which the player must pitch his second with plenty of backspin. Travers began by cutting his tee shot out of bounds and, so it seemed, bang went par for that hole. His prospects seemed even gloomier when he pulled his second drive into long, thick grass. The obvious thing to do was to hack it out short of the water with a niblick and that would probably mean a six, whereas he wanted a four and *must* get a five. He took a big risk and his "jigger" and played what he says was the best shot of his life, the kind of shot with which he used to give his enemies such horrid jolts in a match. The ball just carried the water and ran to within three feet; he holed the putt and he had got his four after all. He had no more adventures, and Jerry was essentially a match player rather than a medal player, apt to have adventures; he stuck to par for the last four holes and he won by a stroke.

Now for another finish which I did see, that by Walter Hagen at Hoylake in 1924. He had to come home in 36 to beat Ernest Whitcombe, and he was playing scrambling golf. He scrambled at the Dee, at the Alps, at the Hilbre, and where most men would have lost three shots he lost only one. Nevertheless, he was now faced with the strictest par for the last six holes, and he plumped his tee shot to the short Rushes into a bunker. That's done him!—such was the general verdict; but it had not, for he pitched out of that bunker stone dead. Even so, when one considered those last five holes at Hoylake, the length of them all and the real fiendishness of the seventeenth, set between the twin perils of the road and the bunkers, 4, 4, 5, 4, 4, was a terrible demand to make. And yet Hagen did it almost easily; he put aside his scrambling mood, he hit every shot in the middle of the club, and doubt had vanished some time before he had finished; he seemed set to do it and nothing could stop him.

GESTURES   153

Cotton's successful pursuit of R. A. Whitcombe at Carnoustie in appalling conditions of rain was, I think, equally fine, but it is hard to think of many such and easy to think of the failures. There has been what old Beldham the cricketer called "many an all-but." Jurado had a great chase after Armour at Carnoustie in 1926, but it just failed. Duncan's chase of Hagen at Sandwich in 1922 would have been the greatest in all history had it succeeded; it failed by a single stroke. And so I might go on. Thrice armed is he who "gets his blow in fust."

GESTURES

HERE is a pleasant little story which has a golfing moral, or at any rate a golfing application. It comes from a seventeenth-century work called "Merry Passages and Jests," by Sir Nicholas Lestrange. It appears that a certain Lord Brookes was "much resorted to by those of the preciser sort" who kept a tight hand over him but "would allow him Christian libertie for his recreations." One day, however, he regrettably overstepped this freedom. "Being at bowles, in much company, and following his cast with much eagerness, he cryed 'Rubbe, rubbe, rubbe, rubbe, rubbe!' His chaplaine (a very strict mann) runns presently to him, and in the hearing of diverse, 'O good my Lord, leave that to God—you must leave that to God!' says he."

No doubt the chaplain was right, in that once the wood or the ball has sped no prayers or adjurations of ours can affect its destiny, which is then in the hands of a higher power. Nevertheless we all, or nearly all, attempt both by word and gesture to amend its course. There are few so icy cool that they can watch their ball skirting the verge of a bunker without trying to make it keep out, and some of us may even be shamefully conscious of putting up silent but heartfelt prayers that in like case our enemy's ball may go in. I once had a caddie whose

154   GOLFING BY-PATHS

prayers were not silent. He was a small boy at a private school and my opponent was one of his masters. His open and fervent urging of my ball into trouble was disconcerting in the extreme and his petitions were too often successful. "Rubbe, rubbe, rubbe!" he cried in effect and in went my ball.

That story of my Lord Brookes has set me thinking of the gestures of great men when they are "following their casts with much eagerness," and a whole series of pictures from the romantic past come before my eyes. A good many of them have their scene on the putting green, for it is there more than anywhere that men indulge in these supplicatory antics. No one used more frequently to egg his ball on to further efforts than Sandy Herd, with little wavings of his putter which began gently and became almost frantic as the crucial moment approached. His manner was, I am bound to say, not so much prayerful as minatory, and his threats were often successful; the ball would drop in at its last gasp, when a cheerful smile would irradiate his face. Then there is a curious movement which I cannot precisely explain but in which many of us, I am sure, indulge. It consists in a sudden thrusting forward of the right foot just as, in a long putt, the ball hesitates between dropping or shivering by on the left of the hole. As I have said before I can clearly see Freddie Tait with an extraordinary clearness making this gesture on the Briars green at Hoylake in a match against Harold Hilton nearly forty-five years ago. A different gesture comes back to me from another match of Harold's at St. Andrews in 1913. He was playing an American invader, "Heinie" Schmidt, and after a desperate struggle, in which he had incidentally putted into the Road bunker, they were on the nineteenth green. Harold was playing his third shot, a good long putt. On and on it came straight for the hole but with barely strength enough to reach it. It hovered and then dropped, and at that instant the striker's chin dropped on his breast in a sympathetic movement. There, very clearly, was a fervent prayer answered.

Another action to which we all treat ourselves now and then is that of walking after the ball as it is making straight for the hole with a view to picking it out triumphantly at the earliest possible instant. It is particularly characteristic of Cyril Tolley; he walks longer and farther than anyone and his judgment is rarely at fault. I have seen him stop, disappointed, half-way as the ball declines to obey, but as a rule the ball knows its duty and does it. The adversary who sees Mr. Tolley beginning to walk had better prepare himself for the worst. It is in the nature of what we should call to-day "the victory roll."

Now, leaving the putting green, whom do I see? My first picture, and it is a very vivid one, will not appeal to many people, for Johnnie Bramston, a great and most picturesque golfer, is long dead. Anybody who remembers him will, I am sure, share my vision of him at the end of a full shot. The ball is showing signs of going too much to the right, and, as he watches it, his right wrist is turning more and more over in an agony of prayerful steering. I can see Harold Hilton doing something of the same sort as his hook, or rather his "draw," shows symptoms of not materialising, but he seems to do it rather with an additional twist of his shoulders. Then there is the converse gesture again made by J. H. with his umbrella. It is the fourth round of the Open Championship at Sandwich in 1934, and Henry Cotton, holding a vast lead, is showing signs of frittering it away. The fours are turning into fives, and most of them from one cause: the player is not holding up his approaches into a right-hand wind, so that the ball is falling away to the left of the green. J. H. is beside himself with anxiety and is thrusting that umbrella out to the right in an unconscious demonstration of how the shot ought to be played. Fortunately all ends happily, for Henry pulls himself together in manful fashion and the umbrella is at rest.

I have been trying to bring this picture gallery of memory up to date and somehow or other I cannot do it. Is it that our modern champions have acquired the frozen impassivity of their counterparts at billiards so that they remain wholly immobile? No, I do not think it is that, for I certainly can recall Cotton giving his putter a sharp rap on the ground, as if to tell it not to do that again. It is rather, I suppose, that the earliest pictures remain the most vivid, because when one first saw them one had a great capacity of hero-worship, and the

156 GOLFING BY-PATHS

tiniest movement of the great impressed itself on the mind. Let me then turn to those other gestures which we make not after the stroke, but before it. It is still in the nature of a prayer, but more likely to be effective than the crying of "Rubbe, rubbe!" It indicates what, with the help of that higher power, we mean to do.

There is one such preliminary gesture which I have seen employed of deliberate purpose by very good players. This happens when they are about to play a brassey shot from rather a close lie, and there is something to carry, so that it is essential to get well down to the ball. They have a practice swing or two in which they are at pains to bring the sole of the club on to the ground with a resounding smack. I remember to have heard Jack White, than whom no man was more deeply versed in useful dodges, recommend this one, and I feel as if I had seen him do it himself. If we could always repeat our practice swing in the shot that follows, golf would be an easy game. Unfortunately we cannot, but now and again this preliminary exercise, with a particular and not a merely general purpose, is very valuable. I think, for instance, that when we are anxious to play a crisp pitch with plenty of bite, a practice shot in which the club makes a purring or fizzing sound is likely to produce the kind of shot required. In old times there was one kind of practice stroke which was eminently practical, namely that in which the player was allowed to test with his niblick the quality of the sand. Nowadays, however, that kind of investigation is denied him. To a skilful niblick player it was no doubt a help, and it did no harm that I know of, but perhaps it is as well to have as few exceptions to rules as possible, and to know quite simply that we must touch nothing in a bunker.

There is one gesture indulged in after the ball has flown which is not in the least in the nature of a prayer, but is rather a defiance of whatever golfing gods there be. That is the throwing of the club, which has been already dealt with. Like many other reprehensible actions, club-throwing can sometimes give great relief. Even Harold Hilton once threw his putter at the tee box and fortunately missed it. It was after he had taken the dreadful eight at the Himalayas which, humanly speaking, robbed him of a third Open Championship. That was cause enough, heaven knows. Who dare throw a stone at him?

TACTICS

IN the nature of things we hear to-day a great deal about strategy and tactics. In happier days we used to hear a great deal about tactics on the links, and I only hope that what we are told about them in war is sounder sense than most of what we were told about them in golf. There are those who would lead us to believe that there is a deep mystery about golfing tactics. This is largely nonsense. Golf is not primarily a game that tends to tactics since one player does not directly attack the other; our actions have only an indirect effect on our opponents. The best tactics at golf are to hit the ball as well as we can.

Of course there is a certain obvious and not at all profound or mysterious wisdom in "playing to the score," in eschewing risks when they are palpably unnecessary and in running them when it appears the only hope. Yet even so in this last case how often should we have done better had we not tried some desperate stroke, because we foolishly deemed our enemy infallible? Nobody has ever had a greater or better deserved reputation as a match player than Mr. John Ball, and he did not appear to watch his opponent very closely. On being told that his enemy was in a bunker he would answer that he had not seen and that anyhow his own job was to get his four. He tried to play as well as he could and let the other fellow look after himself. In modern language he was inclined to play against par, and it was Mr. Bobby Jones's discovery of this plan that made him "break through" and win Amateur Championships instead of just losing them.

Foursomes do give a greater scope for tactics than singles, but here again there is nothing recondite. One example is of

158 GOLFING BY-PATHS

course the question as to which holes each partner is to drive at, and on this point I have heard sound arguments produced by opposite schools of thought. The obvious course is that the better player should take the more difficult tee shots, that is supposing the odd holes are in the aggregate perceptibly harder than the even, and *vice versa*. On the other hand there are those who say that he should take the easier ones. In that case, they argue the side ought to be sure of at least a considerable number of tee shots clear of trouble, whereas the tee shots that are really narrow may catch the good driver as well as the bad.

Again there is the question of the one-shot holes. The majority of them, if there be a majority, are usually given to the stronger player; but the side will thereby lose the advantage of his additional power at the longer holes. Much of course depends on the qualities of the second string. Is he the second string because he lacks accuracy or because he lacks power? If he is, within his limitations, a straight player he had better have the short holes. There is another point not to be forgotten, namely, that the opposing pair have also to make their choice and it may be very important that an easily affected player on *our* side should not either be over-awed by a longer hitter or lured into competition with him. That which was once, I gather, regarded as a classical example of good judgment in this respect is quoted in the Badminton volume. Old Tom Morris was going to play a big match with Bob Anderson against Allan Robertson and Willie Dunn. Anderson's name is now forgotten, but he was apparently in his day just about as good as anyone and in particular a very fine driver. On the other side Dunn was famous for his long driving, which is still commemorated in the "Crescent" or "Dunny" bunker far down the Elysian Fields at St. Andrews, into which he once drove at the Long-hole-in. Tom, convinced that Anderson must not be led into a hitting match with Dunn, persuaded him to drive against Allan, whom he could leave behind with no trouble at all. The plan succeeded and they won the match handsomely.

Another opportunity for tactics, though I maintain it is really a limited one, is given in the deciding of the order in a team match. I remember, a few years ago, whenever the Ryder Cup match was imminent there used to be much tall writing about the great advantage that the American side would enjoy in having Walter Hagen as captain. It was implied that whoever was our leader would be "confoozled and done over" by this marvellous tactician. Now Hagen is an extremely shrewd person and up to every move in the game, but, after all, how many moves were open to him and what could he really do? He was an excellent captain; he could doubtless arrange his side in a sound order and doubtless also make a good guess at the other side's order; but these achievements were not beyond our powers. A good captain can do a great deal for his side in the matter of "jollying" them along, keeping them in good spirits, making them believe in themselves, preventing them from deeming their opponents supermen. All these virtues we saw exhibited in a high degree by our captain, Mr. John Beck, when at last we won the Walker Cup; but here are no sinister and recondite tactics.

Naturally the order of a team does matter, but it is always worth reflecting that one player can only play in one place and win one match; further that what is gained on the swings may be lost on the roundabouts. I remember well an occasion on which I was captain of the England side against Scotland; it was the last time in which I played in the match, at St. Andrews in 1924. After I had decided on our order to the best of my ability, one or two people came to me, very secret and mysterious, and having something black-vizarded and Guy Fawkes-like in their demeanour, telling me that the enemy were going to do something "funny" with their order, that a famous player was to play lower than he ought and that I had better make a counter-move of an equally ingenious character. My answer was something in the nature of the Duke of Wellington's to the blackmailing lady: "Publish and be d——d." We stuck to our order; the famous player won his single, which he might well have done wherever he had played, and we won the match. I may have been guilty of laziness or lack of imagination, but I am inclined to think that I was just ordinarily and prosaically sensible.

160 GOLFING BY-PATHS

There is, so I have been told, a point at which mathematics and philosophy impinge upon one another and only some two men alive are capable of appreciating it. So there comes a point where tactics verge on propaganda and it is hard to tell t'other from which. For example, in that rare but amusing form of golf, the worst ball match, the single player will be well advised to address his two adversaries something in this manner; "I am afraid this will be very dull for you two swells, but if you play a match against each other as well perhaps it will be better fun for you." If they fall into the trap and concentrate on beating each other it is extremely likely that the third insidious serpent will beat their worst ball.

I once played a series of such matches with Mr. de Montmorency and another, also now dead, who had no very great power but went straight and was a magnificent putter. Sometimes we won and sometimes he did, but I observed that when the subsidiary match between my partner and me was closest our worst ball was least successful. When it comes to telling an enemy either that he is driving farther than ever or that he does not seem quite so long as he used to be it is clear that the reign of propaganda has begun, and I did not write this article in order to give immoral advice.

YOU NEVER CAN TELL

SOME missed shots are so clearly of vital importance that they are never forgotten. Such was Padgham's putt on the thirty-fifth green against Cotton at Mid-Surrey in the final of the *News of the World*. Others which are, subject, of course, to the inevitable "if" clause, equally important, are apt to fade, either because they are not "sensational" or else because other more obvious "sensations" follow and blot them from the memory. In thinking of them the mind is apt first to fly to holes beset with terrible and famous bunkers, but I find my mind passing them by and winging its way, a little to my own surprise, to the fourteenth at St. Andrews, the long

YOU NEVER CAN TELL 161

hole in. It would not be surprising if I were thinking of the Open Championship of 1939, when the new tee far back was a destruction for many. There was, for instance, that eight of Bobby Locke's there, when he had arrived on the tee with a score of six under fours. True, he finished most bravely with four fours for a 70, but nevertheless the eight had, I fancy, thrown him out of his triumphant stride to just a small and fatal degree. However, I am thinking of the hole before that distant tee was made, as ordinary mortals play it: when the drive is not really alarming, when there is very little excuse for going either into the Beardies or over the wall. I can recall two occasions when a player went out of bounds over that wall, although it seemed the most improbable thing in the world for him to do, and its importance was past reckoning.

The first was in the Amateur Championship of 1930, and the importance lay in this, that if that most unlikely mistake had not been made I do not believe that Bobby Jones would ever have gained those wonderful four championships in one summer, christened by somebody with a gift of picturesque language "the impregnable quadrilateral." Bobby was playing that excellent American golfer, George Voight, and he was in rather a bad way; Voight was playing well and confidently, and on the fourteenth tee he stood in that position mysteriously believed to be unlucky, two up with five to play. I do not remember that anyone then invoked this fallacious belief on Bobby's behalf; nearly everybody thought sorrowfully that he was going to be beaten, and then Voight made a gratuitous and fatal mistake; with no violent wind to make him do it he cut his tee shot over the wall out of bounds. It gave Bobby a practically certain win at that hole, and it gave him heart and breathing space. From that moment he always looked like winning, and he did win on the last green, though I seem to remember that he had to hole a very nasty putt at the Road hole. I doubt if he could have won if George Voight had not made that slip at the fourteenth, and it was a slip the possibility of which cannot have entered the player's head before he made the shot, nor would it have entered the heads of much humbler players.

162 GOLFING BY-PATHS

Nevertheless a few years later I saw the very same mistake made by another very good golfer with obviously, as I should say, a great effect on the ultimate result. This was in the final of 1936 between Hector Thomson and that most formidable Australian, Jim Ferrier, which Thomson won on the thirty-sixth green. In the morning round Ferrier was going great guns; he was three up after the Hole o' Cross and clearly full of confidence. For no ostensible reason he too cut his drive over the wall and gave his adversary the piece of encouragement that he so badly needed. It did look the most unnecessary of errors, and I remember saying, perhaps rather stupidly, to Mr. Tony Torrance, with whom I was walking, that if I had been three up at such a moment I would have taken good care not to go out of bounds. He answered, and I think truly, that a player who is "on top of the world" in a vein of fine golf and of winning holes, does not, at least in the matter of tee shots, envisage that kind of mistake, or indeed any mistake; he just goes ahead, and as a rule it pays him handsomely. On rare occasions, of course, the unexpected happens and the unthinkable mistake is made; in Ben Sayers's words, "it's no' possible but it's a fact." These things will happen, and they make all the more difference because a minute before they would have appeared almost incredible. All there is to say about them is that they happen least often to those with the longest and coolest heads.

And now, apropos of these things which could not possibly occur save for the painful fact that they do, a little scene comes suddenly back to me from Muirfield. It had no ultimate importance, but it was amusing and instructive. I go back to the Open Championship of 1912, and the fourteenth hole as it was before Muirfield was altered. This was then a short hole, a pitch of no great difficulty over a big cross-bunker. There was plenty of room on the green, but there was a pot bunker some way to the right of the hole. Ray was playing his last round; he had a winning lead and a winner's crowd with him. It was encroaching far on to the green and had completely masked the small pot bunker. Mr. John Ball, armed with a red flag, was trying to clear the green, and insisted on moving back from that bunker a knot of young professionals. They got out of the way with some reluctance, conveying clearly by their manner that this was a piece of unnecessary fussiness and that professionals did not put pitches into bunkers off the line. A moment later Ray played his shot and his ball came plump down into that very bunker. Mr. Ball is not of demonstrative nature, but it was palpable that he was not displeased. Never was there a clearer case of "I told you so" or a better illustration of "You never can tell."

The truth is, no doubt, that there is nothing that cannot happen, and we ought to be well aware of it by this time. It is not either easy or common to putt into a bunker, though nowadays bunkers are so smooth and well raked that it is comparatively common to putt out of them. Nevertheless, consider the case of the little Road bunker nestling under the edge of the seventeenth green at St. Andrews. There is, I will make bold to say, no golfer who has played at all regularly on the Old Course and has not putted into it. If anyone says that he has not done so he is like the young man who told W. G. that he never made a duck and received the answer: "Then you go in last. You can't have played much cricket." I only remember to have seen it done once on an important occasion, by Mr. Hilton against Mr. Heinrich Schmidt, and then it was not, after all, so important, because, as before narrated, Mr. Hilton won at the nineteenth hole. In ordinary games I have seen it often, and need scarcely add that I have done it myself. Yet to the stranger not acquainted with the devilish and magnetic curve of the green the thing appears absurd and impossible. I once knew a golfer whose side in a foursome had three or four for the hole on a sloping green at Brancaster. "Let's give it them," said one of the opponents. "No," said the other, "D might putt into the bunker." And poor D, rather hot and flustered, and very apprehensive of jokes at his expense, did putt into the bunker. However, the story has a happy ending, for the opponents then, like true, chivalrous gentlemen, gave up the hole.

BACK TO SCHOOL

HERE is a little story, entirely mild and entirely egotistical, which may yet waken some sympathetic chords in the breasts of other golfers. It seems unlikely that any of them should be so childish as I am, and yet I dare say a few are. In the golfless land in which I am now living I am wholly dependent on fields; most of them have been very properly ploughed up and the others bear crops of hay, However, there is one which is not always occupied by sheep. and the other day, feeling a sudden passionate desire to play some shots, I set out with an iron for that field. Of course those confounded sheep were there, but I was not going to be deprived of my shots, and climbed over a stile into another field which possessed a few clear spaces among its rank, long patches. With trembling eagerness I teed my ball on a tuft and hit it, to my surprise, straight as Robin Hood's arrow and as far as I contemptibly can. I pursued and found it and was going to hit it back again when a herd of large horses came prancing aggressively into the field. That would never do, and I crept through a fence into the next, which proved wholly unplayable. Then I was confronted by a barbed-wire entanglement, and only got through it, being stiff and clumsy, by falling into a mixed bed of thistles and nettles. I had to stumble round two sides of a plough and finally arrived home limping, perspiring—but happy.

And why was I happy? So a popular preacher might go on, asking his congregation a rhetorical question. The answer is as obvious as the answers to such questions usually are. Because the one shot I had hit had been a good one. If it had been a bad one I might have worried myself to death in wondering what I had "done wrong"; I might have even sacrificed a valuable ball by hitting it away into a field of corn, with no hope of redeeming it, just to quiet my uneasy soul. As it was I was perfectly content and had slaked my thirst for practice.

FRANCIS OUIMET AT GARDEN CITY, 1913
A fortnight before he beat Vardon and Ray

CYRIL TOLLEY IN 1938

Central Press Photos, Ltd.

BACK TO SCHOOL 165

Probably few people who are as old as I am are also as foolish, and yet at the root of my ridiculous behaviour there is a profound truth, namely that if you go out to practise your shots you *must* end with a good one. Of course, this is no new revelation. Circumstances had, till a few days ago, divided me for a whole year from my dear old battered first edition of the *Badminton* book. On being reunited we fell metaphorically into one another's arms, and on the very day after my one shot I was reading the chapter called "Hints on Match and Medal Play." There were the very words of Mr. Horace Hutchinson, which justified my absurdity: "Whatever the particular species of stroke you may be practising, never leave off after making a bad one. Keep on at it until you make a good impression and the confidence in your skill strong in your mind. It is like the final glance which a beauty gives at the most becoming glass in her dressing-room before descending to the triumphs of the evening—it gives her strength in the consciousness of her power." I cannot affirm that I felt like a triumphant beauty when I came home a melting object, but the principle is the same. Incidentally, though it has nothing to do with the question of practising, there is in that excellent chapter one piece of advice now completely out of date, which may show how much in some respects golf has changed. Mr. Hutchinson says that golfers have the habit of husbanding up some wonderful club against the great occasion. " 'Where's that club you were driving with the other day?' you ask one of these worthies. 'Oh,' he will answer, 'I'm saving it for the medal day'; and on the medal day out comes the precious club—and ten chances to one he cannot hit a ball with it!" Mr. Hutchinson rightly stigmatises this as "the height of folly," since clubs are capricious things and you must make the most of them when they are in good humour. But it is a folly that no one would dream of committing now, because clubs are not the fragile things they once were. To-day we might as soon expect a man to put away a precious putter lest in the interval before the medal he should break it over his knee in a tantrum. Once upon a time, however, the life of a driver hung, figuratively speaking, by a thread. There was always the lurking fear of the head splitting at the

M

GOLFING BY-PATHS

end of the horn or of the face suffering irreparable damage on a wet day. To have permanently in the bag two drivers, as like one another as possible, for fear of accidents, was no more than common prudence. Shafts were, of course, less vulnerable, but still horrid accidents did happen. I remember that in one of my University matches my opponent of Oxford was unlucky enough to break his driver, a fact which probably put some holes in my pocket. Clubs are now by comparison indestructible and we need not be afraid of working them as hard as we like. We are far more likely to get tired of them than to break them.

As my dear *Badminton* and I have only just met again after so long a separation perhaps I may say one more thing about it. It refers to the picture called "Modern Golf Clubs," and I ought to add that my book bears the date 1890. That picture always used to puzzle me (I had been playing my juvenile golf for some six years in 1890), and it puzzles me still. There are depicted eleven clubs standing in a row, and I would give anyone who did not know the answer a good many guesses as to the proportion which wood bore to iron. Well, the answer is that there are seven wooden clubs and only four iron ones. It puzzled me because I had never seen anyone carrying anything like so many wooden clubs as that, and I don't believe they did at that time. The irons make easy guessing—a cleek, an iron, a niblick and an iron putter. The mashie was beginning to come in and Mr. Laidlay's skill with it is mentioned in the book, but I suppose it was still something of a hybrid interloper. The wooden clubs are more difficult. I take them to be a driver, a "grassed" driver, long, mid and short spoons, and a wooden putter, which make six; but there is a club rather longer than the putter as to which I am not clear. It must have been, I fancy, a club which was then, in the elegant language which I learned in the Royal Army Ordnance Corps, "obsolescent." It was called the driving putter and was deemed useful against a high wind. I have seen Mr. Tom Simpson, that lover of all things old, use one, but I fancy there were very few of them to be seen in 1890. I dare to say that even then this picture was not up-to-date, and already the "grassed" driver

NOISES WITHOUT 167

and its attendant satellites of the spoon family had been largely
superseded by a single brassey. In fact I believe that some
golfers carry more wooden clubs to-day in their vast bags than
people did then. Only the other day a charming lady wrote
me a postcard to tell me that her husband, a very old friend
and contemporary of mine, had holed a certain hole in one
with his "No. 4 wood." I replied with congratulations, but
added rudely and irrelevantly that the last time I had seen him
use his No. 4 wood he had holed out in the bottom of a deep
pit, while I got on to the green with my iron. Of course I was
jealous!

NOISES WITHOUT

I HAVE heard it alleged and I have also seen it in print (in
Fairway and Hazard) that a club near London has now
this local rule: "A player whose stroke is affected by
a simultaneous explosion of a bomb or shell or by machine-gun
fire may play another ball from the same place. Penalty one
stroke." I sincerely hope it is true, and more so as the rule
shows a proper mixture of the Spartan and the modern spirit.
It acknowledges that bombs are altogether out of the common
and that some allowance is to be made for them; at the same
time, to have a second shot is so outrageous that the player
must be prepared to pay for it; no number of wild Germans
is to be allowed to make the game wholly farcical.

There may possibly be some difficulty in deciding whether
or not the shot and the bomb were actually simultaneous.
When an unfortunate gentleman, chilly and breakfastless,
appears on the first tee at St. Andrews to drive himself into
his office as captain that which strikes terror into him is the
thought that the celebrating gun will go off before he has reached
the ball. My own impression is that when I was in this position,
so honourable and so unenviable, I just beat the cannon. If so,

168   GOLFING BY-PATHS

I was lucky, because I understand that the gunner has a fixed principle; he waits until he sees over the heads of the crowds the captain's club at the top of the swing, and then he lets go. So it is bound to be an uncommonly near thing. On that occasion it does not much matter, except to his own vanity, whether the captain hits the ball or not; but on others it may matter a good deal. I hope there are at least some of my readers who know that beloved old book "Frank Fairlegh." If so they will remember the scene in the billiard room where the heroic Oaklands is being fleeced by the villainous Cumberland. The game is at a critical stage. Oaklands is about to make the decisive stroke when, just as the cue approaches the ball, there comes a resounding sneeze from the confederate marker. The stroke is missed; Cumberland, with great apparent reluctance, says that he *thinks* Oaklands has already struck the ball before the sneeze, and proceeds to run out and win the money.

Are there many historic noises in golf which have disturbed or, more often, failed to disturb eminent players at important moments? I can think of one, connected with the name not of Oaklands but of Oakmont. It was here in 1919, when he was very young, that Bobby Jones reached the final of the American Amateur Championship and played Davison Herron. At a certain hole a steward shouted through his megaphone exactly as Bobby was playing a brassey shot; he went into a bunker and that sealed his fate. The hole, for some reason or other, perhaps through the inspiration of some "brilliant" journalist, became known as the Ghost Hole. When the Championship was at Oakmont six years later, Bobby was in the final again, now as a holder, and was making comparatively heavy weather of it against Watts Gunn, when he came to that very hole and went, I think, into that very same bunker. This time, however, the ghost was a beneficent one, for he got out very well, won the hole, and from that moment went away like a streak to win by 8 and 7. Another distinguished noise is that of the engine that puffed and snorted just behind Miss Wethered, with the only result that, after she had played her shot and been congratulated on her nonchalence, she remarked, "What engine?" So, at least, the story goes; but where exactly did it happen? I have heard it of Troon and, I think, Shering-ham, and also of other courses where there is a railway near the course. It would certainly take more than a puff or a snort to discompose either Miss Wethered or Lady Amory, but I have sometimes wondered whether this was not a ghost train that haunted her admirers wherever she played.

I have been trying to remember noises in my own humble career, and singularly enough, for I am a fussy and pernickety golfer, they seem to have been propitious. I have a distinct recollection of machine-gun practice at St. Andrews when I was playing in an international against Mr. Edward Blackwell. I had hit my tee shot wide to the left at the eighth hole, and that infernal machine seemed to be going off immediately behind me, whereupon I laid a very long putt stone dead. Of course, there was a continuous noise rather than a "simultaneous" one within the meaning of the local rule, and it may perhaps help one to concentrate one's attention ferociously. So may the hideous whirring of a cinema camera, and I have personally the greatest cause to be grateful to one. Three down after three holes in a Walker Cup match and your adversary on the green at a difficult short hole—here is one of the least enjoyable of situations, and it was at this moment that a cinema beast whirred at me. But why call him a beast? He made me, I am sure, put the ball on the green, and after that all was, comparatively speaking, right with the world. Once, too, I positively emulated Miss Wethered. I was playing the late Clyde Pearce, the Champion of Australia and a very good golfer, who was killed in the first war, in the Amateur Championship at Prest-wick. I had just lost two consecutive holes to be one down with four to play (I had lost the first three in that match like-wise); my state of mind was anything but angelic, and the tee shot to the fifteenth hole at Prestwick is generally recognised as the narrowest in all golf. After I had hit a straight one somebody pointed out that the cinema man had been playing his tune all the time, and I had never seen or heard him. I won the hole and, in the end, the match, and so now, when photo-graphers will never trouble me again, I feel very kindly towards them.

170 GOLFING BY-PATHS

Yet how I have hated them before now, not the whirrers but the clickers. The click of a camera really can be "simultaneous" and most destructive. There was a certain camera that clicked at Taylor at Prestwick in 1914, when he and Vardon were drawn together, with the whole vast crowd after them and the Championship a certainty for one or other. It was Taylor's disastrous seven at the fourth hole that settled the issue, but the click at the hole before may have paved the way, for J. H., who had been playing magnificently, was wrought up to a high pitch at the time.

On the whole, I think that distinguished golfers are wonderfully impervious both to movement and noises, but there will always be some great men who are also men on wires. I have read somewhere an account of the famous Squire, George Osbaldeston, shooting pigeons. This was one of the many pursuits in which he was *primus inter pares*, and it appears that he was, as a shot, extremely fussy so that it was as much as anyone's life was worth to make a sound. I don't think that I have often laughed more than I did years ago when staying in a pleasant house in Ayrshire; I have told the story in another place, but all is fair in war. Mr. Laidlay was suddenly moved to give an imitation of Mr. Leslie Balfour-Melville playing a stroke in a crucial match. First he shouted a furious and stentorian "Fore," then he turned with smiles and gentleness to an imaginary lady who was standing in the wrong place behind him; then he shouted again, and just as he was going to begin the lady had alas! done something else that she ought not. It was a truly admirable impersonation and I have never forgotten it. Pretty ladies standing " behind your eye " are better than bombs.

THE ILLUSTRIOUS OBSCURE

ALL readers of Boswell are familiar with the young gentleman who is described as "a clergyman" but has attained everlasting fame because he was so savagely tossed and gored by the great lexicographer. "Were not Dr. Dodd's sermons addressed to the passions?" he innocently asked, glad perhaps of an opportunity for a telling question. "They were nothing, Sir, be they addressed to what they may," replied Dr. Johnson, and there was an end of him. It was an end only for that evening however, for he has since enjoyed a celebrity which has been, if possible, enhanced by a charming essay of Sir Max Beerbohm's.

I was reminded of that young man a little while ago when skimming, as I often do, over the list of "Feats, Interesting Facts and Extraordinary Occurrences" which fills many pages of the *Golfer's Handbook*. There I came across one who is also immortal and anonymous, and his anonymity seems really a little hard on him. Here is his story: "1889. In the Open Championship at Musselburgh an amateur, who partnered Andrew Kirkaldy, holed the last hole in one. It was almost dark when the championship finished and when the player hit his cleek shot the green could scarcely be made out from the tee." A similar darkness has descended on the hero of that feat. It sticks in my head that somewhere else I have read who he was, but as far as this semi-official record is concerned his name, like that of the last Lord of Ravenswood, "shall be lost evermo'." I cannot help reflecting how Andrew must have envied the cleek shot, since on that occasion he tied with Willie Park for the Championship and lost on playing off the tie. Perhaps he expressed himself strongly on the point, but that is by the way. It is surely cruel that the poor man should be nameless, for he must have been greeted with shouting and with laughter; all Musselburgh must have rung with him and many a time doubtless in subsequent years was he called upon to tell the tale anew. Now a wave of oblivion has passed over his name and he is simply "an amateur," a P.B.A.

As I mused upon that man's untoward fate it occurred to me to wonder whether there were in the same record many other of the "illustrious obscure" whose names had been by ill chance or injustice withheld from the world. I found quite a number of them, as to some of whom one would like to know more. Who for instance was "a girl" who played an important part in another Championship, that of 1878 at Prestwick? The story of the finish of that Championship is well known, how Jamie Anderson with four holes to go first holed a full iron shot, next a putt of fifteen yards or so and at the seventeenth, then a short hole, his tee shot. It is at that seventeenth that the young lady comes into the story. Anderson had teed the ball for his shot when she pointed out that it was outside the marks, whereupon he teed again and holed out in one, and even so he only won the Championship in the end by a single shot. Who was his unknown benefactress? She must have known the game and had all her wits about her. Beyond that all is hidden and yet she did what very few of us have done, she changed the course of history.

Turning on a page or two I find another lady who has possibly some cause of complaint. She lost the final of a certain tournament at Paterson in New Jersey at the one hundred and sixth hole. She and her adversary halved an eighteen-hole match, and at intervals of a few days they continued to try to reach a decision, but it was only after six weeks and eighty-eight holes that they were able to do so. Then the other lady won and her name is duly given, Mrs. Edwin Labaugh, but the poor loser who equally contributed to the record is left in outer darkness. Having gone so far and worked so hard she deserved more specific mention. I protest against this pandering to mere success.

There are plenty of anonymous gentlemen likewise, particularly among those who have hit and killed birds and beasts with their shots. The slayers of several sea-gulls, a weasel, a young hare, a fine trout, a sparrow-hawk and one of a covey of partridges will all themselves rest in unvisited tombs as far as this

THE ILLUSTRIOUS OBSCURE 173

record is concerned, since there is no clue to their identities. On the other hand the Rev. Davies Jones of Bala, who apparently aimed a mashie shot at a ball at the mouth of a rabbit hole and killed the rabbit instead, has his title set out at full length, perhaps out of respect for his cloth. There seems some unfairness here; "its unekal" as Mr. Weller Senior used to say when his grog was not made half and half.

Apart from the question of justice there is another and perhaps a wider one, namely whether a golfer would wish to be remembered for ever by some absurd performance or whether it would be better for him to be wholly forgotten. I myself provide an example. On another page of the book I am most deservedly gibbeted for having hit three balls out of bounds at a certain nineteenth hole after my opponent had hit two. It is implied, and no doubt rightly, that so many balls were never hit jointly out of bounds before. Here is fame which is hardly to be distinguished from infamy. I am mentioned in one or two other parts of the book in a rather more honourable context, but I suspect that this lamentable achievement will survive when I have elsewhere been blotted out to make room for younger persons. I have always believed that the minor murderers in the Chamber of Horrors are after a time melted down in favour of more topical successors, but the really great ones, such as William Palmer and Dr. Crippen, remain. So in respect of my shots out of bounds I may be remembered with the greater criminals. Having therefore some sympathy with the unfortunately immortal I feel a little sorry for one who is named as the winner of a certain "Duffers' Medal" at Biarritz which took the traditional form of a large wooden spoon. There are, or were, some holes at Biarritz, especially one up a cliff, which could prove expensive: so it is not surprising to know that the winner's score was 316. He was the Chevalier von Cittern, and even if he had never played before and never did so again—and both seem probable—he has attained his niche. Most people, save possibly those who played behind him, will think that he well earned it by his perseverance, and, more or less apropos, a kind of correspondent has just sent me a copy of a Scottish paper in which there is an extract from the

174 GOLFING BY-PATHS

New York World of fifty years ago. "In the women's tournament won by Mrs. Ford," thus it reads, "the average number of strokes to each hole was 121; the average for the men was 92." With such scoring as that even the Chevalier could not compete.

There are, of course, cases in which the reason for concealment is obvious. The gentleman who at 8 a.m. on a Sunday morning drove off from Piccadilly Circus and holed out at the Royal Exchange, might to-day safely disclose his identity but at the time he may have distrusted the police. So he is for ever veiled as "a golfer." Similarly the two players who were driven off the seventh green by an obdurate ram to take refuge behind a tree, and ultimately had to give up the game, may have preferred what Zero, the Dynamiter, called an "anonymous infernal glory." We may feel tolerably certain that we should have imitated their caution, but when in safety ourselves we might be inclined to laugh at them.

There are various other instances that I might give, such as that of the golfer who had to resign in the semi-final of a tournament because his pince-nez got so wet that he could not see the ball. His name hardly seems essential and many other spectacled golfers, who have suffered in the rain, may be jealous of his pre-eminence. At any rate, with the aid of that invaluable book, to which all my thanks, I have said enough to show that there are other ways of gaining renown besides that of winning championships, even if it be only nameless renown. Some of the greatest in other walks of life remain anonymous as anyone may discover from the *Oxford Dictionary of Quotations*. Who was it who described his head master in those transcendent words, "A beast but a just beast"? He lives for us only as a Rugby boy and so will "An amateur" and "A girl."

THE YOUNG IDEA

WHEN we read of the sports and pastimes of elder days we do not as a rule imagine the players talking the shop of their particular game with that fervour and occasional tiresomeness which marks their successors. When for instance we re-read "Ivanhoe" yet again and find the beloved Locksley cleaving the willow wand we are apt to think of him as a natural or supernatural genius; we do not fancy all the best archers of Needwood and Charnwood analysing his methods and discussing how he did it. And yet no doubt they did and wanted to feel his bow and wondered if they could emulate him if they had just such another, even as we wonder if the clubs of some great golfer would improve our game. No doubt they said that X was a natural archer, whereas Y had striven and agonised and managed to teach himself an artificial style which might forsake him at a crisis.

This small notion came into my head when I was reading with intense pleasure Dr. G. M. Trevelyan's book, "English Social History." There I found one, Hugh Latimer, describing his initiation into archery by his father, a yeoman in the reign of Henry VII. His father, he wrote, "taught me how to draw, how to lay my body in my bow. . . . I had my bows bought me according to my age and strength; as I increased in them, so my bows were made bigger and bigger. For men shall never shoot well unless they be brought up to it." That is an engaging phrase, "to lay my body in my bow," with quite a golfing turn to it, and Hugh Latimer gave a further elucidation of it. He was taught, he went on, "not to draw with strength of arms as divers other nations do, but with the strength of the body." Dr. Trevelyan, in a note, cites another and later authority, W. Gilpin in "Remarks on Forest Scenery," and this too I will take the liberty of quoting: "the Englishman did not keep his left hand steady, and draw his bow with his right; but keeping his right at rest upon the nerve, he pressed the

175

176   GOLFING BY-PATHS

whole weight of his body into the horns of his bow. Hence probably arose the phrase 'bending a bow' and the French of 'drawing' one." Here, also, at any rate to my warped mind, is golf again, for how often have we had it pointed out to us not to swing with the arms alone, and, for that matter, how often have we tried to "get the body into it" and got it in in the wrong way!

There is much learning common to all games. I am wholly unlearned in archery, but I once watched some skilful archers and I remember noticing one point in the method of him who was by common consent the best there; indeed I was told that there was no better in England. He stood wonderfully immobile and his right hand was still at his ear when the arrow hit the target. I have no doubt he "laid his body in his bow," but that I do not recall, not having the knowledge to look out for it. Generally speaking, whatever game we watch we can see that the best players obey, *mutatis mutandis*, some rule that we have been taught in golf. "Keep your eye on the ball" is a rule of almost universal application, for instance, and we sometimes see it flagrantly neglected even by eminent persons. When, as sometimes happens in the highest circles, we see a poor wretch miss a place kick at goal from bang in front of the posts we can often observe the cause of his lapse from grace in the head that has come up palpably too soon.

Hugh Latimer's remark that "men shall never shoot well unless they be brought up to it" is one that is as nearly true of golf as such generalisations can be. There are exceptions, of course, men of great natural game-playing ability who take to golf as grown-ups and work very hard at it, but they are very few, and even so they are not quite so good as the best of those who have been "brought up to it." This bringing-up, in the case of great golfers, does not always imply that careful teaching which Hugh Latimer had from his father, nor that equally careful provision of their clubs. Indeed it may be said that most of the best golfers have never been deliberately taught in their lives; they have followed Mr. Robert Harris's aphorism that "the right way to learn golf is to learn it first and think about it afterwards." As for clubs, many of them have not in

THE YOUNG IDEA 177

early youth been able to have their clubs "bought according to their age and strength." They have not been able to buy any at all, but have had to subsist on a casual old club or two given them by a kind employer or picked up anyhow or nohow. I think I remember to have read that the great Bob Ferguson never possessed a regular set of clubs until he had won his first tournament, a triumph which he achieved with a "job lot," some of which had been lent him for the occasion. Hugh Latimer in the fifteenth century started his career in more auspicious circumstances than did several Open Champions in the nineteenth.

No doubt boys in this country are coached much more and much earlier than they used to be, and I imagine that this is still more true of America, but perhaps we incline to exaggerate the studiousness of American youth. There is a general impression that Bobby Jones was taught by Stewart Maiden, but in fact the teaching chiefly consisted in Bobby as a small boy following his idol round the course and imitating him. Too careful coaching in youth may, I venture to think, do at least as much harm as good in cramping natural ability. I once had an interesting talk with the golf coach at an American college and he said that when he taught his pupils indoors during the winter he concentrated on teaching them to swing and did not let them care overmuch where the ball went. They had a ball to hit, but its destiny was of secondary importance.

The other day I chanced to be on a golf course, and sitting in the veranda I watched with some interest a boy of perhaps eleven or twelve years old having a lesson from the professional. He was by no means a complete beginner, having already the rudiments of a good, free swing as most small boys have, and I wanted to see what his teacher would do with him. I thought the boy was rather sternly used in that only at the very end of his lesson was he allowed to hit a real shot with a real ball. All the rest of the time he was kept at more theoretical learning, being put into attitudes and swinging, so to speak, by numbers. I thought that if I had been that boy I should have yearned for a shot or two, but he did not seem to mind, for, when he was released, I saw him still swinging thoughtfully and stopping

178   GOLFING BY-PATHS

every now and then to verify his pose at the top of the swing.
I dare say the professional knew best and I do not wish to teach
my grandmother, but I did wonder whether quite so much
pensiveness was good for aspiring youth. I remember a remark
of Mr. John Ball's that he did not like to see a young one too
careful, and it seemed to me a wise one.

Once or twice I have tried to coach children, and it then
seemed to me that one of the difficulties was to know when to
point out a definite mistake and when to say no more than, in
effect, "Never mind. You missed that one. Now hit this
one." A child will in the nature of things miss a certain number
of shots from very childishness and not from having anything
radically wrong with the swing. The good coach will know
when to interpose definite instruction and when to be merely
and generally encouraging. That at least is how it strikes me,
though I do not claim any great skill or experience. I heard
the other day of a fully grown-up player who declared with
pride that he had reduced the number of things he had to
remember in the course of his swing to six. I should have
thought that was about five too many, but, however that may
be, it is not a frame of mind to be recommended to the quite
young golfer.

ASSORTED ROUGH

I WAS counting my few golf balls, considering how precious
they were likely to be and how unpopular in days of
dearth would become courses possessed of very thick
and ball-concealing rough. Then my mind wandered all over
the different kinds of rough that are sent to tease poor golfers,
and I reflected how very modern was this division into "fairway" and "rough" and how when I first played golf I never
heard of such things. There was simply the course, described
in the *Badminton* glossary in 1890 as "That portion of the links
on which the game ought to be played, generally bounded on
either side by rough ground or other hazard." The correct

ASSORTED ROUGH 179

technical term for "rough" was, I suppose, "fog," defined as "moss, rank grass." To-day we are apt to think of the course or fairway as an avenue strictly enclosed on either side by a border of rough, but that would certainly be no fair description of the courses on which I played juvenile golf. Felixstowe, Aberdovey, Eastbourne, Royston—no, there were bunkers, whins and, by the sea, bents dotted about; but there was no hard or fast line, and indeed at Royston in those days if you avoided the bunkers, which were small and far between, you could go entirely where you pleased. There are still seaside courses which may be said to have only hazards and no definite rough—St. Andrews for example—and I confess I like them best thus. I feel as if I had only come across these parallel lines of rough, now such old enemies, when I, as a comparatively seasoned golfer, joined the Woking Club in 1897 and tried to keep out of the heather on either hand.

With how many varieties of rough are we now familiar? There is that heather, for instance, on many of the best inland courses, especially near London, to be found perhaps in its richest, most tangled profusion at Walton Heath. To transfer the epithet from the ball to the rough, there are spots there which are truly inextricable. It was into one of these that Densmore Shute put his ball in his match with Cotton when Braid remarked with a placid venom, "He'll need all his dynamiters there." For myself I prefer my heather drawn a little milder and I always thought that Ashdown Forest had a very good brand. True, one could get into some horrid places in it and quite right too, places where prayer and the heaviest niblick were the only resource. Yet it was not always so fierce; it was possible very often to do something more than merely hack and hew. It was noteworthy that both Mr. Hutchinson and Jack Rowe used to take spoons in it rather than irons and would witch the ball away with wonderful skill.

Then there are trees, which I presume come under the generic title of rough; not an occasional lone tree, but lines of woodland. The thought of them brings back memories of New Zealand, which is Byfleet, and of Mr. Mure Fergusson crashing into them, only to find a gap, recover by a miraculous shot and add insult to injury by holing the putt. The two dark lines closed formidably in on you and made it at first very hard to keep straight, but when once you were used to them you grew to like the feeling and to deem them not only an incentive but also an aid to accuracy. That was, and is still no doubt, a snug and charming course when the wind was blowing hard over the more open country and there was a friendly intimate feeling about the Sundays in the old days there, which I since have met with in perfection only at Swinley, and on that course of pine trees, Mougins, near Cannes.

Gorse, or let me rather be properly Scottified and say whins, is another definite variety of rough on certain courses. The whins make a fairly solid line on our right going out at St. Andrews, all the way from the third hole to the seventh. At the tenth they threaten us on our left, and then cross over and hang on our right flank at the thirteenth and fifteenth. They are, of course, but a remnant, a pale shadow of what they were in the days before we were born, and that is what we must always remember when we consider, let us say, Allan Robertson's famous 79, the first round of under 80 ever played there nearly eighty-four years ago. Nowadays to summon up the image of a double menace of whins on either hand is for me, and I am sure for many other people besides, to think nostalgically of delightful Aldeburgh. I used incidentally to find those whins very expensive in the matter of balls when my young family was learning golf there. They will always flourish I hope, though it is wonderful what the niblicks of the erratic can accomplish in the course of years. I cherish memories of a screen of gorse that once guarded the old sixth hole at Aberdovey. That hole, now played from another quarter, is to-day the fifth, and if there is one stumpy little whin bush it is about all there is. There were many similar patches on other courses which are to-day only represented by their ghosts.

We must by no means forget the rough which consists simply of rough grass, for it is the commonest, though by no means the most distinguished of all. Among celebrated courses Muirfield comes to mind as being well endowed, though not so richly as of yore. There was a time when to get into the rough

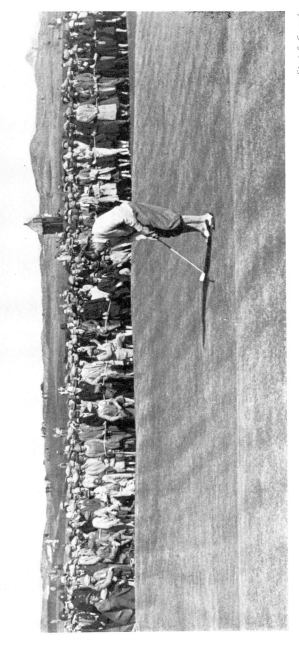

THE LAST PUTT
Walter Hagen winning the Championship at St. George's in 1928

LADY HEATHCOAT-AMORY (MISS JOYCE WETHERED) DRIVING

On the left, Miss Pam Barton, Miss Enid Wilson, Mlle Simone de la Chaume and Henry Cotton

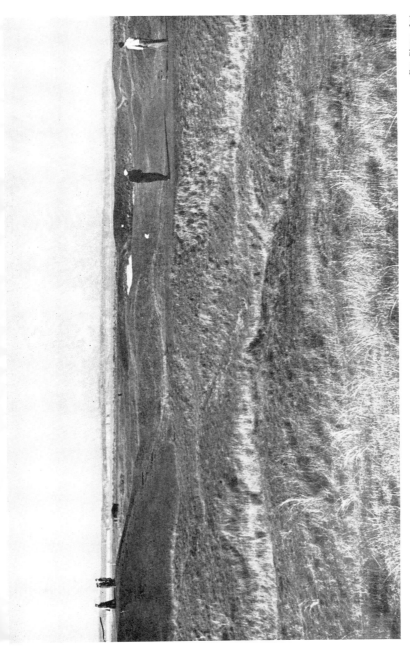

DRIVING TO THE 7TH HOLE AT SANDWICH
With Pegwell Bay and the White Cliffs in the distance

Fox Photos, Ltd.

NORTH BERWICK LAW LOOKING DOWN ON THE LINKS

Jas. C. H. Balmain.

at Muirfield was, as Mr. John Ball might have said, to have to scratch your head and be thankful to get back on to the course by the shortest way. There were exceptions, and I shall always remember my old friend, Mr. Herman de Zoete, when he reached the semi-final there in 1903 and only lost to Mr. Maxwell at the nineteenth. He was like the exit of the waiter in Calverley's alphabet "not rigidly straight," but he constantly made splendid and incredible recoveries from that rough with a little, short-shafted lofting cleek. To-day, even the mildest of men can sometimes get quite a respectable distance out of the stuff, but then it was the job for a giant.

Common or garden hay scarcely deserves to be included among golfing difficulties; and yet I have seen it play an important part in important competitions on courses of unquestioned eminence. One of these was the Amateur Championship at Sandwich in 1904 won by the first of our American conquerors, the late Mr. Walter Travis. The hay was really worthy of the name and fringed the fairway, as I recall it, in a terrifying manner. People are apt to talk as if Mr. Travis had putted his way to victory and his putting was magnificent; but a word is also due to the accuracy of his long game, which was not so very long perhaps but kept him out of the deadly grass. In the final Mr. Blackwell hit some of his mightiest shots, but they availed little if they finished in the hay, with Mr. Travis a good long way behind, but bang in the middle of the course.

The other was an Open Championship at Hoylake; I think it must have been that in 1924, which Walter Hagen just won from Ernest Whitcombe by a glorious spurt in the last lap. There had been a combination of rain and hot sun which had caught even the Royal Liverpool Golf Club unawares; the hay had come on so fast that you might almost have seen it growing, and there were tangled groves of it not merely on the edges of the fairway but on the edges of the greens. I remember watching one player who had just overrun the green of the Long hole, which is the third. His ball was only a yard or two off the mown expanse, but he had to hack and hack again before he reached it. Fortunately, grass of such ferocious length and consistency is rare, for it is a most un-golfing form of difficulty. It gives scope for little or no skill in recovery, for nothing in short but brute force and qualified ignorance. I must apologise to several other kinds of rough in which I have passed strenuous minutes with the niblick; to a particular yellow-flowered brand at Brancaster; to the bracken of Broadstone and many other agreeable courses; to some thorny undergrowth which my memory connects with Seacroft and also with Blundellsands, to my dear old friends the "leeks" of Aberdovey. I have not more room to dilate on them, but I love to see my opponents in them one and all.

GOLFING VIEWS

THE discussion about the view of Durham (which to me stands for the pleasant, long-drawn-out expectancy of a journey by day to St. Andrews) has set me ruminating on golfing views. It is one of golf's oldest jokes that only the man who is several holes up draws his partner's attention to the view and that his remarks are, as a rule, coldly received. I am afraid we do not always look at the scenery from the links quite as often as we might, and it is very un-grateful of us, for in this respect golf can give points to any other game. It would not be true to say that the view of every cricket ground is the same; Worcester and Canterbury differ from Bramall Lane; but golf has a variety and beauty of prospect which the other games cannot boast, and to go over them in the mind's eye makes an agreeable and sentimental retrospect.

The best views are by no means always from the best courses, and for this there is at least one good reason. A noble prospect often implies the crest of a rise and a stiff climb to reach it, and there is no hole quite so tiresome as that which consists of a long slog up a hill, a hole that the architect must make in order to get to the top, however much he may loathe it. There is one such view from the mountain-top at Royston, which, though

GOLFING VIEWS

183

a beloved is not strictly a great course. Another which comes to mind I have only seen once, but it remains vividly in my memory, namely that at Stinchcombe Hill in Gloucestershire. As I recall it, one plays along a rocky peninsula, and the epithet is no exaggerated one, since in some places the holes had, I believe, to be bored out of the rock. This peninsula seems to jut out into space and far below is the gorgeous stretch of the Vale of Berkeley. There is another Gloucestershire course too with the same wonderful extent of view, at Cheltenham. I clambered there one day with a kind friend in a high wind, to a point which he declared to be the highest in the Cotswolds, and I saw no reason whatever to disbelieve his statement, even if I had had enough breath to dispute it. Tewkesbury, Gloucester, the Severn—what did I not see? It was as vast a view as that of the "coloured counties" from Bredon Hill, where there is no golf course, but some pleasant turf which tempted me.

For steepness of climb and immensity of prospect combined Mont Agel, behind Monte Carlo, doubtless takes some beating, and the climbing is done by a funicular railway. But let me come to that which I like best of all—I have not the least doubt about it. "Place me on Sunium's marbled steep" exclaimed Lord Byron, but I am content with something nearer home; place me on Gullane Hill. Here is the best of golf, and I can never deny that it is an added attraction, but leaving it on one side, the noble expanse of green and the loneliness—yes, loneliness, despite three courses—and the sea and the giant pattern of the Forth Bridge in the distance and the crying of the gulls make up an unequalled and unforgettable vision. I am in the middle of reading "The Pavilion on the Links" again, which no doubt accentuates my yearning. Never again do I want to play that hole up the hill, but I do desperately want once more to see that view from the top of it.

So much for the mountains, and now down to the flatter country on which as a rule is the better golf. It is a regrettable fact that Nature in disposing of her sandhills has not been very kind in the matter of views; the hills too often blot out the sea. It is rare to find a first-class seaside course where, as at Porthcawl which is one of the exceptions, one can watch the creamy waves without interruption. All the more precious, therefore, become those occasional glimpses between the sand-hills or from a high tee on the top of them. No one has ever gone so far as to call Hoylake beautiful, and I am not prepared to assert that the view across the water to Hilbre Island is worthy of that name. Perhaps it is only relatively beautiful—I cannot say; I only know that I am fond of it.

At Sandwich, on the other hand, I think the view of Pegwell Bay, with the white cliffs beyond and the sea glittering in the sun is positively beautiful. It strikes one "all of a heap" as after wandering amid tall and secret hills one comes suddenly upon it by the broad strath of turf leading to the seventh hole. Deal is not quite so kind, and to see the water and the ships at their best one must ascend to the first floor of the club-house and flatten the nose against its magnificent plate-glass window. At St. Andrews the best sea view comes at the beginning, where the bay comes curving in, but there is a view of the Eden, a little secret view, from the short hole at the end of the New Course, which runs it hard in my affections.

Of such secret sea-views I know none more attractive than at Archerfield. That at North Berwick has more of width and splendour, and the Bass shining white in the sun must appeal even to one who is several holes down and has just been laid yet another stymie. Nevertheless give me Archerfield, where for a while one is wholly curtained by woods, until at the far end comes the narrow but exquisite view of the sea and its islets. One seems to have it all to oneself, just as one is apt to have that most engaging of little links.

Newcastle in County Down must never be forgotten, with the waves on one side and Slieve Donard on the other "sweeping down to the sea"; and then there is Portmarnock and the hole, the fourteenth unless my mind is going, that is called Ireland's Eye. It is one of the very best of holes, and I can still feel tingling in my finger-tips a certain iron shot I once played up to that green, so defiant and so girt about with trouble. And when one has reached it there is the islet of Ireland's Eye in the distance, on which, an added charm, one of the most interesting of murders was committed. *A propos* of murders I had forgotten Arran, where there was one not to be despised, and I had likewise forgotten the view of Arran from Prestwick. The Ayrshire views can hold up their heads in any company.

Scotland seems to be much richer in sea-woods than is England. I can think of few English ones comparable to Archerfield Wood. Formby has, it is true, plenty of fir trees on its sand-hills, but I think I liked the hills barer, as they were when I first knew them. Woods suggest to me rather the many courses, both pretty and good, round London. I have always loved a certain avenue down which I used to drive or attempt to drive at Cassiobury Park, and I have an old affection too for the charming glades of New Zealand. I know no background to a green of which I am fonder than that at the fifth hole at Woking. The green seems to be set in a bower. So also I can think of no nobler single tree than the big yew which keeps watch and ward, a solitary sentinel, behind the ninth green on the new course at Addington. There are lovely birches on so many Surrey courses that I cannot choose one line of them above the rest, but I know which line of fir trees I love best. For that I must go to Suffolk, for it is the double row of firs which bisects the course at Worlington. For majesty and vastness there are not many golfing views better than Walton Heath on a fine day. I think fierce old Cobbett said it was as vile a spot as he had ever seen in his life, but he took altogether too agricultural a view and I don't think that even the green fairways winding among the pink heather would have mollified him.

No doubt I have left out innumerable views which my readers will think ought to have been included, but the truth is that I have "roamed in a crowded mist" of courses and remembered happily but at random. Perhaps I ought to add one view which comparatively few golfers know. For about a year and a half my only golf was played on a course within sight of Olympus, with its triple peak rising majestic out of the Thessalian plain. It was infinitely impressive, and heavens! how I grew to hate it. One can have too much even of a good thing.

TO THE NINETEENTH

THIS article is not, as might possibly be inferred from its name, a facetious one about taking refreshment. It refers to the much more serious subject of those horrible extra holes which we have all had to play at some time or another in a tournament, whereupon all our friends come out to look at us in ghoulish glee. Horrible they are, and yet in a way stimulating, for we know that it is now or never, victory or Westminster Abbey. As our old friend Mamilius remarked in the *Lays of Ancient Rome:*

> One of us two, Herminius,
> Shall never more go home.

The subject came into my head as I was browsing on a book of reference and came across almost my only title to golfing fame, or rather, perhaps, infamy. I have already suggested that after I have vanished from the scene it will still be recorded that Mr. Horace Hutchinson and I put five balls out of bounds between us at the nineteenth hole at Hoylake, and that I then retired, having no more balls left to slice. I am not going to revert to that painful affair, except to say that many people have told me that they were present and have enlarged hilariously on the details, and that no one of them has ever got the story right. No, I would rather talk about some much more distinguished nineteenth and thirty-seventh holes I have seen or tried to see, for the crowd is usually so thick on these occasions that all one can in fact see is "the 'oofs of the 'orses."

The records of the Amateur Championship show that since 1885 the final has only five times gone beyond the home hole, twice in the days of eighteen-hole finals, and three times since the days of thirty-six holes. The first two were before my time, and both were at St. Andrews. In 1891, Mr. Laidlay beat Mr. Hilton at the twentieth, having saved himself by a miraculous run-up at the nineteenth, and four years later Mr. Balfour-Melville beat Mr. Ball at the nineteenth. The second occasion was unique in that the winner went to that hole in his last three matches and each of his adversaries, first Mr. Willie Greig, next Mr. Laurence Auchterlonie, and finally and incredibly Mr. Ball, pitched his third shot into the narrow waters of the burn: Mr. Ball, so it is always said, because, having first taken out his trusty iron, he put it back and chose a mashie with which he had not played a shot all through the championship. He figures in two out of three matches that went past the thirty-sixth green. He beat Freddie Tait at Prestwick at the thirty-seventh in 1899, and Abe Mitchell at Westward Ho! in 1912. The third instance is Mr. Tolley's win against Mr. Robert Gardner at Muirfield in the first championship after the Great War. For the last twenty years our feelings have not been so harrowed. On all three of those occasions I was there, and how much can I honestly declare that I saw? Well, I did see Mr. Tolley hole that noble putt of his for a two; in fact, I can see it now, and as he walked up to his ball he looked as if he could contemplate no other possible ending. As to the other two, I believe I caught a glimpse of Mr. Ball's legs and his club at Prestwick, but did my eyes behold the ball actually go in for that tremendous three? I could not take my oath one way or the other. Mr. Hilton in his reminiscences says that he could see the player but not the ball, that he liked the look of his attitude as he struck, and was not surprised to hear the ensuing shout. Perhaps that was my case too; there could be no possible mistake about the shout. Of Westward Ho! I have a clear memory. The thirty-seventh had been duly halved in five, both players recovering very well from trouble near the green, and I had rushed ahead down the course towards the second hole. Then came the first ball, right down the middle; that was Mr. Ball's, beyond a doubt, for he had the honour; and then came a long, baffling pause and no other ball. People near the tee signalled to us that all was over, and we ran back, mystified. Poor Abe had topped into a ditch almost in front of his nose, had tried to get out, and then caught

188   GOLFING BY-PATHS

the ball as it was going to fall back into trouble. So of those three culminating holes, two were won in a stroke under par and the other was not holed out at all.

To leave the Championship for a moment, there is another famous series of extra holes at which I was present but which I can hardly say that I saw, for the reason that it was too dark. That was in the final of the President's Putter at Rye in 1926. Never, despite our best endeavours, could we induce the finalists to start *quite* early enough after lunch in that tournament, and so, when Mr. Wethered and Mr. Storey ended all square the light was already very dim. Now one seemed to be about to clinch the matter and now the other, but the last putt would never quite go into the hole, perhaps because the hole was so difficult to see. So they halved and they halved, and when they had halved five holes I, though having no official status, suggested to them that it was time to stop. The idea had not occurred to them, but it seemed rather a good one, and they agreed to play one more hole. Never have I prayed more fervently for a hole to be halved. Halved it was in a highly respectable five; we groped our way home to the lights of the club-house, and the Society funds had that year to provide two medals instead of one. Ever since then we have had a referee.

Another thirty-seventh hole occurs to me for a particular reason, although I did not actually see it. It is unique and historic, since it will be the only thirty-seventh hole played in a Walker Cup match. This was in the first match in the National golf links in 1922, and a certain pleasant casualness in the proceedings is shown by the fact that no one had decided what was to be done in case of a halved match. Mr. Sweetser and Mr. Hooman duly halved, and that was, incidentally, a fine feather in Mr. Hooman's cap, for only a week or so later Mr. Sweetser swept through the American Championship like a devouring flame, beat Mr. Bobby Jones by 9 and 8 and, generally speaking, played the deuce with all his adversaries. Having halved, the pair asked what they should do next: Mr. Fritz Byers decided that they should go on, and Mr. Hooman won with, I think, a three. I, meanwhile, was struggling behind

Central Press Photos, Ltd.

MISS CECIL LEITCH AT TROON

Where was played the greatest of all her matches against Miss Wethered

Sport & General.

THE BIG BUNKER AT THE 4TH HOLE AT WESTWARD HO !

TO THE NINETEENTH 189

with Mr. Fownes, the American captain, and had just holed a
putt at the thirty-fourth to make myself dormy two. At that
moment I heard about this thirty-seventh hole and my mind
was instantly made up. America had won the match in any
case, and I had not toiled and sweated through the live-long
day to be deprived after all of the blessed, fate-defying position
of dormy. So I told my friend Mr. Fownes that no number
of wild presidents should drag me past the thirty-sixth hole.
It may have been a shameful proceeding on my part, but I could
not help it, and fortunately the question did not arise. Since
then it has been decided that a halved match in a Walker Cup
is a halved match, and goodness knows that thirty-six holes
are hard enough work without any more. The same rule now
applies to the University match, in which I have seen some truly
blood-curdling thirty-sevenths, and one which, save for the two
poor players, was a glorious farce. The result of the whole
match was long since decided; these two wretches were the only
two left and they had to go on, while all the rest of their com-
rades, arms linked and in jocose mood, came out to watch the
fun. It did not end till the thirty-ninth.

I have been ungallant enough not to mention any great thirty-
sevenths between ladies, but there is one that nobody who saw
it is at all likely to forget, that between Miss Leitch and Miss
Wethered at Troon in 1925. That *was* a match. First Miss
Leitch, who had rather scrambled her way through to the final,
played magnificently and gained a considerable lead; then Miss
Wethered fought her down and down and had herself a winning
lead, and finally Miss Leitch came with a noble spurt and halved.
As I remember it, both were on the near edge of the green
with their seconds, a long putt distant, and Miss Wethered just
got down in two and Miss Leitch just didn't. Never did I see
two players who had more clearly had enough, and never did
a thirty-seventh seem a crueller necessity. There ought to have
been two medals that year.

O

A CLUB OF CHARACTER

"ON a wild moraine of forgotten books" I lighted the other day on the late Mr. Garden Smith's "The World of Golf" and began to read it again with a lazy pleasure. In it I found one little story which set me, still lazily, thinking. As every golfing schoolboy ought to know, there was once at St. Andrews a golfer called Tom Kidd, who won the Open Championship in 1873 and was one of the long hitters of his day. It appears that towards the end of his career he possessed a very particular driver which came from Tom Morris's shop. It had, of course, a thick handle and a finely tapered shaft, but its great beauty lay in the head. This, says my author, "was long and narrow, as was the fashion in those days, but the face was fairly deep, and there was no lack of wood in its composition. With age the varnish which had been originally applied on the light beechwood without staining had attained a beautiful deep amber colour." On Kidd's death this club fell into the hands of an English golfer, who regarded it presumably as a treasure too great to be used. At any rate, he put it away in a box, where it never saw the light, except such truant rays that may have crept in through the keyhole, for nine long years. He then exchanged it with another golfer, who held different views and took it with him to play at St. Andrews. He was on the first tee with his precious driver in his hand when Tom Morris, who was standing by, asked him where he had got that club. "It once belonged to Tom Kidd," said the new owner, in a tone of nicely blended pride and reverence. "I ken the club fine," answered old Tom. "Whaur did ye get it?"

I like that small story for several reasons. First, it speaks of a cosy, friendly, intimate little world of golf in which a single club could gain such fame for its peculiar characteristics. Secondly, it shows what a fine art was once the club-maker's; and thirdly, how close an observer was Tom Morris and what a long memory he had in that after nine years he could instantly recognise that driver. I cannot help wondering a little sadly whether such a thing could happen nowadays, whether anyone could at a glance know an old friend which had been not his own but somebody else's. I think it might happen in the case of a wooden putter, and, if so, the man to recognise it would be a St. Andrews caddie. I possess one ancient wooden putter myself, bearing the name of Philp, and I enjoyed an unspeakable thrill when I once showed it to Simpson, the professional at Rye, who is a St. Andrews man. He saw a little mark cut in the shaft just below the leather, and said he would bet that the club had once belonged to Young Tommy, since that was the mark he always made on his clubs. The pedigree of the club, as I have it, is that it passed from Bob Kirk, the father, to Bob Kirk the son, and whether or not it went through Tommy's hands I shall never know now, but the possibility that it did and the grounds for such a belief at are least extremely romantic.

Such a thing is very unlikely to occur in the case of modern clubs, which are all so good and, to my eye, seem so dully and dreadfully like one another. I believe I should have a difficulty in knowing my own irons among a crowd of others. Wooden clubs have, as a rule, more individual characters, and yet, apart from the fact that some have silvery shafts and some have dark ones, there is the strongest family likeness between them all. This was not so once upon a time, and there are certain old clubs of mine which I feel I could and would take my oath to wheresoever I found them, even if it involved the gravest imputations upon an apparently respectable person. More than that, I feel, though possibly I exaggerate my powers, that I could recognise some of the clubs with which my friends and opponents used to play long ago. There was, for instance, a little stumpy-headed brassey with a piece of red fibre let into the face, which belonged to Mr. de Montmorency and had before that belonged to Mr. E. H. Buckland. He used to call it "Dumpty," and I am glad to know that it is still alive; I should surely know it anywhere. Mr. Horace Hutchinson's immensely long driver with quite a small head, made by Jack Rowe, is one of my possessions, but if it were buried for ten years I could not fail to know it again. Mr. Croome's clubs,

GOLFING BY-PATHS

rather upright in the lie, with beautifully varnished heads, seem to me very familiar; so do some of Mr. John Low's spoons with light-coloured heads, made by Lorimer or Willie Auchterlonie; I feel that I should know them, and I should, at any rate, strongly suspect Sir Guy Campbell's. Mr. Lionel Munn's clubs seem in recollection to have had rather long heads, of a shape peculiar to an Irish club-maker; and so I could go on, and be doubtless very tiresome.

When, on the other hand, I survey, in my mind's eye, the clubs of my younger friends I am at once lost. I can say, perhaps, that Mr. Oppenheimer has, or had, a set of Bobby Jones clubs, which are rather characteristic in build; but then, so have lots of other people. There is only one club to which I think I could positively swear, a not essentially beautiful driver belonging to Mr. John Morrison. I know that because it is of a very fair complexion, whereas heads of lightest yellow are seldom seen and most gentlemen prefer brunettes. Mr. "Boxer" Cannon's putting cleek, with which he strikes such mighty blows in one-club matches at Worlington, has something of a unique air; so has Miss Doris Park's cleek with the curly neck which belonged to her illustrious father; and of course there was Mr. Allan Graham's brazen serpent of a putter, which was instantly to be recognised when he lent it to Sarazen in an Open Championship at Hoylake. None of those three putters can by any stretching of language be called modern, and modern clubs seem to me a monotonous lot—monotonous in their excellence and shapeliness. It is perfectly natural that they should be, because it is one of the avowed merits of the clubs of to-day that one should differ from the other as little as possible, and we buy them not singly but in sheaves. Turning back to Mr. Garden Smith's book, which was published just over forty years ago, I find "A set of first-rate clubs is not easy to come by, and the beginner will fare better in the end if he acquires his clubs gradually, picking them up from time to time from professional players, even if he pays a fancy price for them." Of course, "set" of clubs meant only seven or eight, and it was great fun picking them up. Each had a cast of countenance of its own, just as each had its own little history, whereas to-day a whole bag-load may have the same history and the owner needs almost a shepherd's power of knowing his sheep. I wonder who has got Tom Kidd's driver now, and whether he prizes it as he ought.

THE HEDGE-GOLFER'S FAREWELL

*N*OS *dulcia linquimus arva*. I have forgotten most of the Latin I ever knew, but I can always remember the remarks of Melibœus to Tityrus in the first five lines of the Eclogues. In them occur the words I have just quoted, and they come a little sadly to my mind now. It so happens that I am leaving a kindly city of refuge and so have been saying good-bye, in a series of p.p.c. visits, to the various fields in which from time to time I have hit golf balls.

There is really quite a large number of them, though one or two and in particular the noblest of them all, fifty-five whole acres of it, has now become plough. There is the charming little field, with the steep climb up to it, perched as it were on the roof of the world, where there is a great stretch of view and the breeze always blows "more snell and caller" than in the valley beneath. The turf there has something more of delicacy and of the true golfing quality; the long line of ashes at one end made admirable signposts by which to mark down the ball; but alas! there were too many thick tufts and tuffets and so too much searching and too much losing. There were over many tuffets, too, in the marshy, rushy meadow by the side of the little river. There were also very often too many cows, but that was a common complaint. I was constantly being evicted by cows, or sheep, or horses. They did not resent me, but I resented them, since they disturbed my concentration on the grim matter in hand. Then there was the narrow field, possibly the best from a severely educational point of view, between a willow-girt stream on one side and the high road on the other. It was rather too fierce and dangerous a test, and so was the one set on so steep a slope that the ball came bounding down

194 GOLFING BY-PATHS

like a chamois from rock to rock and demanded very accurate watching. Once I toiled manfully up to the top of that slope to find, like Professor Challenger and his associates, a lost world on a secret and beautiful plateau, and I did very well there till intrusive persons with guns and dogs drove me away. Finally, there was almost the best of all, which I discovered all too late, very big, reasonably flat, void of all wild beasts, where patches of coarse sand gave here and there an almost golfing air. I ended there by hitting four balls one after the other in a last tremendous burst and limped home uncommonly stiff in the back. Good-bye, one and all, ye hospitable and muddy fields of the Cotswolds. Exercise and good fun have you given me now and then. Several theories have I put to the test on your turf and found them, sooner or later, fallacious. Several balls have I left to moulder lost among your tuffets, or to be eaten by your cows. Now I must seek pastures new—good-bye one and all!

They talk in books of hedge-priests and hedge-taverns and so on, and one who hits balls in fields may surely be called a hedge-golfer. It seems the appropriate name for me, for ever since the war began, save for one or two brief visits to the sea, I have played only by myself and among the hedges. Surely I ought to have learnt some valuable lessons to pass on to my golfing brothers; yet, in fact, I have learnt few, and those of rather a depressing character than otherwise. One thing which has impressed itself upon my mind—probably this does not apply to the young and lusty—is that one's sensations are deceitful and that the ball goes much the same distance every time. The practiser hits a couple of shots which have an unsatisfactory feeling, and then, with the third ball, comes one which suggests the perfection of timing. "Aha!" he exclaims, as did the beginner who holed out a full iron shot. "Aha! Now I'm getting into it." He pursues the three balls expecting to find the last far beyond the other two and behold! they are all together in a clump. Doubtless the third was hit much the best of the three, but doubtless also it has made precious little difference.

I have fallen into the habit of pacing my shots, not in any

hopes of breaking records but simply because it is an aid to finding the ball. When my modest standard has been exceeded by more than a very few yards I know that it is of no avail to look further ahead, and I retrace my steps. This custom of pacing has rubbed into me the lesson that though some shots "feel" better than others, they all end in much the same place. From that fact I draw an inference which may have a certain negative value for other people. The only thing that would make the ball go perceptibly further would be a perceptibly swifter movement of the club head. I, especially with my stiff back, cannot make that head go any faster, no matter what antics I attempt, and I believe that most people come to have a speed of their own which they cannot make any greater. After a while, then, we must each accept our maximum speed as a law of nature, and think merely of hitting the ball as true and clean as we can. Taking thought may make us more accurate and more regular strikers of the ball but, after a certain time, it will not add a cubit to our length. There will be certain days on which we shall enjoy the delusion that it has done so, and I hope to have such days as long as I can hold a club, but a delusion it surely is.

One of the obvious defects of hedge-golf, regarded from any serious standpoint, is that it is too easy. It is not, in the often-quoted words of the old Scottish golfer, "aye fechtin' against ye." There is nothing to put one off. One has all the field to one self; there is nobody to move behind one, nobody to talk at the wrong moment, nobody in front to keep one waiting. Even a cow would have a disciplinary effect, but, as I said before, I have studiously eschewed cows. Then there is the fact that one always gives oneself a good lie, even if one does not actually tee the ball on an inviting lump. I have often resolved to play the ball where it lies, but in the end I have always pampered myself with a tee. Again, there is nothing to mark one's inaccuracy. One aims, let us say, at a distant beech tree and pulls the shot on the line of an oak twenty yards to the left. Thereupon one alters the aim for the next two balls and goes for the oak. If those next two shots are straight, one is apt entirely to forget that the first one was crooked and

GOLFING BY-PATHS

on a golf course would very likely have been bunkered. The three balls are close together and the player exclaims, like Little Jack Horner: "What a good boy am I!" Yet, in fact, one of his shots has been naughty and might have lost a match.

This is particularly true of iron shots, for their main object is accuracy, and to aim at nothing very particular is not the way to test oneself in that respect. Of course, the player ought to drive a peg into the ground and play his iron shots at it, but of course he does not, and indeed any such solemnity seems a little out of keeping with the pleasant casualness of the game. Yes, it is all a little too easy, and so the hedge-golfer quickly discovers when he returns to a real course, with something of a Rip Van Winkle feeling, and sees a perfectly good field shot go into a perfectly good bunker. However, I must not end my valediction on a thankless note, and indeed I am very, very far from being ungrateful.

FORWARD TEES

IN wartime we play golf, if at all, for air and exercise and even for pleasure. It seems to be essentially a time when the game should be made as agreeable and easy-going as possible. It was doubtless with this view that a friend of mine declared in the club-house the other day that he thought everybody would be happier if the tees were put forward. The regular players on this course can hit the ball both clean and straight, but, as is only right in such times as these, they are long past the first flush of youth and cannot hit it very far. So with the turf slow there is a number of admirable "two-shot-holes" which for them—and for me—deserve that name only in cynical inverted commas. I think each of his auditors knew that the speaker was right and yet his proposal was received with rather blank faces and it is doubtful whether it will be carried out. If it is not I think there will be two reasons, and the first of them deserves to be called both unselfish and patriotic. Near the course is an "Octu" from which the young gentlemen

FORWARD TEES

come to play on one hardly-earned afternoon in the week. All are young and lusty and some of them are really good players, and it would perhaps be unkind to give them a course unworthy of their powers. The other reason bespeaks a narrower patriotism. All members of all clubs are proud of their courses and cannot bear them not to be at their best. They are perpetually afraid lest some hypothetical stranger should come and turn up his nose at them.

As I was only a temporary sojourner I did not feel justified in giving an opinion, but I said "Hear, hear!" to the speaker in my heart. It is not, I hope, all vanity that makes people a little "disgruntled" when the two-shot holes are out of their reach, nor is it an unhallowed attachment to scores, which resents the fours turning into fives. In fact, many holes which are admirable as two-shotters are dull when they become two and a bit. The bunkers are, as a rule, clustering round or near the green; he who cannot reach the green often cannot reach the bunkers either, and therefore for him something in the nature of "any old shot" will do for his second. This is no new discovery, though the truth of it becomes more patent as we get on in life and, on a course where all classes of golfers play, the old and short must clearly grin and bear it. It is only perhaps when all are old and short that some concession might be made and that, I think, was what my friend meant by his proposal.

There is an obvious solution, namely, to have alternate sets of tees, the back and the forward, so that players may please themselves. "Obvious" indeed faintly describes it; it cries aloud to be adopted, and in the United States it has long settled the difficulty; but somehow or other it has never been successful in this country. There are exceptions, such as the yellow and blue boxes at Addington, which were habitually used according to the taste and the driving power of the members; but they are few. Too often some insensate pride drives to the back tees those who would be far happier on the front ones. A few years ago at Hoylake some of the strong young men of the club thought that far-back tees would be good for their golf, and accordingly discs were set for them. These were intentionally made small and inconspicuous, so that they should escape the attention of all save the few who needed them, and should not tempt those who did not. And yet, so I was told, the distant tees were constantly used by people for whom that noble links was full long enough from the normal ones. What is there to be said about it except, heartily including ourselves in the condemnation, "Lord, what fools these mortals be?"

I am afraid vanity must have something to do with it, and I am quite sure it has in one particular respect. X and I may each be, in fact, just as short as the other; there is nothing to choose between us in point of driving, and yet each of us at the bottom of his heart believes that when he "really gets hold of one" he is a little the longer. So if X proposes to me that we shall play from forward tees, I think that he is trying to gain an advantage. If I make the same proposal to X he thinks that by accepting it he will sacrifice his superior power. And so we walk back to the tees in the dim distance and both reach the holes in "two of those and one of them."

It may be urged that in war-time green-keeping ought and indeed must be reduced to a minimum, and that the more tees the more work is wanted. That is true, but is it not also true that in war-time we ought to be satisfied with the most rudimentary of teeing grounds, in fact, with any moderately level piece of turf? Sand boxes are no longer necessary, and it is surely not hard to find a place wherein to drive our wooden peg. Of course there are holes at which the teeing ground is in the middle of a sandy waste and really does need regular upkeep, but generally speaking one piece of turf on the course is as good as another.

When we talk thus of putting the tees forward we do not mean, or at least I do not mean, all the tees. Some of the holes would want no cutting down and would be needlessly spoilt by a rule-of-thumb shortening all round. It is only certain of them at which forward tees would make for the greater happiness of by far the greater number. The ladies seem to me to set us a good example; they strike a happy medium. This is so on the only course with which I have been at all familiar in war-time. At a number of holes the ladies' tees are only a few paces in front of the men's; sometimes they are on a level. It is only at those where, owing to the nature of the ground, the men's tees would take all fun and hope out of the shot for the average lady golfer that there is any considerable distance between the two. Fun and hope I say, picking my words with some care. Where there is neither golf is, to say the least of it, not a very good game.

The fact that winter is now upon us ought to make my friend's proposal all the more acceptable. His is a seaside course where the turf is slow, but there are many inland ones where to slowness is added muddiness. I have told before of the dear old gentleman I used to know who, as soon as November came, was seen busily practising with his wooden clubs on the ground that he had unaccountably lost his length. Some of us may be rather more clear-sighted than he was as to the cause, but our plight is the same. I confess that one of the minor and utterly unimportant pleasures that I look forward to after the war (in a good hour be it spoken) is to play once again on a ground that is keen and hard and full of running, so that my "shotties" will almost turn into shots. No doubt I shall suffer from the converse delusion of that of my dear old gentleman, namely, that I have unaccountably recovered my driving. However preposterous that would be very pleasant, and meanwhile if anyone will make a kindly forward tee I will promise to pocket any pride I have left and drive from it.

ON GIVING UP

WHO are the mysterious people who, according to the advertisements which I read daily, are prepared to sell me a series of numbered irons, with a wooden club or two and sometimes a bag thrown in, for more money than I ever possessed? Who, if any, are the "mugs" who buy them? The last is, however, but a supplementary question. It is the sellers as to whom I feel curious. They may be sinister figures from the black market travestied by false whiskers or blue spectacles, but that seems hardly likely. They may simply be persons who, like most of us, wish to turn an honest penny. Again they may have determined—and this is what makes me anxious—to give up golf once and for all. The offer of a bag has an ominous sound. Some years ago I was playing at Addington and, in timid apology for my bag, which was in the last stages of disintegration, said to my caddie that I meant to buy a new one. He replied that he thought the old one would last me as long as I could play golf. It depressed me at the moment, but I cheered up and bought the new bag nevertheless.

To-day I am not merely depressed by these offers but by the letters I get from my friends. They one and all protest that they have not played for years. One, a very good player indeed, says that hitting an old ball into a thick heather bush and then hunting for it for ages does not amuse him in the least and that he seriously doubts whether he will ever begin again. Another says that he cannot walk there and back and carry his own clubs. Both of them live near famous courses and their remarks, even though they be not taken at the foot of the letter, are yet symptomatic. I believe that there is a very large number of people who from lack of heart for it or lack of transport or lack of golf balls have got almost entirely out of the way of playing the game. I myself have not hit a ball for several months and before that I had not played on a real golf course, as distinguished from practice shots in a field, for two mortal years. I have a certain amount of confidence in myself because, despite disabilities, I do not believe I have the power, however wise it might be, to give up the game, but as to some of these others I really and truly do feel anxious. About our young warriors there need not be this particular anxiety; they will come back to the links all the keener, but their elders, who were already getting a little lazy before the war, may refuse, like poor Mrs. Dombey, to make an effort.

It does require a certain effort to start again, the more so because we are not used to it. It was otherwise with cricket and football, which each had its appointed season. It was natural to put away the well-oiled bat and get horribly stiff over the first game of football in the winter term and *vice versa*;

ON GIVING UP 201

but golf in this country we never wholly give up. I have sometimes wondered whether in this respect the Americans are not
more enviable than we are in having a close season. Save for
those who go south in the winter there comes a snowy time
when clubs must be put away. On my first visit to the United
States I played a round with a very good golfer on a Chicago
course and can still remember the tone in which he spoke of
beginning again in the spring time, the joy of playing once
more mingled with the agony of restlessness till he could break
eighty. There is a freshness of enthusiasm about that which
the British player does not often taste; he does not take a long
enough rest. Young Tommy Morris used to say that he could
not understand how Mr. Mitchell Innes, when playing as fine a
game as anyone had ever played, could bear to go away to the
highlands in pursuit of "a wheen stinking beasts" and then
"come back no able to hit a ba'." That is the opposite point
of view to that of my Chicago friend, due no doubt to different
climate and circumstances.

I have been trying to think of any distinguished golfers who
have habitually or indeed ever given up the game for really
long periods, except in war-time, and the only one who comes
into my head is Mr. Edward Blackwell in his youth. Then he
would disappear into California for several years and never see
or touch a club, since that was in days before the great American
golfing empire had arisen. He would return to win a St.
Andrews medal and play great matches with Freddie Tait,
Andrew Kirkaldy and Willie Auchterlonie and then leave his
clubs behind him and return to the wilderness. I suppose he
might have been an even better player than he was—he could
scarcely have driven farther—had it not been for those long
blank gaps, but at any rate he did not lose his keenness. However, he was young then and these depressing creatures who
talk of never playing again are past the first flush. For such as
them it is a great thing not to have an interregnum, as witness
the schoolmasters who go on playing football and playing very
well too when they are more than old enough to know better.

That there can be good and valid reasons for giving up golf
I am not prepared to deny. A much-loved relation of mine,

202   GOLFING BY-PATHS

now dead, gave it up under peculiar circumstances. He was
suddenly attacked by a strange disease of the golfing nerves;
he could get his club up to the top of the swing with his usual
painstaking and elaborate swing but once there it stuck; not
all the King's horses and all the King's men could get it down
again. Like Horatius he "twice and three times tugged amain."
and when, as happened sometimes, the club-head did come
down at last, it did so in a series of jerks and the ball trickled
along the ground for an inconsiderable distance. Thereupon
with perfect serenity he put his clubs away for ever and he was
probably wise.

He, to be sure, had no brilliant golfing past to look back
upon with the bitterness of contrast, and it is not as to such as
he, not as to the rank and file that I am afraid but rather as to
those who have been really good golfers. The former do not
suffer from such sensitive feelings and for them, moreover, hope
springs eternal; it is possible even for an octogenarian to have
his handicap reduced, if only it be high enough to begin with.
It is otherwise with such as have once been somewhere near the
top of the tree but have now for some time been tumbling
down it branch by branch. I once asked one of the greatest
of cricketers whether he ever played nowadays and he answered:
"No. I don't play so well as I used to and I don't like it."
That was an answer compelling admiration by its complete
honesty, and it represents, I imagine, the feeling of a number
of golfers. For a good many years towards the end of his life
John Low lived hard by the course at Woking. He took the
greatest possible interest in the new bunkers; he was always
ready to watch his friends playing the mildest of foursomes,
and he carried a spoon under his arm; but that was as far as
he would go. Now and again I used to see him, in the dim
distance and complete solitude, playing a shot with that spoon,
but, as far as I know, he never played a single hole, much less
a round. If that was the course which made him happiest he
was entirely right to pursue it, but it seemed rather a pity.
Clearly there is something to be said for never having been up
in the world since there is then no pain of coming down.

It may well be, and I hope it is, that I am making myself

ON GIVING UP 203

quite unnecessarily unhappy about these faint-hearts. Circumstances do so alter cases. For instance, I am writing these words very close to the fire, with a snow-clad world outside the window. These are emphatically not the circumstances to make anyone think of beginning again. Just about fifty years ago this day I won a scratch medal at Cambridge (whence I write) with red balls on a course covered with snow, except for the greens, which were frozen as hard as a brick and had been swept for a small area round each hole. Even that thrilling memory does not fill me with any markedly enthusiastic desire to repeat the experience. But will there not come a fine and sunny day bringing with it a sudden longing to surge out on to the course once more? For my part I firmly believe there will.